ASCENT
AFTER DECLINE

ASCENT
AFTER DECLINE

Regrowing Global Economies
after the Great Recession

OTAVIANO CANUTO
AND
DANNY M. LEIPZIGER

THE WORLD BANK
Washington, D.C.

THE
GROWTH
DIALOGUE

ISBN: 978-0-8213-8942-3
eISBN: 978-0-8213-8943-0
DOI: 10.1596/978-0-8213-8942-3

Library of Congress Cataloging-in-Publication Data
Ascent after decline: regrowing global economies after the great recession / edited by Otaviano Canuto and Danny Leipziger.
    p. cm.
 Includes bibliographical references and index.
 ISBN 978-0-8213-8942-3—ISBN 978-0-8213-8943-0 (electronic)
 1. Economic policy. 2. Economic development. 3. Recessions. 4. Global Financial Crisis, 2008–2009. I. Canuto, Otaviano. II. Leipziger, Danny M. III. World Bank.
 HD87.A754 2011
 338.9—dc23

2011040045

Cover illustration: Michael S. Geller, *An Idea of Order*, 2010, oil on canvas, 36" × 36"
Cover design: Drew Fasick
Photo credit: David Scavone

Contents

About the Editors and Contributors   xi
Preface   xv
Acknowledgments   xix
Abbreviations   xxi

Part 1   Diagnosing the Challenges   1

  1   The Challenges of Growth   3
       by Otaviano Canuto, Danny M. Leipziger, and Brian Pinto

  2   Rebalancing Global Growth   35
       Menzie Chinn, Barry Eichengreen, and Hiro Ito

  **3   Fiscal Policy and Growth:
       Overcoming the Constraints   87**
       Carlo Cottarelli and Michael Keen

  **4   Infrastructure Policy for Shared
       Growth Post-2008: More and Better,
       or Simply More Complex?   135**
       Antonio Estache

Part 2   The Way Forward   179

  5   Rethinking Growth and the State   181
       Philippe Aghion and Julia Cagé

6   **Financial Shocks and the Labor Markets: Should Economic Policy Save Jobs?**   **201**
    Tito Boeri and Pietro Garibaldi

7   **Information Technology, Globalization, and Growth: The Roles of Scale Economies, Terms of Trade, and Variety**   **219**
    Catherine L. Mann

8   **Innovation-Driven Growth: Analytical Issues and Policy Implications**   **247**
    Paolo Guerrieri and Pier Carlo Padoan

    Index   **281**

Box

1.1   Policy Challenges for the G-20   9

Figures

2.1   Current Account Balances, 1996–2016   37
2.2   U.S. Saving, Investment, and Current Account, 1968–2011   38
2.3 · Current Account Balance as a Percentage of Euro Area GDP, 1995–2010   41
2.4   Out-of-Sample Current Account Predictions for Selected Countries, 2011–15   63
2.5   Out-of-Sample Current Account Predictions for Selected Countries, 2006–08 and 2011–15   66
2.6   U.S. Current Account Projections under Three Scenarios   70
2.7   Chinese Current Account Projections under Liberalization of Financial Markets   71
2.8   Chinese Current Account Projections under Liberalization and Development of Financial Markets   73
3.1   General Government Balances in Group of Seven Economies, 1998–2007   90

3.2   General Government Debt in Group of Seven
      Economies, 1950–2007   92
3.3   Predicted Old-Age Dependency Ratio, 2009–50   93
3.4   Projected Pension Spending with and
      without Reforms, 2010–30   93
3.5   General Government Debt in Emerging Economies,
      1998–2007   94
3.6   General Government Balances and Debt in
      Advanced vs. Emerging Economies, 2007–15   95
3.7   General Government Net Debt Projections for
      Advanced Economies, Projected to 2030   96
3.8   Precrisis and Postcrisis Output in Advanced
      Economies, Projected to 2014   97
3.9   Actual and Debt-Stabilizing General Government
      Primary Balances, by Debt Ratio, 2010   98
3.10 Scenarios for Primary Balance Adjustment and Debt
      in Advanced and Emerging Economies, 2007–30   101
3.11 Corporate Income Tax Statutory Rates and
      Revenue in OECD Countries, 1985–2008   122
4.1   PPI Commitments to Infrastructure Projects in
      Developing Countries, by Implementation Status,
      1990–2009   150
5.1   Relation between University Output and
      Autonomy in Selected European Countries   183
5.2   Relation between Changes in Inherited Trust and
      Per Capita Income, 1935–2000   191
5.3   Relation between Distrust and Extent of
      Entry Regulation   192
5.4   General Government Balances of Selected
      Countries, 2007 vs. 2009   194
5.5   Gross Government Debt of Selected Countries,
      2007 vs. 2009   195
5.6   Relation between Taxation and Growth in
      High-Corruption OECD Countries   196
5.7   Relation between Taxation and Growth in
      Low-Corruption OECD Countries   197
6.1   U.S. and Euro Area Unemployment Rates, 2000–10   202

6.2   Stock Market Capitalization and Unemployment,
       Euro Area and United States, 2000–10   204
6.3   Unemployment-to-Output Response in G-7 Countries   206
6.4   Employment-to-Output Elasticities in Advanced
       Countries, by Recession Type   208
7.1   Transformative Technology and Social Surplus   223
7.2   Growth and International IT Trade: The Hypotheses   232
7.3   Growth and International Trade in IT: The Calculations   233
7.4   Social Surplus and IT Trade in Selected Economies,
       2000–07   235
7.5   Variety vs. Concentration in Product Trade,
       Selected Countries   239
8.1   Real Income Sources in Europe and Japan
       Compared with the United States, 2007   255
8.2   Effects of Deregulation and Harmonization on
       Selected Variables   268
8.3   Effect of a 5 Percent Increase in Human Capital on
       Selected Variables   269
8.4   Comparative Effects of Policy Scenarios on Output   270
8.5   Impact of Structural Changes on Selected Variables   272
8.6   Cost of Delaying Deregulation   273
8.7   Aggregate Effect of Coordinated Policies:
       Increasing Human Capital and Deregulation   274

Tables

2.1   Fiscal Adjustment in the Euro Area, 2010–11   42
2.2   Actual and Projected Current Account Balances
       in the Euro Area, 2008–16   43
2.3   Current Account Regression without Institutional
       Variables   55
2.4   National Saving and Investment Regression without
       Institutional Variables   57
2.5   Current Account Regression with Institutional Variables   59
2.6   National Saving and Investment Regression with
       Institutional Variables   60
2A.1   Mnemonics for Variables in Analysis   79

2A.2   Assumptions of Out-of-Sample Forecasting Variables   80
3.1   Key Features of the Value Added Tax in
       Selected Countries   115
4.1   Annual Infrastructure Investment Needs, Globally and
       by Developing Region, 2010–15   139
4.2   Precrisis Risk-Adjusted Infrastructure Performance in
       Australia, 1995Q3–2006Q2   158
5.1   Welfare Costs of Delayed Intervention as a
       Function of the Elasticity of Substitution and
       the Discount Rate   186
6.1   Okun's Betas (Employment-to-Output),
       Average Period   209
7.1   Global IT Trade Patterns, by Economy, 1990–2004   225
7.2   Global IT Expenditure Patterns, by Economy, 2000–08   228
7.3   Country Deviation from Trend Line and Export and
       Import Concentration   241
8.1   Dynamic Model Equations   263

About the Editors and Contributors

Editors

Otaviano Canuto is vice president and head of the World Bank's Poverty Reduction and Economic Management (PREM) Network, a division of more than 700 economists and other professionals working on economic policy, poverty reduction, and analytic work for the Bank's client countries.

Previously, Dr. Canuto served as the vice president for countries at the Inter-American Development Bank. He was executive director of the Board of the World Bank in 2004–07. He also served in the Brazilian Ministry of Finance as secretary for international affairs and has been a professor of economics at the University of São Paulo and University of Campinas (UNICAMP) in Brazil, from which he holds a Ph.D. in economics.

Danny M. Leipziger is professor of international business at George Washington University's School of Business. Previously (2004–09), he served as vice president and head of the Poverty Reduction and Economic Management (PREM) Network, as well as in other managerial positions in the World Bank. He currently manages The Growth Dialogue.

Dr. Leipziger also was vice chair of the Commission on Growth and Development, chaired by Nobel Laureate Michael Spence, which produced the Growth Report in 2008. Dr. Leipziger, who holds a Ph.D. in economics from Brown University, has authored books on the Republic of Korea, Chile, banking crises, globalization, and the middle class and has published widely in development economics.

Contributors

Philippe Aghion is Robert C. Waggoner Professor of Economics at Harvard University and an invited professor at the Institute of International Economic Studies in Stockholm.

Tito Boeri is a professor of economics at Bocconi University, Milan, and acts as scientific director of the Fondazione Rodolfo Debenedetti.

Julia Cagé is an economist at Harvard University and the Paris School of Economics, where she is a doctoral candidate.

Menzie Chinn is a professor of public affairs and economics at the Robert M. LaFollette School of Public Affairs, University of Wisconsin, Madison.

Carlo Cottarelli is director of the Fiscal Affairs Department of the International Monetary Fund, Washington, DC.

Barry Eichengreen is Charles C. Pardee and Helen N. Pardee Professor of Economics and Political Science at the University of California, Berkeley.

Antonio Estache is a professor of economics at the Université Libre de Bruxelles, Brussels.

Pietro Garibaldi is a professor of economics at the University of Turin, Italy; director and fellow of the Collegio Carlo Alberto; and head of labor studies at the Fondazione Rodolfo Debenedetti.

Paolo Guerrieri is a professor of international economics at the University of Rome "La Sapienza"; visiting professor of international economics and business at the College of Europe, Bruges, Belgium; and vice president of the Institute for Foreign Affairs, Rome.

Hiro Ito is associate professor of economics at Portland State University, Portland, Oregon.

Michael Keen is assistant director in the Fiscal Affairs Department of the International Monetary Fund, Washington, D.C.

Catherine L. Mann is Barbara and Richard M. Rosenberg Professor of Global Finance at the International Business School, Brandeis University, Waltham, Massachusetts.

Pier Carlo Padoan is deputy secretary-general and chief economist of the Organisation for Economic Co-operation and Development, Paris.

Brian Pinto is senior adviser in the Poverty Reduction and Economic Management Network of the World Bank Group, Washington, D.C.

Preface

The state of the global economy as of 2012 is much more troubled than most pundits had predicted. The recovery from the Great Recession has lost steam, and we have moved into more uncertain territory. There is increasing talk of a possible "double-dip," financial volatility continues, and policy makers around the world are scrambling to restore stability and confidence.

In the industrialized world, the Euro Area is struggling to save its common currency, strengthen its banks, and avert an even larger debt crisis. Across the Atlantic, the United States, after an over-extended use of unconventional monetary policies, continues to face damaged household balance sheets, depressed consumption, and persistent unemployment. Japan continues its battle for economic rebirth. Against this backdrop, the role that developing countries had played in 2010-11, as growth engines for the global economy, may no longer be adequate as an antidote for a sluggish industrialized world. In sum, the ascent after decline, foreseen earlier in 2011, has been delayed.

This dismal state of the world economy makes *Ascent after Decline* more relevant and timely as policy makers and their economic advisers strive to find tools that will work not only in jump-starting sluggish economies, but also in sustaining growth when many factors are now more challenging, if not adverse. Unless a vigorous recovery ensues and economic growth becomes stronger, the dangers to the global economy and to economic development will only worsen. This global concern extends beyond simple measures of gross domestic product; continuation on the current path poses significant risks to social cohesion, as persistent unemployment and economic hardships increase. The sacrifices necessary to maintain the open trading system may become too onerous for some governments;

nationalistic policies on exchange rates, import protection, and industrial support may once again become commonplace—hence the need to try any and all measures to restart the global growth engine.

This volume combines the analyses of leading experts on the various elements affecting economic growth and the policies required to spur that growth. *Ascent after Decline: Regrowing Global Economies after the Great Recession* identifies the main challenges to the economic recovery, such as rising debt levels, reduced trade prospects, and global imbalances, as well as the obstacles to growth posed by fiscal conundrums and lagging infrastructure. It also examines the way forward, beginning with the role of the state and then covering labor markets, information technology, and innovation. The common thread throughout the book is the view that economic regrowth will depend in large measure on smart policy choices and that the role of government has never been more crucial than at any time since the Great Depression.

In a way, the view that government is at the core of the ascent may seem at odds with some ideologies. It is, however, very much at the heart of what the Commission on Growth and Development opined in its 2008 and 2009 *Growth Reports*. Although the findings of that Spence Commission were framed in the context of policies to produce high levels of sustained economic progress, the admonition is even more acute in a world economy lacking confidence. Housing, debt, and asset markets are under siege in many industrialized countries, and emerging market economies are not immune to these trends. We live in a world where neither single policy interventions nor single country interventions are sufficient. What are needed are smart and coordinated policies across many fronts.

As members of the World Bank community, these issues are of particular importance to us, since without a resurrection of strong economic growth in major economies, the likelihood of rapid economic development in poorer developing countries is dampened. This is troubling because we have seen progress in many parts of the globe in the past decade, including in Africa, and these gains will be arrested as long as the global economy is in disarray. Donors will withdraw, investment will retrench, and prospects will dim. This immiserizing welfare outcome is to be avoided. The volume is intended to shed light on those areas of policy that reduce the prospects of a prolonged period of stress and decline by "regrowing growth." We believe the collection of papers could not be more timely.

Otaviano Canuto
Vice President and Head
Poverty Reduction and Economic Management (PREM) Network
The World Bank

Danny M. Leipziger
Professor of International Business,
George Washington University, and
Managing Director of The Growth Dialogue

Acknowledgments

This work grew out of the conference, "Ascent after Decline: Re-Growing Economic Growth," a joint venture of The Growth Dialogue and the World Bank's Poverty Reduction and Economic Management (PREM) Network. The event convened influential scholars to exchange their views and latest research about the future contours of economic growth in the wake of the Great Recession of 2009–10. Many of those conference participants contributed to this volume, the successor to the 2010 book, *The Day after Tomorrow: A Handbook on the Future of Economic Policy in the Developing World.*

Therefore, we are first indebted to each of our chapter authors as well as the following discussants and commentators of the Ascent after Decline workshop: Stijn Claessens (deputy director, research department, International Monetary Fund); William Cline (senior fellow, Peterson Institute for International Economics and Center for Global Development); Uri Dadush (senior associate and director of the International Economics Program, Carnegie Endowment for International Peace); Jaana Remes (senior fellow, McKinsey Global Institute); and Norman Loayza (lead economist, Development Research Group, World Bank). We also particularly thank Diana Manevskaya, who organized the conference.

Special thanks to Catherine Mathieu for her indispensable advice and support, as well as to editor Mary A. Anderson and PREM Senior Communications Officer Alejandra Viveros, the project manager who shepherded the manuscript to completion.

Last but not least, this book could not have been produced without the expertise and professionalism of several key people in the World Bank's Office of the Publisher—notably, Stephen McGroarty, Mary Fisk, and Andres

Meneses, who managed the overall production and dissemination of the volume. Thanks also to Michael S. Geller for generously allowing the use of his painting for the cover art.

To all of these contributors, advisers, and supporters, our sincere gratitude.

Otaviano Canuto
Vice President and Head, Poverty Reduction and Economic
Management Network
The World Bank

Danny M. Leipziger
Managing Director, The Growth Dialogue
Professor of International Business, School of Business
The George Washington University

January 2012

Abbreviations

ACE	allowance for corporate equity [taxation]
ASEAN	Association of Southeast Asian Nations
BNDES	Brazilian Development Bank
EMDE	emerging-market and developing economy
EMG	emerging-market economies
EPEC	European PPP Expertise Centre
EPL	employment protection legislation
EU	European Union
FAT	financial activities tax
GDP	gross domestic product
GERD	government expenditure on research and development
GNI	gross national income
GPT	general purpose technology
G-20	Group of 20 Finance Ministers and Central Bank Governors
ICT	information and communication technology
IDC	industrial countries
IMF	International Monetary Fund
IP	intellectual property
IT	information technology
LDC	less-developed countries
MECTR	marginal effective corporate tax rate
MNE	multinational enterprise
NEPAD	New Partnership for Africa's Development [of the African Union]
OECD	Organisation for Economic Co-operation and Development
PCGDP	ratio of private credit creation to GDP [proxy measure of financial development]
PIIGS	Portugal, Italy, Ireland, Greece, and Spain

PPI	private participation in infrastructure, public-private investment
PPP	public-private partnership
QE	quantitative easing
R&D	research and development
SAR	special administrative region
SOE	state-owned enterprise
TFP	total factor productivity
TOT	terms of trade
TT	transformative technology
VAT	value added tax

Diagnosing the Challenges

The Challenges of Growth

by Otaviano Canuto, Danny M. Leipziger,
and Brian Pinto

This volume examines one of the most fundamental questions to emerge from the Great Recession of 2007–09. What happens to economic growth going forward? Although all are painfully aware that some major economies are significantly below their growth potential and that it may be 2013 or 2014 before the global economy returns to normalcy, no one is sanguine about medium- to long-term growth prospects. For this reason, the challenging task of "regrowing growth" will take center stage for politicians and policy makers alike.

The core concerns surround the damage to balance sheets, employment, and confidence worldwide. Moreover, other elements of the future international economic landscape may fundamentally change the outlook for economic growth: Will international flows of capital be encouraged or discouraged? How open will export markets be, given the potentially substantial structural changes underway and their implications for employment? And how much reliance will there be on market solutions when governments—now overly indebted and wary of additional relief expenditures—are expected to deliver on the promise of economic growth? How these pressing policy questions are answered will, in large measure, determine the future face of globalization.[1]

One point is clear: without a resurrection of strong economic growth in major economies, the likelihood of rapid economic development in poor developing countries is dampened.[2] And even among the richer nations, the ability to manage debt is a direct consequence of overall economic robustness as epitomized by economic growth. The nature of that ascent is the subject of this volume. That the ascent will be a steep one can be surmised. How various elements will affect growth prospects is less clear but vitally important. In the terminology of Hausmann and Rodrik (2003), this is a process of discovery and we are in somewhat uncharted territory.

Varying Challenges

A sharp cleavage has become evident between the prospects and challenges facing advanced economies and those facing emerging and developing economies.

Advanced Economies

Attention in the advanced economies has been focused on the financial sector, where the global crisis originated, and on government balance sheets, which have been affected by bailout costs and the need for massive fiscal stimulus. At the same time, to avert another Great Depression, monetary policy has been pressed into service in an unprecedented manner—from a coordinated cut in policy interest rates in October 2008 to operations aimed at increasing liquidity in the nonfinancial corporate sector and, so far, two rounds of quantitative easing (QE) in the United States.

The Euro Area faces serious difficulty from its dependence upon bank credit and a sovereign debt problem in vulnerable Euro Area countries that has compounded the problems of banks holding government securities. These problems began with the bailout of Greece in April 2010 and have since spread to involve Ireland, Portugal, and Spain despite the creation of a €750 billion stabilization fund and substantial purchases of government bonds by the European Central Bank.

An added wrinkle is the urgent need for fiscal consolidation, which the International Monetary Fund (IMF) recommended should begin in 2011 to rein in unsustainable debt levels.[3] Consolidation will require reductions in fiscal deficits, which could take a toll on growth and exacerbate the problems banks are facing.

Another layer of uncertainty is provided by proposals to revamp prudential regulations and capital adequacy requirements, which could adversely affect loans extended by banks in the short run even as they reduce volatility and bolster the health of the financial system over the long run. Finally, of course, there are always unforeseen exogenous shocks, such as oil price developments, that can profoundly affect growth prospects.

Emerging and Developing Economies

In contrast, with a few exceptions, emerging and developing economies remain robust sources of growth.[4] In most, the recovery has moved beyond the replenishment of inventories and toward consumption and investment, with large increases in industrial production having used up excess capacity. Capital flows have resumed and credit growth is increasing except in some countries in Central and Eastern Europe, which was the epicenter of the emerging-markets crisis.

As discussed further below, however, the relatively weak growth prospects in the advanced economies and interdependence between the two sets of economies pose serious coordination challenges, which the Group of 20 (G-20) is seeking to address.

Obstacles to Global Recovery

The main obstacles to recovery include uncertainty in financial markets, which stems from many sources: mounting sovereign indebtedness, growing solvency concerns in the Euro Area periphery, a huge amount of maturing bank debt, and exposure of both households and banks to stagnation in the real estate sector. The real estate sector will pose a drag on the recovery and will continue to be a source of risk to the financial sector for a while (Roubini 2010; Shiller 2010).

With respect to household balance sheets, although there has been some improvement as savings recover and new borrowing begins to reverse its decline, these rebounds are as tentative and fragile as the recovery itself.[5] Even though deleveraging has begun, it has a long way to go, particularly in the vulnerable Euro Area periphery, as the ratio of debt to income remains highly elevated compared with a decade ago.

Against the above background, limited room remains for monetary and fiscal policy maneuvering in the advanced countries. A delicate balancing act is called for—in particular, how to manage the hand-off to private demand as fiscal stimulus fades, while also ensuring that fiscal consolidation itself does not worsen recovery prospects to the point where sustaining public finances slows growth and reduces fiscal revenues.

In the medium term, the return to strong growth is threatened by

- *Rising debt levels.* The significant impact of increased, albeit slow, growth on medium-term public debt sustainability, was shown vividly in an exercise carried out for the October 2010 IMF "Global Financial Stability Report" (IMF 2010a): If growth is 1 percent less than in the IMF *World Economic Outlook* baseline between 2010 and 2015, gross government debt in the advanced economies will exceed 120 percent of gross domestic product (GDP) compared with less than 110 percent in the baseline. For individual countries, the baseline versus slow-growth scenario in 2015 is eye opening: 250 percent versus 269 percent of GDP for Japan; 110 percent versus 122 percent for the United States; and 86 percent versus 99 percent for the United Kingdom.[6]
- *Reduced trade prospects.* Whether the movement of nominal and real effective exchange rates is enough in magnitude and direction to achieve a global rebalancing of demand has become a controversial topic. In the absence of coordinated actions to facilitate global adjustment, pressures for protectionist measures could arise. The failure of the Doha Round may well portend greater future trade friction as countries grapple with high rates of joblessness.
- *Global imbalances.* A related concern is that, after initially shrinking, trade deficits have been widening in external-deficit countries where significant output gaps exist; that is, these economies have excess capacity, with GDP in some cases significantly below potential. The opposite is happening in external-surplus countries, and if this situation persists, it could end up derailing the global recovery. As the IMF *World Economic Outlook* warns, "Over the medium term . . . domestic demand [in emerging economies] is unlikely to be strong enough to offset weaker demand in advanced economies, and global demand rebalancing is therefore projected to stall" (IMF 2010c, 8).

Rebalancing Global Demand

The "strong, sustained, and balanced growth" sought by the G-20 (2010) rests on two feats of rebalancing: (a) *internal rebalancing* in advanced countries, with private demand stepping into the breach as fiscal consolidation occurs, and (b) *external rebalancing*, involving a reduction in current account deficits in countries like the United States and a corresponding reduction in current account surpluses, particularly in emerging Asia and in China.

The big questions are, first, to what extent will uncertainty in financial markets, problems in the real estate sector and on private balance sheets, and the end of restocking impede private demand from firing in the advanced economies, and second, whether the domestic demand in emerging economies, while robust in many, will compensate for weaker aggregate demand in the advanced economies.[7]

A crucial consideration, as noted above, is that the room for fiscal and monetary policy maneuvering in the advanced countries is now limited. A second round of quantitative easing (QE2) in the United States ignited a fierce debate about a return to currency wars and the perceived negative collateral damage to emerging economies as the money created spills over via the carry trade. One view is that such easing is more of an attempt to avoid a slide into deflation than to surreptitiously engineer a devaluation of the dollar; with monetary policy rates close to zero and a political impasse over further fiscal stimulus, this easing is the only available option.[8]

Estimates of potential output growth and output gaps for the United States and Euro Area reported by the IMF point to three conclusions: "(1) a sizable and persistent reduction in potential output relative to the precrisis trend; (2) substantial excess supply—that is, large negative output gaps—for both regions; and (3) considerable imprecision in the estimates, suggesting that the distribution of possible outcomes is a matter of substance for policymakers" (IMF 2010c, 29).[9]

The trend of decreasing output levels in advanced economies will have significant negative repercussions for fiscal revenues relative to the precrisis situation, with adverse consequences for public debt dynamics unless public expenditures are cut or taxes are increased. Capital and labor will need to be reallocated from declining to expanding sectors, posing major social challenges. This shift also means that the demand for consumer durables and investment-goods imports by advanced economies will be below precrisis trends during the transition. Emerging economies that rely heavily on such demand will have little choice but to augment domestic sources of demand to achieve growth rates similar to those that prevailed before the crisis.

All of these trends mean that, globally speaking, emerging economies will have a difficult time compensating fully for the fall in potential output and demand in the advanced economies. For developing Asia, where the large surpluses reside, the IMF forecasts an excessively high and unchanged savings rate of about 45 percent in 2012–15, with little change in investment ratios. In other words, global imbalances are likely to persist (IMF 2010c).

G-20 to the Rescue?

The G-20 envisages three kinds of policy responses in pursuit of global economic growth (G-20 2010):

- Policies that support *strong* growth by closing output and employment gaps and raising potential growth
- Policies that support *sustainable* growth by enabling sustainable public finances, prices, and financial stability; opening markets; and promoting social and environmental goals
- Policies that support *balanced* growth by reducing global imbalances and promoting international development.

Box 1.1 summarizes the challenges the G-20 faces in achieving these policy goals.

The IMF, which supports the G-20 Mutual Assessment Process, finds serious challenges to achieving the G-20's growth goals and is not encouraging.[10] The IMF (2010b, 6) report notes that although exchange rate adjustment is crucial for global rebalancing, "major surplus countries have intervened to limit appreciation."

Growth and unemployment projections in the G-20 country submissions are far more optimistic than what past recoveries suggest. Projected improvements in fiscal sustainability are based on optimistic growth and interest rate projections, posing serious risk should the global recovery stall. Surprisingly—and perhaps illustrating the controversial nature of

Box 1.1 Policy Challenges for the G-20

Fiscal Policy

Fiscal policy should aim to support recovery in the near term while ensuring sustainability over the medium term. Tax reform can boost supply and potential output by shifting the burden from factor income to consumption. Expenditure cuts and reforms focused on reining in pension liabilities, wages, and administrative costs are preferable to revenue increases while cutting deficits. The challenge is twofold: (a) design growth-friendly fiscal consolidation through suitable expenditure and tax reforms along the above lines, and (b) develop and announce credible medium-term consolidation programs to reduce macroeconomic uncertainty and associated risk premia.

Financial Sector Reform

Financial sector reform poses a huge challenge, involving first the resumption of bank credit, especially in the Euro Area, and second, the strengthening of prudential frameworks with a macro focus on systemic risk to complement the traditional focus on individual financial institutions. Nonbank institutions will need greater scrutiny and supervision, and the preferential tax treatment of debt may need to be eliminated to avoid a bias toward leverage. The Basel Committee on Banking Supervision has recommended increased equity in the capital structure of banks. Although this proposal could increase the cost of bank credit in the short run, it is expected to promote resilience in the long run.

Monetary and Exchange Rate Policies

The stance on monetary policy will vary from country to country depending upon the pace of the recovery and inflation pressures. Exchange rate adjustment among major economies has so far been insufficient to make a dent in global rebalancing, and the prospects do not look great. At the same time, the extraordinary monetary easing in some advanced countries has stimulated capital flows to emerging economies, adding to volatility and creating complications for monetary policy.

Structural Reforms

Structural reforms are needed to promote the flexibility and resilience of economies, thereby promoting growth that is

- *strong*, by raising growth potential through better resource allocation;
- *sustained*, by facilitating fiscal consolidation through faster growth and tax and expenditure reform, reducing inflationary pressure by eliminating supply bottlenecks; and
- *balanced*, by raising productivity and competitiveness in external-deficit countries and strengthening social safety nets to reduce excess household saving in external-surplus countries.

Policy Coordination

This is the heart of the matter. Coordination is needed for strong, sustained, and balanced growth through two rebalancing feats: (a) *internal rebalancing* in major advanced economies by strengthening private demand even as public support is withdrawn, and (b) *external rebalancing* to achieve a shift toward domestic demand in external-surplus countries and toward external demand in external-deficit countries. Exchange rate adjustment is a crucial and controversial component of the needed rebalancing.

the challenge—little external rebalancing is incorporated, with current account positions expected to widen.

Given the limited room for maneuvering in fiscal and monetary policy, structural reform is critical for sustained growth. But the IMF (2010b, 2) assessment notes that, in this context, "Major challenges remain to develop more ambitious and detailed reform agendas with specific roadmaps; to target deeper and broader product and labor market reforms that strengthen competition, or enhance flexibility in key market segments in advanced economies; and to boost infrastructure investment and strengthen social safety nets in emerging economies."

On the crucial topic of coordination, the IMF (2010b) posits three layers, taking into account the scope for policy maneuvering and the initial conditions:

- The *first layer* applies to emerging surplus countries, where boosting internal demand is urgently needed to compensate for the slowdown in the advanced economies. The policy menu includes stronger social safety nets, including pensions and health insurance; increased exchange rate flexibility to increase consumption and thereby shift global demand toward internal sources in these countries; and higher infrastructure spending in fast-growing economies, including oil exporters.

- The *second layer* involves fiscal adjustment in the advanced economies (particularly those with external deficits) to restore sound public finances and to achieve the G-20's own growth baseline. In the United States, for example, fiscal adjustment could be made growth-friendly through tax reform and by limiting the growth of public transfers. Sizable adjustments are called for, and in some cases (as in the United States), the adjustment may have to be back-loaded to avoid a slide into deflation. A crucial success factor is the preparation and announcement of credible, medium-term fiscal plans to instill confidence in the private sector and keep interest rate risk premia in check.

- The *third layer* consists of structural reforms across the G-20 aimed at gradually increasing employment and reversing the contractionary effects of the crisis on potential output to boost long-run growth. These include product and labor market reforms and would need to be tailored to individual country contexts and priorities.

In sum, the coordination challenge is daunting but necessary to ensure the steady recovery and the strong, sustained, and balanced growth the G-20 seeks. This goal depends not only on policy determination and coordination but also on changes in the global growth picture facing policy makers.

The Changing Landscape for Growth

It is rather difficult to move beyond the immediate reactions to the Great Recession because the severity of the shock has been so dramatic. The damage to household balance sheets in the United States, combined with the unprecedented stress inside the Euro Area, has meant that the ramifications of the current policy mix are relegated to a second order of importance.

Many developing countries were mercifully spared the worst of the initial shock because their financial sectors are too poorly developed to take on high-risk transactions. In addition, the normally precarious external environment was such that those countries tended to manage their macroeconomic policy more cautiously. For them, the other shoe has yet to drop.

The Lay of the Land

What can the changing landscape mean for medium-term growth in developing- and emerging-market economies? And can the past talk of delinking, multipolarity of growth, and the rise of Asia fundamentally alter their policy options?

At one basic level, the domestic policy imperatives remain the same—namely, to save more, invest better, and derive more value added from exports while increasing human and physical capital to raise long-term productivity. Those challenges remain, as ever, the basic task of development.

Still, although the Growth Commission's Supplemental Report (CGD 2009) left the essential recommendations of its 2008 Growth Report (CGD 2008) unchanged, the returns once expected from the export-oriented, outward-looking strategy may have declined. This is an important finding. It is revealing because countries have increasingly found that the standard prescriptions attached to the basic growth paradigm do entail variations, especially concerning the role of government in the development process. If the landscape has fundamentally changed, perhaps their policies need to adapt further as well.

The issue of policy formation revolves around a number of questions whose answers are not yet totally clear. How fundamentally, for example, has the economic landscape changed? Mohamed El-Erian (2009) describes a "new normal" in which fiscal imbalances and rising debt will take their toll and raise the cost of borrowing. Others point to the continuing rise of income inequality as a major threat to the open trading system and also cite the strong asymmetries between job creation and job destruction that drive global externalities of national policies (Leipziger, forthcoming; Spence 2011a; Stiglitz 2011).

According to Menzie Chinn, Barry Eichengreen, and Hiro Ito in chapter 2 of this volume, we can expect imbalances between China and the United States to reemerge. And in chapter 5, Philippe Aghion and Julia Cagé examine how the role of government in the production of innovation must fundamentally change as well. How might these new trends play themselves out?

On the side of fiscal imbalances, debt, and capital flows, there has been a short-run enthusiasm for emerging markets because of the abnormally low yields in the United States and the precarious state of the euro. This situation has prompted some countries, like Brazil, to impose ever-increasing capital import taxes. Still, the lure of an appreciating currency combined with excessively high domestic real interest rates makes Brazil appealing. But will this allure last when rates normalize in the Organisation for Economic Co-operation and Development (OECD) countries and when domestic debt must be financed and yields rise? If not, the new steady state facing emerging-market and developing economies (EMDEs) will be capital shortage, not capital surplus. The policy conclusion is that domestic resource mobilization efforts may need to be strengthened because international flows may be more selective and less inclined toward the short term. That EMDEs should be wary of volatile short-term flows is correct, and some have been proponents of the Chilean disincentives of the 1990s toward hot flows (Perry and Leipziger 1999); however, with large infrastructure needs and high social expenditures in many countries, capital may still be in short supply.

Related to capital flows and the need to maintain a competitive exchange rate without subsidizing exports (either explicitly or implicitly), there is the issue of how far to rely on exports as the growth engine. The economic environment that faced the Republic of Korea and original East Asian tigers served them well, and they in turn have benefited from the incredible growth performance of China. But what about this triangularity as it affects other, newer entrants into global markets, and how has the new landscape affected the trade prospects of EMDEs more generally?

China's rise has been unprecedented. Along with its dramatic export performance has come a new scale of demand for natural resources from poorer countries, and this is beneficial overall, although there are some legitimate questions surrounding the terms and conditions of Chinese foreign aid and natural resource contracts. But when will China relinquish its dominance of low-end manufactures and allow what William Cline (2010) referred to as the "adding-up problem" to absorb new producers? The answer: as soon as China can move up-market and capture further higher-value-added export markets.

This is where the problem becomes dicier, because developed economies, faced with an unprecedented combination of joblessness and offshoring (Blinder 2005, 2007, 2009), may not be politically able to maintain open markets for countries that run persistent imbalances while also subsidizing their exports. Hence emerges (a) the argument that poorer countries need open markets more than do emerging-market economies that can actively promote shifts to what Rodrik (2010) calls "modern tradables" to gain a foothold in global markets, and (b) the concern that poorer countries' turn in the queue may be jeopardized by China's ambitious export goals.

If what Chinn, Eichengreen, and Ito predict (in chapter 2 of this volume) is accurate about the lack of adjustment by the two great imbalancers (China and the United States), and if these persistent imbalances lead importers to push back trade openness, then the prospects for poorer developing countries may become the ultimate casualty. All this may then lead to a change in the prevailing growth paradigm, as Rodrik (2011) has highlighted, and to a reconsideration of more domestically led growth strategies (Lin 2010).

Paradigm Shifts

The growth and development paradigm has been debated for decades. The "Growth in the 1990s" project at the World Bank was, in a sense, a compilation of evidence to support the beyond-the-Washington-consensus view of development policy (World Bank 2005). That bold and heterodox view was an accurate description of the 1990s. The subsequent decade was truncated, for policy purposes, by the continuing crisis in 2008–10, but the first 7.5 years of the decade were a bonanza. Low interest rates enabled cheap borrowing. Massively increasing trade volumes allowed not only China but also other economies in East and South Asia to capture market shares, and even Latin America improved its performance. In Sub-Saharan Africa, one-third of the continent's economies managed for the first time to grow at rates surpassing 5 percent in real terms, a truly remarkable performance (Gelb, Ramachandran, and Turner 2007). However, all this growth was based on the prevailing paradigm of relatively open global markets, access to credit, and few shocks.

The benign external environment started to change in 2007 with the higher fuel prices and then higher food prices, both of which the international community was ill-equipped to manage. These shocks were not paradigm changers, however. The Great Recession of 2007–09 revealed that the global economy was even less able to manage a systemic shock that simultaneously affected (a) *financial markets*; (b) *housing markets* in the major economy, accounting for 25 percent of global gross national product and a large part of global demand; and (c) *equity markets* that relied on housing, exports, and banking for their success.

Trade finance was among the first lines cut in the crisis, not because of its risk but because it was the easiest way to conserve liquidity. The global community lacked an adequate response, although the World Bank Group's International Finance Corporation and some export credit agencies attempted to stem the tide. But this abrupt financial retrenchment made trade an early casualty of the crisis. As a result, developing countries were forced to dig into their own reserves to provide credit, not only for trade finance but also subsequently for rollover of normal debt that businesses had assumed was available. Even some central banks had to seek additional funds, and the U.S. Federal Reserve loaned funds to Brazil, Korea, and Mexico—all of which had already been holding larger than "normal" levels of reserves. Reliance on external capital became a liability, even for the innocent.

As a consequence, many emerging markets began providing more domestic credit through state banks and entities. This was a model previously associated with East Asia, but it is now practiced to a larger extent in Brazil, India, and elsewhere. State financing was no longer a dirty word. That said, the increase in government-led financing by entities such as the Brazilian Development Bank (BNDES) increased dramatically and, some would argue, irreversibly during the crisis (Parra-Bernal and Alves 2010).

Along with state financing come allocation decisions that go beyond creditworthiness and stray into the realm of another sometimes dirty word: "industrial policy." To be fair, economists like Dani Rodrik (2008) had previously debunked the notion that governments would have no role in resources allocation. Indeed, the Growth Report of the Commission on Growth and Development was clear that government's role was not only indispensable but also strongly positive in the highly successful, fast-growing economies on which the commission had focused (CGD 2008).

Exporting countries also realized that they needed to accelerate diversification. Some major export powers, such as Korea, had already made the shift and had made China the major new market segment. However, with China's growth persevering during the crisis while most of the OECD economies faltered, these diversification efforts became more urgent.

The strategic aspect of this shifting focus is dramatic because China's import demand is largely for unfinished products, and even its foreign direct investment entails the employment of Chinese labor that is sent to the exporting country. Thus, in terms of competitive advantage, developing countries relying on the China market are, in a way, mortgaging their own development because their factor endowments more closely resemble China's than they do those of the OECD economies.

This fact plus the lower risk appetites of capital-surplus countries emerging from banking and financial crises has led some analysts to shed further light on the views of Rodrik and Subramanian (2009), who say the paradigm shift entails a great need for countries to create domestic demand to fuel their growth aspirations. Combined with Rodrik's (2011) view that countries cannot simultaneously satisfy democratic principles, national social commitments, and globalization obligations, the world is unfortunately left with a multilateral system under considerable stress and with few champions for globalization (Leipziger 2011).

Forging the Link between Medium- and Long-Term Growth

It is as incorrect to assume that all is already written in stone that the global economy will be "mean reverting." If the crisis has taught one lesson, it is that when fundamental shifts occur, the outcomes will entail new elements that shape future directions and affect policy choices. Given higher debt service costs in the medium term—inevitable in light of not only crisis management but also, more notably, demographic shifts and social policy requirements (see Cottarelli and Keen in chapter 3 of this volume)—risk capital will be scarcer. This shortage has implications for inherently risky projects in developing countries: namely, self-financing may become a necessity rather than merely an option.

To increase financing for infrastructure in particular, countries will need to use resources more efficiently and reduce leaks (see Estache in chapter 4). Consequently, they will be increasing the government share of project finance and will need increased official development assistance for growth-producing activities. These changes will have implications for donors, who often prefer soft expenditures that command domestic support in rich country capitals, but are not the highest-return uses for scarce capital. To make social expenditures sustainable, countries need growth—hard-core economic growth that can create employment and income opportunities.

Joblessness, in the United States in particular, will persist over the medium term given the long recovery period forecast by the IMF (2010c) and also seen in the historical work of Reinhart and Rogoff (2008, 2009, 2010), although historical trends may underestimate the magnitude of the current, once-in-a-century crisis. If true, the added delay in job recovery will make offshoring and the exporting of jobs a major political liability, and even the most-open economies, such as the United States, may resort to forms of industrial policy that they had, up to this time, eschewed.

Faced with low-value-added markets in China (where middle-class demand will take a decade to emerge) and less-welcoming OECD markets, EMDEs may need to be more self-reliant. The risk of this approach, of course, is that countries will also resort to implicit forms of protection that are unwarranted and will not subject their producers to the efficiency rigors of the market—an unfortunate result that would ignore the lessons of economic history.

At the same time, new opportunities may need nurturing, and whether in the information and communication technology (ICT) area (see Mann in chapter 7) or through technological innovation (see Aghion and Cagé in chapter 5), government policy may emerge as vitally important to move growth rates back toward their previous levels. With the medium-term outlook depressed—namely, with Japan and the United States considerably below their potential output levels for years—others will need to pick up the slack. And in so doing, if successful, EMDEs may become more like China as new growth drivers. Such a positive outcome requires action not only by developing countries but also, notably, by some major emerging-market economies that need to become custodians, along with the OECD-member countries, of global institutions and global rules (Leipziger 2011).

As Leipziger and O'Boyle (2009) noted, major new economic players hoping to quickly join the OECD ranks will increasingly see it in their self-interest to foster more-rapid convergence, not through the decline of the existing global powers, but by growing faster in a growth-conducive environment. That environment requires greater commitment from the new economic powers. A rapidly declining U.S. economy serves no one's interests, for example, and a too-rapid takeover of European markets by East Asia will leave a large part of the global market depressed (Leipziger 2010a).

Therefore, the longer-term outlook for EMDEs depends largely on how the medium term is handled. Paradigm shifts are inevitable, but unless they are accompanied by renewed attention to multilateralism, the road ahead will be much tougher for all concerned.

Contributions of This Volume

The volume raises some key issues facing the global economy during the coming decade. The synopses below provide a brief snapshot of those issues while allowing the subsequent chapters of this volume to speak for themselves.

Part I: Diagnosing the Challenges

The first part of this volume includes three diagnostic chapters examining crucial elements of the post-Great Recession growth challenge.

Chapter 2: Rebalancing Global Growth. Menzie Chinn, Barry Eichengreen, and Hiro Ito examine how quickly global imbalances can be reduced as a basis for sustainable and stronger global growth. They make a key point: that it was not current account imbalances per se but the capital inflows into the United States that magnified the problem by destabilizing the banking sector and the financial system more generally.

One school of thought is that the imbalance—captured, to a large extent, by the U.S.-China bilateral current account—will tend to automatically and permanently shrink because private consumption is 70 percent of U.S. GDP, a figure that will perforce decline as households increase savings to help heal their balance sheets. But the authors argue that the real depreciation of the U.S. dollar required to halve the country's current account deficit is unlikely to happen unless (a) the United States loses its luster as a safe haven (so capital inflows subside) or (b) there is a large increase in aggregate demand in the rest of the world, China in particular.

The authors use annual data on 23 industrial and 86 developing countries over 1970–2008 to estimate a simple model determining current account balances, national saving, and investment. The estimated relationships are used to project current account balances over 2011–15. For the United States, the results suggest little movement in favor of rebalancing—consistent with the idea that the United States' special status as the issuer of the international reserve currency enables it to run larger current account deficits.

So what can be done to insulate growth from the pernicious effects of only slowly declining current account imbalances combined with capital flows searching for yield? The authors focus on several venues for action:

- *Financial regulation.* Regulatory reform, including countercyclical macroprudential regulation, is vital to prevent a repeat of events such as the subprime crisis, the authors contend. In particular, they emphasize that national-level financial reform is not enough; cross-boundary coordination is needed to deal with big financial conglomerates and regulatory arbitrage.
- *Central bank policy.* These banks may have to take more explicit account of imbalances and asset prices in formulating monetary policy and minimizing threats to growth.

- *Fiscal policy.* When current account deficits grow and capital flows in, countries may need to tighten fiscal policy proactively to help prevent financial vulnerability and threats to growth. For advanced economies, the authors recommend that fiscal policy target a cyclically adjusted budget balance of close to zero, including contingent liabilities from guarantees.
- *Cross-border coordination.* Because global imbalances will atrophy only slowly on their own, countries must coordinate actions—with Germany and China urged to run higher fiscal deficits, and countries with large deficits or uncertain financing urged to consolidate. Such coordination would support global aggregate demand as imbalances slowly shrink. Greater currency flexibility in China would speed things up as part of a broader package.
- *International financial architecture.* Changes that increase emerging markets' access to emergency financing through pooled reserve arrangements, bilateral swap lines, or quick-disbursing monies from a special facility at the IMF would be a plus—reducing the pressure for self-insurance and ideally tilting policies away from the dogged pursuit of high current account surpluses.

Chapter 3: Fiscal Policy and Growth. Carlo Cottarelli and Michael Keen grapple with the fiscal and public-debt consequences of the Great Recession. In addition to spelling out the new fiscal reality, they discuss how to make the imperative reduction of public indebtedness as "growth-friendly" as possible. Infrastructure investment, in particular, can bolster aggregate demand, while serving as a critical complement to private investment.

The pressing question of how to adjust fiscal policy while maximizing the positive benefits for growth has no easy solution. As the authors point out, the fiscal fallout from the global crisis presents daunting challenges, both for restoring fiscal sustainability and for creating the best possible climate for private investment and faster growth while doing so.

The Great Recession led to a fiscal deterioration and rise in government indebtedness worldwide because of slowing growth and rising deficits linked to falling revenues, automatic stabilizers, and discretionary spending to boost aggregate demand. The most dramatic effect has occurred in the advanced economies. The policy response should not merely aim to compensate for the setbacks associated with the global crisis but should also take into account the profound challenges posed by aging, climate change, and globalization. The authors' analysis and recommendations fall into two categories: (a) macroeconomic, concerning public indebtedness and its dynamics; and (b) microeconomic, concerning the intricacies of tax policy and expenditure composition.

Although fiscal deficits in advanced economies were not exactly out of control ahead of the crisis, there was an insufficient attempt to run surpluses during the precrisis, high-growth period—something that prudence would have dictated, given the adverse demographics of aging populations. Besides, public debt had reached unprecedented peacetime levels by 2007 in the three largest advanced economies: Germany, Japan, and the United States.

The situation worsened with the advent of the crisis, during which deficits increased because of revenue shortfalls and automatic stabilizers, even without the countercyclical stimulus packages considered. As a result, general government gross debt in the advanced economies rose from a little over 70 percent of GDP in 2007 to 100 percent by 2010, and the level is projected to reach 115 percent by 2015. This debt level could get even worse because of higher interest costs in the postcrisis period, of course, or if losses from the financial sector mount. The authors highlight this important factor: the crisis caused a large, long-lasting loss in output, especially in advanced economies.

Public indebtedness, especially in advanced economies, is already so high that merely stabilizing it may have highly negative consequences for potential growth. Lowering indebtedness to thresholds that empirical studies indicate are "safe," from the growth perspective, would take a Herculean effort. The authors calculate that reducing public debt in advanced and emerging economies to 60 percent and 40 percent of GDP, respectively, by 2030 would involve a staggering increase in cyclically adjusted primary fiscal surpluses—by 8.25 percentage points of GDP for advanced economies and by 3 percentage points for emerging economies during 2011–20, with the primary surplus then kept at this level until 2030. The big question then is whether an adjustment of this magnitude will not itself have adverse consequences for growth because of the aggregate demand effects.[11]

Cottarelli and Keen conclude with a broad review of expenditure reforms (for example, regarding welfare programs, infrastructure, and innovation spending, the latter of which can potentially aid growth prospects) as well as subsidies and tax expenditures, which can harm the growth outlook. The authors also offer specific recommendations about smarter taxation. Given the bleak fiscal picture and the need for some public spending that is pro-growth, there is much to be gleaned from these tax reforms.

Chapter 4: Infrastructure Policy for Shared Growth. How will the crisis affect the financing of infrastructure and the relative roles of the public and private sectors? Antonio Estache revisits these questions, which have profound implications for the productivity of private investment and fiscal accounts.

The infrastructure sector attracted attention as a quick fix during the global crisis. In G-20 countries, for instance, infrastructure accounted for 20–30 percent of the average fiscal stimulus package. Policy makers and politicians have glommed on to the idea that publicly financed infrastructure projects might be the silver bullet to create jobs and keep up aggregate demand.

Not so fast, Estache reminds us. First, well-executed infrastructure projects take a long time to put together. Second, their job effects may take a long time to materialize. Third, the long-run fiscal implications are likely to be serious, with operating and maintenance costs—often conveniently ignored when infrastructure investments are proposed to keep the economy going—being a sizable part of the capital expenditures themselves.

Estache uses the global crisis as an opportunity to take a hard look at developments in infrastructure. His key point is that although the financial sector and its regulation have received most of the attention in the aftermath of the global crisis, infrastructure (which accounts for 12–18 percent of GDP) warrants a similar level of scrutiny. Policy makers tend to focus on what they perceive as the growth and jobs benefits of infrastructure, paying little heed to the rents extracted by construction firms, bankers, and operators—the burden of which ultimately falls on taxpayers. The importance of tightening regulation and the management of the public role in infrastructure is reinforced by three observations:

- The crisis is not likely to have a major impact on the demand trend for infrastructure in either the developing or developed world.

- Private finance for infrastructure is likely to witness a sharp retrenchment because of the deterioration in its risk-return calculus.[12]
- The political economy of infrastructure has been undergoing sharp shifts, with the burden of infrastructure shifting back to current and future taxpayers.

Estache cautions that the issues will not be easy to deal with. Regulation must restore balance among the key stakeholders—namely, operators, users, and taxpayers. So far, investors and operators have been the big winners, and there has been increasing political reluctance to get users to pay fully.

The first step, Estache contends, is to reduce costs through greater transparency and better procurement. Given the long-term nature of the assets involved, restoring planning to anticipate fiscal effects is paramount. Second, public-private partnerships should not be used to circumvent fiscal constraints. Third, a harder line must be taken against the tendency to let large infrastructure operators renegotiate contracts to permit an increase in tariffs or subsidies—which Estache identifies as the infrastructure analogy of the "too big to fail" feature of the financial sector. And, fourth, guarantees have to be carefully designed to limit fiscal risks.

The chapter concludes with a discussion of two upcoming challenges: (a) the greening of infrastructure, especially in the energy and transport sectors; and (b) the growing role of infrastructure in regional integration efforts around the world. The first challenge will call for policy and regulatory coherence across finance, infrastructure, and environment ministries as well as appropriate demand management through prices (because the existing infrastructure stock will last for a long time). The second challenge, a topic of interest not just in Europe but also in Africa, involves immense issues going beyond the creation of regional markets and extending to coordination of policies, including regulation.

Part II: The Way Forward

Having diagnosed the challenges to restoring high rates of growth, this volume proceeds in the second part to provide some insights into the way forward.

Chapter 5: Rethinking Growth and the State. Against the challenges of global imbalances, deteriorating fiscal and public-debt situations, vast infrastructure needs (exacerbated by greening and regional integration challenges), and tightening global credit constraints, what should governments do? No one will seriously challenge the idea that regulation, whether in finance or infrastructure, is a fundamental government role that, if anything, needs strengthening. Philippe Aghion and Julia Cagé argue that the issue is not so much *size* but *smarts* when it comes to defining the government's role, especially against the backdrop of the global crisis.

The authors examine the need to redefine and sharpen the role of the government in two particular areas: (a) *as an investor in the knowledge economy*, a critical underpinning to faster growth; and (b) *as a guarantor of the social contract* at a time when coping with the social costs of the crisis and creating jobs must go in tandem with reducing indebtedness. In these areas, the authors contend, government intervention could spur innovation and growth if the state is noncorrupt and trustworthy.

Aghion and Cagé consider the following aspects of the state's policy role in knowledge investment:

- *Education funding.* Countries closer to the technological frontier will benefit from increased research funding, provided universities are autonomous and grants are awarded competitively.
- *Worker retraining.* State subsidies are likely to be needed to retrain workers in firms far from the technological frontier as part of a broader strategy of *liberalization* of trade or entry, the potential losers of which include workers who need retraining from labor-shedding firms with little incentive to act on their own.
- *R&D spending.* Over the business cycle, research and development (R&D) is critical to firms' long-run growth, but difficult to maintain during downturns, when firms are credit-constrained. Public support for R&D could be a useful approach to macroeconomic stabilization through countercyclical fiscal policies that shore up aggregate demand.
- *Climate-related innovation.* Climate change presents a particular challenge for the state. The authors suggest a two-pronged approach: carbon pricing to discourage dirty technology, combined with subsidies to simultaneously encourage clean innovation. The basic argument is that heavy path dependence in innovation makes it difficult to break free from the stock of dirty technology, where the expected profits

from innovation are highest. In this case, a laissez-faire approach is not the right policy.

- *Industrial policy.* The authors advocate competition-compatible industrial policy, arguing that industrial policy need not be opposed to competition policy. For example, it could be designed in the form of targeted subsidies to several firms in a given sector instead of picking individual winners. Such targeting of sectors could spur innovation as firms within the sector compete with each other, leading to higher productivity and spurring new product creation, as confirmed by a study using Chinese firm-level data.

The state's role in guaranteeing the social contract in the aftermath of the crisis has acquired new significance because of the need to restore sustainability to public finances while maintaining social peace until the global economy returns to normal, which might take a long time. The authors explore the following aspects of the state as guarantor of the social contract:

- *Investment in trust.* Empirical studies show that trust exerts a causal effect on growth by striking an appropriate balance in regulation and encouraging the emergence of social actors and collective negotiations with labor unions. Distrust increases the demand for regulation, which in turn hurts economic growth.
- *Redistribution while cutting fiscal deficits.* This effort brings with it many additional benefits, such as promoting trust and encouraging innovation and risk taking. The authors present strong evidence from OECD countries that low-corruption countries, as measured by the *International Country Risk Guide*, exhibit a positive relationship between GDP growth and the top marginal rate of corporate taxation.

In short, Aghion and Cagé argue that the role of the state needs to be rethought beyond the regulation of the financial sector. The state can spur innovation and growth by investing in knowledge and earning the trust of the people to efficiently guarantee the social contract.

Chapter 6: Financial Shocks and the Labor Markets. One of the most politically sensitive issues is what to do about the socially wrenching unemployment effects of the global crisis, exacerbated by the fact that the unemployment consequences of the Great Recession have been far more severe than those of other recessions. Tito Boeri and Pietro Garibaldi take up this question in chapter 6.

The authors provide a *tour d'horizon* of the policy questions involved. As one would expect, there are sharp differences between the United States and Europe. In the United States, unemployment virtually doubled from peak to trough within a few quarters and is receding only very slowly. Unemployment rates changed much less in Europe, but there is considerable heterogeneity across countries. Part of the difference is explicable by differences in labor market institutions, but the major impact is clearly related to the disruptions in the financial sector, where the global crisis originated. A widely documented credit crunch persisted well into 2009 on both sides of the Atlantic, and this likely played a major role in labor market outcomes.

Boeri and Garibaldi capture changes in unemployment over the business cycle as linked to output changes by calculating Okun's elasticity while differentiating between recessions linked to financial crises versus other causes. They find that unemployment has responded much more strongly to the output decline associated with the Great Recession than during earlier contractionary periods. To capture interactions between the financial sector and labor market, the authors undertake empirics that find that financial crises lead to the largest impact of changes in output on employment.

The authors focus on two channels whereby financial distress can be transmitted to the labor market: the *job destruction* effect and the *labor mobility* effect. The first effect gets exerted when leveraged firms face a credit crunch and lay off workers, destroying jobs—an effect that operates through the *demand* for labor. The second effect occurs when workers who need to move to new jobs or respond to a new spatial allocation of jobs following a crisis find that they are stuck because of financial constraints (such as mortgages)—an effect transmitted through the *supply* of labor. Empirical evidence confirms both effects: conditional on a financial shock, the more-leveraged sectors display larger employment-output elasticities ("volatility"), and micro survey data indicate that workers with mortgages find it more difficult to move to job opportunities elsewhere.

Against this background, the authors ask whether, in the context of the Great Recession, financial institutions or jobs should be saved. The usual answer is that saving jobs might require saving financial institutions first. But so far, in spite of the vast sums spent to bail out and shore up the financial sector, unemployment remains high, and there is a risk that the Great Recession may translate into a much bigger structural unemployment pool; in fact, some 30 million workers in G-20 countries have fallen into unemployment as a consequence of the global crisis. The employment losses have not only been much larger than anticipated, based on past estimates of Okun's elasticity, but have also been bigger in more-leveraged sectors.

The authors favor policies that focus on saving financial institutions because of their systemic significance, the difficulty in deciding which sectors to pick for saving jobs, and the standard moral hazard arguments, which might predispose firms to build up leverage in anticipation of being helped. Going forward, they advocate a strong focus on job-creating competition policy and easing barriers to entry based on the compelling evidence that the lion's share of net job creation is in startup firms.

Chapter 7: Information Technology, Globalization, and Growth. Chapters 7 and 8 delve into a particular aspect of the knowledge economy: how information technology (IT) can be used to boost a given country's growth prospects.

Every so often, a transformative technology comes along that radically alters the way things are done, thus raising productivity and growth: for example, the steam engine, automobile, airplane and, in our age, IT. In contrast to the gloom attending the medium-term policy challenges posed by the global crisis, Catherine Mann in chapter 7 discusses the opportunities for economic growth created by IT.

What are the links to growth? The standard channel through which IT would increase growth rates is its positive impact on total factor productivity (TFP) growth as a result of innovation. Given the special features of IT, Mann applies a concept called social surplus (an extension of the notion of consumer surplus) to calculate the overall economic gains from the falling prices associated with an innovation. Social surplus attempts to capture the gains from intermediate inputs and production in addition to the benefits to the final consumer.

From a policy angle, three key variables influence economic welfare and growth: terms of trade, economies of scale, and variety. The secular fall in the quality-adjusted prices of IT products (and hence, a potential decline in the terms of trade) would tend to favor consumers and importers, but the terms of trade are not so easy to measure because of the fragmentation of IT production along a global supply chain. At the same time, economies of scale combined with the ability to import inputs (which also benefit from scale economies) could benefit exporting countries. Variety could result in considerable growth benefits to the extent that it is positively related to prices and profits.

Mann then turns to the empirical evidence. A striking finding is that TFP growth in ICT-*using* industries tends to be far higher than in ICT-*producing* industries. A likely channel applicable particularly to services is that the ICT-enabled networking, backward to suppliers and forward to customers, has led to significant cost reductions. But there is considerable variation across countries driven by the standard correlates of growth: institutions, human capital, flexible labor markets, and product market competition.

Businesses must have an incentive to do existing things much better as a result of ICT, and this is where the real benefits lie. For developing countries in particular, large investments in human capital are likely to be needed to capitalize on ICT as a source of productivity and growth. Variety also helps, by increasing the chances that firms find good matches for their needs. On the policy front, a good strategy for a developing country might be to start off by joining the global supply chain and eventually create better conditions for using IT at home, which is where the growth potential of IT lies.

Chapter 8: Innovation-Driven Growth. Paolo Guerrieri and Pier Carlo Padoan expand on the theme of IT-related growth in the context of pursuing "new sources of growth" in the postcrisis world. Their quest is motivated by explaining—and remedying—the slowdown in growth in the Euro Area relative to the United States after 1995, until which it was rapidly catching up with the United States. They ascribe the slowdown to the relative neglect of innovation in Europe. Although the idea that innovation and productivity drive growth is not new, Guerrieri and Padoan argue that the process of innovation itself has undergone fundamental change because of the Internet. They present results from a simulation model to define a corrective policy package for Europe.

The need for new growth sources is urgent because both potential output and growth will be heavily weighed down by structural unemployment and loss of skills, reduced investment as a consequence of rising risk aversion, and higher real interest rates and adverse effects on TFP as companies close and knowledge is lost.

One thing is clear: innovation must be a key component of the new growth strategy—which in itself is not a novel idea. What *is* novel is that the process of innovation is undergoing radical change through open innovation, global innovation chains, and the facilitating role of new technology platforms such as the Internet. The authors highlight those features of the new innovation process, which have also contributed to greater tradability of services.

The authors illustrate the power of the new innovation process to propel growth by applying their ideas to Europe. After World War II and until the early 1990s, Europe displayed strong catch-up growth relative to the United States, but it has since stagnated. For example, per capita GDP growth in Europe over 1996–2005 was only 1.8 percent in the Euro Area compared with 2.3 percent in the United States. The relative European slowdown can be largely explained by slower growth in labor productivity (GDP per hour worked) compared with the United States. A particular source of concern has been the observation that TFP growth has steadily declined in Europe since the 1970s, with TFP growth over 1995–2005 just half the prevailing rate during the 1980s and 1990s. In contrast, TFP growth in the United States accelerated since 1995 to twice that of the Euro Area.

What could explain this slowdown in Europe? The slow pace of structural reform relative to the United States in areas such as labor markets, competition policy, and taxes is an obvious candidate. However, studies show that the main factor may be the inability to exploit the "new economy" linked to ICT diffusion. In fact, OECD data show that during 1996–2006, more than two-thirds of productivity growth in the advanced economies came from innovation and related investment in intangible assets. Besides, much of the innovation in the United States was in service areas such as retail distribution, transport, construction, and financial and professional services, and this accounts for the bulk of the difference between the United States and the Euro Area.[13]

Guerrieri and Padoan's analysis concludes with these main findings:

- An increase in human capital operating through technology has a bigger impact on GDP than deregulation, which operates through a positive impact on services (but note that service sector liberalization is crucial for catching up with the United States).
- Although a decrease in regulation and an increase in harmonization of regulation (meaning greater integration) have similar effects, harmonization has a bigger beneficial impact on services (especially imported services), while technology benefits more from deregulation.
- The ultimate driver of growth is technology accumulation, and this is strongly supported by human capital accumulation.
- Delay in implementing policy change will be costly for productivity and growth.

Economic Regrowth Depends on Policy Choices

The Great Recession of 2007–09 was not simply a severe business cycle slowdown or even a combined collapse in credit, housing, and asset markets of the kind described by Claessens, Kose, and Terrones (2008). The global economy's preceding boom, though unbalanced and eventually unsustainable, also revealed deep structural changes in the global economic dynamic and these are irreversible.

Thanks to improved policies in much of the developing world and the corresponding opening of avenues toward convergence with advanced economies, the former acquired increasing weight and relevance. There is ground for a reasoned optimism regarding the maintenance of such policies and thus for the continuation of those changes in the future (Canuto and Giugale 2010).

At the same time, as mentioned by Leipziger and O'Boyle (2009), the emergence of the "New Economic Powers" also entails some risks if the NEPs are inclined to seek convergence through high growth rates without incrementally taking on new responsibilities for maintenance of the system. Spence (2011b) argues persuasively that there is a new path of convergence between emerging and advanced countries, and if he is correct, the path of global reform will surely need to be accelerated and the distribution of responsibilities reexamined in earnest.

On the other hand, as noted before, nothing is already written in stone. The global economy will not be "mean reverting." And when fundamental shifts occur, the outcomes will entail some new elements that will shape future directions and affect policy choices. The responses to those policy choices will largely determine the future face of globalization.

Of course, one may speculate. Perhaps there will be a bifurcation of possible scenarios ahead: The first is a path by which advanced economies reacquire the ability to grow, there is a simultaneous global rebalancing of demand and supply, and global growth can facilitate rather than hamper necessary structural change. The second is a path by which the global economy remains trapped in a suboptimal trajectory, considerably below potential output, with the attendant strains in terms of political economy that make convergence more disorderly.

We humbly hope the contributions in this volume might help to avoid policies conducive to the latter scenario and rather encourage the former. After all, even more-rapid convergence can have multiple paths, each with its own implication for global welfare.

Notes

1. Leipziger (2010b) draws out some early trends and inflection points of the current debate around globalization but acknowledges that much is yet to be determined depending on the emerging international economic environment and the degree to which nations see it in their interests to cooperate, even in tough times.
2. Canuto (2010) posits several sources of "autonomous growth" in developing countries, through which many developing economies will be able to keep growing even if advanced economies remain trapped in their current doldrums. As time passes, he sees a switchover of global locomotives taking place. However, a growth differential between developing and advanced economies may still emerge with higher or lower global growth rates, depending on the growth pace of the latter.
3. See, for example, IMF (2010c, 35), which asserts that "fiscal consolidation needs to start in 2011," as well as the supporting arguments in favor of medium-run consolidation.
4. See Canuto and Giugale (2010) for a three- to five-year perspective.
5. Former IMF Managing Director Dominique Strauss-Kahn stated, during a February 2011 panel discussion at the IMF in Washington, D.C., "Global imbal-

ances are back, and issues that worried us before the crisis—large and volatile capital flows, exchange rate pressures, rapidly growing excess reserves—are on the front burner once again" (IMF 2011).

6. Presumably, the effects would be even more adverse if interest rates rise.

7. As developing countries tap "autonomous" sources of growth, they may keep growth at rates comparable with those prevailing before the crisis and thereby partially rescue advanced economies from their low-growth trends (Canuto 2010). There are limits to this phenomenon, however, given that a rebalancing of global demand and supply happens gradually, and interdependencies still exist even in a more multipolar economic world.

8. William Dudley (2010) recently stated, "Currently, my assessment is that both the current levels of unemployment and inflation and the time frame over which they are likely to return to levels consistent with our mandate are unacceptable. I conclude that further action is likely to be warranted unless the economic outlook evolves in a way that makes me more confident that we will see better outcomes for both employment and inflation before too long." About QE 2, see also Brahmbhatt, Canuto, and Ghosh (2010).

9. The World Bank's "Global Economic Prospects 2011" report also points out several persistent tensions and pitfalls in the global economy, which in the short run could derail the recovery to varying degrees (World Bank 2011).

10. A full-fledged framework for such a peer process is still far from a reality and, as World Bank President Robert Zoellick (2009) said early on, "Peer review of a new Framework for Strong, Sustainable, and Balanced Growth agreed at [the Pittsburgh] G-20 Summit is a good start, but it will require a new level of international cooperation and coordination, including a new willingness to take the findings of global monitoring seriously. Peer review will need to be peer pressure."

11. Some literature argues that fiscal adjustments can be growth-enhancing through the familiar channels of lower real interest rates, reduced uncertainty about future tax rates, and so on. At the same time, fiscal consolidation based on spending cuts, especially current spending, tends to be less contractionary than tax-based adjustments. This suggests that the nature of the fiscal adjustment could be extremely important, although one should recognize the special circumstances associated with the Great Recession: for instance, that real interest rates are already low.

12. For example, in 2009, the S&P 500 Utilities Index and S&P Global Infrastructure Index showed a 25 percent return compared with the 38 percent return for global equities measured by the S&P Global Broad Market Index (BMI). At the same time, costs of bonds and fees associated with public-private partnerships have almost doubled, raising the cost of capital for that sector. Owing to lags, the full impact of the likely pullback by the private sector will be felt only in 2011 and after.

13. It might be worth cautioning, however, that in some areas such as finance, innovation stayed ahead of regulation with disastrous consequences.

References

Blinder, Alan S. 2005. "Fear of Offshoring." Working Paper 119, Center for Economic Policy Studies, Princeton University, Princeton, NJ.

———. 2007. "How Many U.S. Jobs Might Be Offshorable?" Working Paper 142, Center for Policy Studies, Princeton University, Princeton, NJ.

———. 2009. "Offshoring: Big Deal, or Business as Usual?" In *Offshoring of American Jobs: What Response from U.S. Economic Policy?*, ed. Jagdish Bhagwati and Alan S. Blinder, 19–60. Cambridge, MA: MIT Press.

Brahmbhatt, Milan, Otaviano Canuto, and Swati Ghosh. 2010. "Currency Wars Yesterday and Today." *Economic Premise* 43, World Bank, Washington, DC. http://siteresources.worldbank.org/EXTPREMNET/Resources/EP43.pdf.

Canuto, Otaviano. 2010. "Toward a Switchover of Locomotives in the Global Economy." *Economic Premise* 33, World Bank, Washington, DC. http://siteresources.worldbank.org/INTPREMNET/Resources/EP33.pdf.

Canuto, Otaviano, and Marcelo Giugale, eds. 2010. *The Day after Tomorrow: A Handbook on the Future of Economic Policy in the Developing World.* Washington, DC: World Bank.

CGD (Commission on Growth and Development). 2008. "The Growth Report: Strategies for Sustained Growth and Inclusive Development." CGD, Washington, DC.

———. 2009. "Special Report: Post-Crisis Growth in Developing Countries." CGD, Washington, DC.

Claessens, Stijn, M. Ayhan Kose, and Marco E. Terrones. 2008. "What Happens during Recessions, Crunches, and Busts?" Working Paper 08/274, International Monetary Fund, Washington, DC.

Cline, William R. 2010. "Exports of Manufactures and Economic Growth: Fallacy of Composition Revisited." Working Paper 36, Commission on Growth and Development, Washington, DC.

Dudley, William C. 2010. "The Outlook, Policy Choices, and Our Mandate." Speech at City University of New York, October 1.

El-Erian, Mohamed A. 2009. "Europe's Adjustment to a New Normal." Pimco.com article, Pacific Investment Management Co. (PIMCO), Newport Beach, CA.

Gelb, Alan, Vijaya Ramachandran, and Ginger Turner. 2007." Stimulating Growth and Investment in Africa: From Macro to Micro Reforms." *African Development Review* 19 (1): 26–51.

G-20 (Group of 20 Finance Ministers and Central Bank Governors). 2010. "Seoul Summit Document: Framework for Strong, Sustainable and Balanced Growth." G-20 Seoul Summit, November 12. http://www.economicsummits.info/2010/11/seoul-summit-document.

Hausmann, Ricardo, and Dani Rodrik. 2003. "Economic Development as Self-Discovery." *Journal of Development Economics* 72 (2): 603–33.

IMF (International Monetary Fund). 2010a. "Global Financial Stability Report." October 2010, IMF, Washington, DC.

————. 2010b. "G-20 Mutual Assessment Process—IMF Staff Assessment of G-20 Policies." Report for the G-20 Summit of Leaders, Seoul, November 11–12, IMF, Washington, DC.

————. 2010c. *World Economic Outlook October 2010: Recovery, Risk, and Rebalancing.* Washington, DC: IMF.

————. 2011. "IMF Managing Director Dominique Strauss-Kahn Calls for Strengthening the International Monetary System." Press Release 11/36, February 10. http://www.imf.org/external/np/sec/pr/2011/pr1136.htm.

Leipziger, Danny M. 2010a. "The Global Growth Outlook: Does Pessimism Dominate?" *Economic Viewpoint* 23, George Washington University School of Business, Washington, DC. http://business.gwu.edu/files/economic-viewpoint-23.pdf.

————. 2010b. "Globalization Revisited." In *Globalization and Growth: Implications for a Post-Crisis World*, ed. Michael Spence and Danny M. Leipziger, 3–33.- Washington, DC: Commission on Growth and Development.

————. Forthcoming. "The Distributional Consequences of the Economic and Financial Crisis of 2008–2009." In *Unequal Losers*, ed. Ambar Narayan and Carolina Sanchez-Paramo. Washington, DC: World Bank.

————. Forthcoming 2011. "Multilateralism, the Shifting Global Economic Order, and Development Policy." *Canadian Development Report*. North-South Institute, Ottawa, Canada.

Leipziger, Danny M., and William O'Boyle. 2009. "The New Economic Powers (NEPs): Leadership Opportunities Post-Crisis." *World Economics* 10 (3): 43–79.

Lin, Justin. 2010. "New Structural Economics: A Framework for Rethinking Development." Policy Research Working Paper 5197, World Bank, Washington, DC. http://siteresources.worldbank.org/INTMOZAMBIQUE/Resources/New _Structural_Economics.pdf.

Parra-Bernal, Guillermo, and Aluisio Alves. 2010. "BNDES Looks to Stimulate Brazil Credit." Reuters, November 22. http://www.reuters.com/article/2010/11 /22/us-brazil-summit-bndes-idUSTRE6AL3F720101122.

Perry, Guillermo, and Danny M. Leipziger, eds. 1999. *Chile: Recent Policy Lessons and Emerging Challenges.* Washington, DC: World Bank.

Reinhart, Carmen, and Kenneth Rogoff. 2008. "This Time Is Different! A Panoramic View of Eight Centuries of Financial Crisis." Working Paper 13882, National Bureau of Economic Research, Cambridge, MA.

————. 2009. "The Aftermath of the Financial Crisis." Working Paper 14656, National Bureau of Economic Research, Cambridge, MA.

————. 2010. "Growth in a Time of Debt." Working Paper 15639, National Bureau of Economic Research, Cambridge, MA.

Rodrik, Dani. 2008. "Normalization Industrial Policy." Working Paper 3, Commission on Growth and Development, Washington, DC.

————. 2010. "Growth after Crisis." In *Globalization and Growth: Implications for a Post-Crisis World*, ed. Michael Spence and Danny M. Leipziger, 125–150. Washington, DC: Commission on Growth and Development.

————. 2011. *The Globalization Paradox: Democracy and the Future of the World Economy.* New York: W.W. Norton & Co.

Rodrik, Dani, and Arvind Subramanian. 2009. "Why Did Financial Globalization Disappoint?" *IMF Staff Papers* 56 (1): 112–38.

Roubini, Nouriel. 2010. "Dr. Doom Predicts Another $1 Trillion in Housing Losses." Dealbook article, *New York Times*, December 6.

Shiller, Robert J. 2010. "Don't Bet the Farm on the Housing Recovery." *New York Times*, April 10.

Spence, Michael. 2011a. "The Impact of Globalization on Income and Employment: The Downside of Integrating Markets." *Foreign Affairs* 90 (4): 28–41.

————. 2011b. *The Next Convergence: The Future of Economic Growth in a Multispeed World.* New York: Farrar, Straus and Giroux.

Stiglitz, Joseph. 2011. "Monetary Policy." Remarks at the "Macro and Growth Policies in the Wake of the Crisis" conference, International Monetary Fund, Washington, DC, March 7–8.

World Bank. 2005. *Economic Growth in the 1990s: Learning from a Decade of Reform.* Washington, DC: World Bank.

————. 2011. "Global Economic Prospects 2011: Navigating Strong Currents." Semiannual report (January), World Bank, Washington, DC.

Zoellick, Robert B. 2009. "After the Crisis?" Speech at the Paul H. Nitze School of Advanced International Studies, Johns Hopkins University, September 28.

2

Rebalancing Global Growth

Menzie Chinn, Barry Eichengreen,
and Hiro Ito

The global imbalances of the last decade were, everyone now realizes, a decidedly mixed blessing. They enabled China and other emerging-market economies to export their way to higher incomes. They allowed those economies' central banks to protect themselves from capital flow volatility by accumulating vast war chests of foreign reserves. They supported buoyant asset markets and rising consumption in the advanced economies despite what were, in many cases, slowly growing or stagnant real wages. By 2004, observers were characterizing this situation as a happy complementarity of interests—as a stable and socially desirable equilibrium that might run for another 10 or 20 years (Dooley, Folkerts-Landau, and Garber 2003; Dooley and Garber 2005).

With benefit of hindsight, we now know that the prospects were not so happy.[1] Capital inflows fed excesses in U.S. financial markets that ultimately destabilized banking systems and economies on both sides of the Atlantic (Darvas and Pisani-Ferry 2010; Obstfeld and Rogoff 2009). Those excesses bequeathed an overhang of debt and financial problems that now create the prospect of a decade of no growth or slow growth across much of the advanced industrial world.

Although the implications for emerging markets have been more positive, there, too, are indications that what worked in the past won't work in the future. Large export surpluses and low consumption rates are likely to give way in the face of demands for higher wages and living standards, and not just in China. A manufacturing-centered growth model that makes heavy use of cheap labor, voraciously consumes raw materials, and has a large carbon footprint is unlikely to be sustainable for another 10 or 20 years (Roach 2009).

That it is now necessary to rebalance the global economy to create a sustainable basis for economic growth is a commonplace. But this frequent observation is too infrequently accompanied by specifics. This chapter attempts to provide some.

Its first half describes the specific policy challenges facing the principal national and regional economies. The second half adds some numerical precision by analyzing how much adjustment in current account imbalances to expect in the short and long run. Given the finding that emerges from this analysis—that rebalancing is likely to be an extended process, with significant imbalances persisting in the short term—the chapter concludes by suggesting measures that can make imbalances safe for growth during the transitional period while they are being resolved.

Policy Challenges and Responses

A first observation is that global imbalances do not merely involve the United States and China. As figure 2.1 shows, China was responsible for only a relatively small fraction of total global current account surpluses, especially toward the beginning of the decade. Even at its peak in 2007–08, the Chinese surplus accounted for only about one-fourth of total global surpluses. More important previously were the European surplus countries, led by Germany.

Equally important in the critical 2005–08 period were the oil-exporting surplus countries. The other surplus countries of emerging Asia made a smaller but still persistent and visible contribution. In this period as well, there was again a significant contribution from Northern Europe (primarily Germany).

On the deficit side, in contrast, one country—the United States—consistently dominates. Given recent events, however, it is impossible to

Figure 2.1 Current Account Balances, 1996–2016

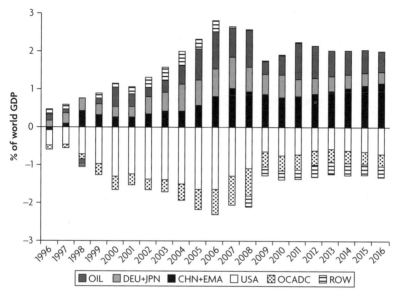

Source: IMF 2011.

Note: Data for 2010–16 are projections. OIL = oil-exporting countries. DEU+JPN = Germany and Japan.
CHN+EMA = China and other emerging Asia. USA = United States. OCADC = other current account deficit
countries. ROW = rest of the world.

ignore the evidence in figure 2.1 of substantial deficits (in recent years, approaching half of U.S. levels) in the now-troubled Southern European bloc. In hindsight, again, more attention should have been paid to this aspect of the problem before 2010.

The same basic message emerges from the top and bottom halves of figure 2.1. Although the United States plays a disproportionately large role in the problem of global imbalances, the task of rebalancing global growth is not simply a U.S. story or even a U.S. and China story. A substantial number of countries, advanced and emerging, participated in the development of these imbalances. Therefore, a substantial number, advanced and emerging, will also have to contribute if rebalancing is to be compatible with the resumption of economic growth in the advanced countries and its maintenance in emerging markets.

United States

The U.S. current account deficit has fallen from its peak of 6 percent of gross domestic product (GDP) in 2006 to 5 percent in 2008 and 3 percent in 2009. With the onset of the financial crisis and recession, there has been a sharp swing in the private savings-investment balance, as shown in figure 2.2.

Measured household saving has risen from near zero to close to 8 percent. Private investment, meanwhile, has dropped sharply because of recession and financial distress. The partially offsetting factor (also shown in figure 2.2) is the public saving-investment balance, or the mirror image of the fiscal stimulus that has been used to stabilize demand in the face of the crisis. In an arithmetic sense, the change in the current account balance is the difference between the rise in the net private savings ratio and the fall in its public counterpart, all expressed as shares of GDP.

The argument that this shift in the current account is more than transitory goes like this: First and foremost, given that consumption is 70 percent of U.S. GDP, the change in household saving is likely to be permanent or at least persistent. Deleveraging by the financial sector will

Figure 2.2 U.S. Saving, Investment, and Current Account, 1968–2011

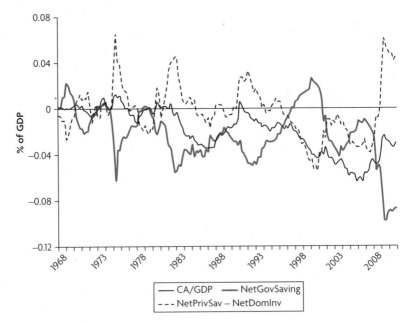

Sources: U.S. Bureau of Economic Analysis; authors' calculations.
Note: Data normalized by GDP. CA = current account. NetGovSaving = net government saving. NetPrivSav −
NetDomInv = net private saving − net domestic investment.

make access to credit more difficult. Households will face a continuing need to rebuild their retirement wealth; they are unlikely to see again anytime soon the large capital gains on real estate and equity portfolios on which they banked in the low-savings years. With the end of the Great Moderation, Americans have been reminded that the world is a risky place, encouraging more to engage in more precautionary saving. Recent research provides some support for this view (for example, Carroll and Slacalek 2009; Mody and Ohnsorge 2010).

Second, a public sector deficit on the order of 10 percent of GDP cannot persist indefinitely. Exactly how and when that deficit will be narrowed is to be seen, but it is hard to dispute that it is subject to Stein's Law.[2] One thing on which it is possible to agree is that there is no single solution to the problem of restoring fiscal balance. A combination of tax increases, entitlement reforms, and reductions in discretionary spending surely will be required.[3]

There has been substantial debate about the impact of fiscal restraint on the current account. The results presented here, and discussed in the next section, suggest that there is indeed a noticeable (and statistically significant) impact—on the order of 0.3 to 0.4 percentage points' current account improvement for each percentage point of increase in the budget balance. This result suggests that fiscal consolidation over the medium to long term can contribute significantly to global rebalancing.

Third and finally, one can imagine a subsidiary contribution to restoring current account balance from a modestly lower investment rate if, as some observers suspect, the crisis has permanently damaged the growth potential of the economy and rate of return on capital.[4] Financial regulation that increases the cost of intermediation, and thereby the cost of capital, will work in the same direction.

With the United States saving more relative to what it produces, its net exports will have to rise. The historical rule of thumb, neglecting autonomous changes in foreign demand, is that a 1 percent improvement in the U.S. current account requires a 10 percent fall in the real trade-weighted dollar exchange rate to price the additional U.S. goods into foreign markets and shift domestic spending away from imports. This is the result that obtains in the Organisation for Economic Co-operation and Development's economic model.[5] Some will say that the requisite shift is now larger because the U.S. manufacturing sector has been allowed to atrophy, reducing the country's export base.[6]

Stronger growth in the demand abroad for U.S. goods (think China) would moderate the magnitude of the necessary fall, while weaker growth in such demand abroad (think Europe) would accentuate it. Obstfeld and Rogoff (2007) and Eichengreen and Rua (2010) simulate these adjustments, distinguishing demands for traded and nontraded goods and making different assumptions about the rate of growth of foreign demand. According to Eichengreen and Rua (2010), halving the size of the U.S. current account deficit requires a 15 percent fall in the dollar real exchange rate, assuming an increase in demand in the rest of the world that offsets the posited reduction in U.S. demand equaling 3 percent of U.S. GDP (which is the posited change in the U.S. saving-investment balance). As the increase in foreign demand grows smaller, or even as the same increase in foreign demand is concentrated in a smaller subset of countries, the requisite depreciation of the dollar grows larger.

On balance, it is hard to avoid the conclusion that more is needed to achieve a sustainable reduction in the U.S. current account deficit. As of early summer 2011, the fall from the November 2005 local peak in the Federal Reserve's Price-Adjusted Major Currencies Dollar Index was around 19 percent.[7] Following the outbreak of the subprime crisis and then the Bear Stearns and Lehman Brothers shocks, the dollar strengthened as investors fled to the safe haven of the U.S. Treasury market. With the outbreak of financial turbulence in Europe in 2010, this experience was repeated: the dollar strengthened again, both against the euro and on an effective basis.[8]

So long as the dollar exchange rate continues to be driven more by capital flows than by the correlates of the current account, and so long as the U.S. Treasury market continues to be seen as a safe haven, it is hard to see how the halving of the U.S. current account deficit can be sustained. One can imagine that, as continued capital inflows lead to mounting U.S. external indebtedness, the dollar's safe-haven status will be called into question.[9] But it is hard to know when.

In the short run, then, it seems all but inevitable that as U.S. investment picks up and as additional investment feeds more growth and demand, the U.S. current account deficit will widen again. The International Monetary Fund (IMF) forecasts that this widening will be limited to no more than half a percent of GDP over the next five years (IMF 2010a). That projection is either overly optimistic or it is making additional, unspecified assumptions about dollar decline or strong demand growth abroad.[10]

Europe

For present purposes, the European continent can be divided into two parts: Northern Europe (primarily Germany) and Southern Europe (Greece, Italy, Portugal, Spain, and the honorary member, Ireland)—each of which will have to make very different contributions to rebalancing.[11] As figure 2.3 shows, Germany's surplus and the PIIGS'[12] deficits are now more or less offsetting (as they also were, more or less, for much of the preceding decade).

Because Europe as a whole has not been in large current account surplus or deficit, it is hard to argue that the continent played a major role in the buildup of global imbalances.[13] Where this pattern of intra-European

Figure 2.3 Current Account Balance as a Percentage of Euro Area GDP, 1995–2010

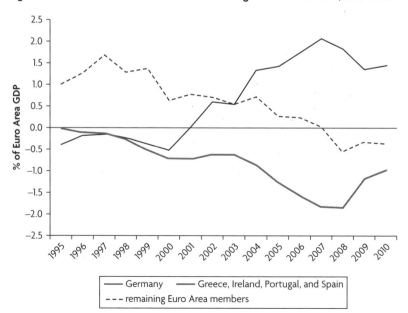

Source: IMF 2011.

imbalances clearly did play a role was in the buildup of vulnerabilities within Europe (which, as already seen, will have implications for what happens going forward).

With the decline in borrowing costs attendant on the European Monetary Union, there was a large rise in consumption spending across Southern Europe (see, for example, Jaumotte and Sodsriwiboon 2010). In some countries (such as Spain), this spending was mainly private dissaving; in others (Greece and Portugal), government took an active part. Partly as a result of the concurrent shift to current account surplus in Germany, the resulting Southern European deficits were freely financed. The 2008–09 crisis was then the straw that broke the camel's back. Governments had no choice but to support demand with additional public spending, even while employment and export supply declined. The result was the growth of twin deficits, culminating in 2010 in fears of a regionwide sovereign debt crisis.

Euro Area Deficit Countries. One consequence is the need now for significant fiscal consolidation across the crisis countries. Table 2.1 shows that planned budget reductions in 2010 ranged from 7 percent of GDP in Greece to 3 percent in Ireland and 2.5 percent in Portugal and Spain.

Table 2.1 Fiscal Adjustment in the Euro Area, 2010–11

	Proportion of Euro Area GDP (%)	Discretionary budget cuts (% of GDP)	
	2010	2010	2011
France	21.3	0.0	0.6
Germany	26.8	−1.5	0.4
Greece	2.6	7.0	4.0
Ireland	1.8	3.0	2.0
Italy	16.9	0.5	0.8
Portugal	1.8	2.5	3.1
Spain	11.7	2.5	2.9
Others	16.9	−0.4	0.5
Euro Area	**100.0**	**0.2**	**1.0**

Source: Economist 2010, drawing on Barclay's Capital.

These reductions were to be followed by somewhat smaller adjustments in the same direction in 2011 (except in Spain and Portugal at the time of writing, where the projected fiscal adjustments are projected to increase). With not just public but also private spending likely to be weak, current account deficits will tend to narrow.

Were Southern Europe to swing sharply toward current account balance, that would increase the difficulty of engineering the same shift in the United States. In fact, the IMF expects the current account deficits across Southern Europe to shrink only gradually: table 2.2 shows that of Greece falling only from 10 percent of GDP in 2010 to the 7–8 percent range thereafter, that of Italy falling by barely 1 percent of GDP, that of Portugal falling not at all before 2012 and after that by only 1 percentage point of GDP, and that of Spain falling by barely a fourth of a percentage point of GDP.

Table 2.2 Actual and Projected Current Account Balances in the Euro Area, 2008–16
percentage of GDP

Country	2008	2009	2010	2011	2012	2013	2014	2015	2016
Austria	4.86	2.91	3.17	3.06	3.11	3.31	3.33	3.28	3.15
Belgium	−1.90	0.84	1.20	1.02	1.20	1.50	1.88	2.31	2.40
Cyprus	−17.20	−7.55	−7.03	−8.86	−8.66	−8.45	−8.35	−8.01	−7.99
Finland	2.85	2.35	3.13	2.76	2.57	2.63	2.74	2.80	2.84
France	−1.91	−1.93	−2.05	−2.78	−2.70	−2.42	−2.25	−2.22	−2.19
Germany	6.73	5.00	5.31	5.14	4.56	4.34	4.26	3.99	3.62
Greece	−14.69	−10.99	−10.45	−8.16	−7.06	−6.64	−5.49	−4.39	−3.85
Ireland	−5.65	−3.04	−0.72	0.19	0.59	0.24	0.16	0.13	0.13
Italy	−2.93	−2.08	−3.50	−3.37	−2.96	−2.97	−2.98	−2.73	−2.41
Luxembourg	5.26	6.70	7.72	8.54	8.70	8.93	9.15	9.24	9.29
Malta	−5.56	−6.94	−0.62	−1.05	−2.31	−3.24	−3.84	−3.63	−3.30
Netherlands	4.26	4.57	7.13	7.88	8.23	7.84	7.24	6.60	6.05
Portugal	−12.61	−10.93	−9.87	−8.73	−8.53	−6.62	−6.43	−6.03	−5.65
Slovak Republic	−6.62	−3.59	−3.45	−2.83	−2.74	−2.55	−2.66	−2.60	−3.13
Slovenia	−6.67	−1.49	−1.16	−2.00	−2.10	−2.10	−2.20	−2.42	−2.62
Spain	−9.74	−5.53	−4.49	−4.78	−4.55	−4.11	−3.89	−3.68	−3.47

Source: IMF 2011; data for 2011–16 are staff projections.
Note: The table does not include figures for Estonia, which was admitted to the Euro Area in 2011.

These April 2011 forecasts assume that private spending and growth will be maintained and that investment (the current account deficit being the excess of investment over saving) will not take a sustained hit.

Subsequent events however, call these rosy forecasts into question.[14] To reassure financial markets, governments have been compelled to adopt even larger discretionary cuts to their budgets. Uncertainty about implementation and about the prospects for European economic growth is likely to have a more powerful negative impact on private spending. With deeper recessions, current accounts will move toward balance more quickly. They will move not as a result of Southern European countries exporting more (the absence of a national exchange rate ruling out devaluation to jump-start exports, and the dependence of these economies on intra-European exports limiting the benefits of euro depreciation) but as a result of their importing *less*. Deeper recessions and less spending on imports will mean less support for global rebalancing.

Measures to reduce uncertainty and otherwise limit the depth of the recessions associated with these fiscal consolidation measures would encourage investment. More investment would both help the countries in question and contribute to global rebalancing—objectives that point to the importance of solidifying political support for fiscal consolidation where it is fragile. It means making the necessary consolidation as growth-friendly as possible by relying more heavily on cutting public expenditure than on increasing taxes. It means relying more on cuts to current, rather than capital, expenditure (where the latter often proves temporary) and, where tax increases are needed, relying on less-distortionary taxes (increases in value added taxes and sin taxes).[15] It means restructuring debts where they are unsustainable (such as in Greece). It means coming clean about the adequacy of the capitalization of European banks holding the debts that must be restructured. It means supplementing fiscal consolidation with structural (labor-market and other regulatory) reform to address these economies' supply-side weaknesses and attract the foreign capital needed to finance current account deficits that will only be wound down slowly.

And it means reiterating the commitment of other European countries to temporarily provide this finance if markets fail. Alas, these seem like formidable prerequisites for ensuring mild recessions and modest support from this region for global rebalancing.

Euro Area Surplus Countries. Support from the Euro Area surplus countries—Germany and its smaller compatriots (Austria, Finland, and the Netherlands)—would make life for Southern Europe easier and also contribute to global rebalancing. According to the forecasts shown above in table 2.2, the current account surplus of the dominant member of this group, Germany, will remain stable through 2011, the government doing little if any budget cutting until then (and the economy still feeling a positive discretionary impulse in 2010, reflecting the phased implementation of earlier stimulus measures). Subsequently, the projection shows Germany's current account surplus shrinking by 1 percent of its GDP by 2013 and another 1 percent by 2015. Even then, however, German current account surpluses remain substantial. The euro now having fallen significantly, further boosting German exports, one can reasonably ask whether this vision of a progressively narrowing German surplus is overly optimistic.[16]

This adjustment would be aided by measures that boosted German investment relative to saving. German commentators regularly bemoan the country's low rate of domestic investment, which is running at only 16 percent of GDP—lower than in France, lower than in Italy, and lower than the Euro Area average (19 percent, according to European Central Bank data for the first quarter of 2010). Investment tax credits can be used to encourage investment at home. Product market deregulation and the elimination of red tape can encourage investment in the underdeveloped service sector. These measures would be consistent with the pro-growth agenda of the German government and also contribute to global and intra-European rebalancing.

Operating on the savings side of the savings-investment imbalance would be harder. Standing in the way of continued public dissaving in Germany are (a) a constitutional amendment requiring the government to run a quasi-balanced budget and (b) a powerful collective psychology. If policy initiatives to promote investment result in faster economic growth, this could lead to a temporary decline in saving and increased household spending in anticipation of higher future incomes. But the experience of the last decade does not suggest that this mechanism works powerfully in Germany.

Non–Euro Area Countries. What about non–Euro Area Europe? In terms of global imbalances, non–Euro Area Europe means mainly the United

Kingdom. (Denmark, Norway, and Sweden have been running surpluses, but they are small economies. In Eastern Europe, only the Southeastern European economies, which are even smaller, are now running substantial current account deficits.)

The United Kingdom is running a current account deficit of 1.7 percent of GDP, which the IMF foresees as shrinking only marginally. The question is whether that external deficit could now fall more sharply because of the weakness of sterling and because of the new government's deep budget cuts, which could slow public spending, private investment, and growth. Such a result would not be helpful from the rebalancing point of view.

In sum, the picture in Europe is mixed because Europe is mixed. That Southern Europe and possibly the United Kingdom will substantially reduce their current account deficits seems fairly certain. Whether Germany and other countries will take up the slack is less clear.

China

Most of the attention devoted to China's high savings rate (approaching 45 percent of GDP and producing a substantial current account surplus despite the country's high level of investment) focuses on household saving. Chinese households have good reason for precautionary saving. The structure of the economy is changing rapidly, with uncertain implications for people's livelihoods. With the declining relative importance of state companies, the social safety net has been effectively downsized. There is limited scope for borrowing to pay for health care, education, and other costs. Public support for retirees is similarly limited.[17]

The policy recommendations that flow from this analysis are familiar: China should develop its financial markets as well as its education, rural health care, and public pension systems. Those recommendations also have implications for global rebalancing. Building financial markets and a social safety net will take time; these are not institutional reforms that can be carried out in a few years. With the determinants of household savings rates changing only gradually, China's current account surplus will narrow only gradually.[18] There may be hope for a contribution to global rebalancing in the medium term but not much in the short run.

In fact, household savings rates in China have been declining in recent years, which makes it hard to blame them for the growth of the Chinese surplus (Prasad 2009). They are not unusually high by the standards of other emerging markets. Savings, as conventionally measured, amount to only some 35 percent of household income, which is not extraordinary. Moreover, household saving accounts for, at most, half of national saving. The other half is undertaken by enterprises and (until recently) government.

One explanation for the high level of corporate saving is that the strong performance of Chinese exports has given export-oriented enterprises more profits than they can productively invest.[19] Some commentators move from this observation to the conclusion that the government should revalue the currency to reduce this profitability. This is an uncomfortable argument; it suggests that the authorities should want to make the leading sector of their economy less profitable and efficient—and especially that they would want to subject that sector to a sharp shock to profitability in the form of a step revaluation. From this point of view, it is understandable that Chinese officialdom has been reluctant to see more than gradual appreciation of the renminbi, which, other things equal, would be unlikely to make more than a gradual impact on global imbalances.

On the other hand, if the 2010 upsurge in labor unrest and double-digit wage increases (prominently at Foxconn and Honda but also more broadly) indicate that previous policy amounted to an effort to artificially hold down the real exchange rate that is now abruptly unraveling, there could be a more discontinuous adjustment. Wage increases of 20 percent would not be unlike a 20 percent revaluation in their effect on exporters' competitiveness. If the upsurge in labor militancy is general, the impact on global imbalances could be significant (see also Kroeber 2010). Deutsche Bank (2010) uses a multisector computable general equilibrium model to estimate the impact of a 20 percent wage increase and concludes that this would raise consumption and investment by 3.9 percent of domestic production (equivalently, net exports fall by 3.9 percent of GDP). In other words, a 20 percent wage increase would be enough to cut the Chinese surplus by about half.

But the high savings of Chinese enterprises is more than simply a matter of the real exchange rate. In addition, it likely reflects the underdevelopment of financial markets as borrowing-constrained enterprises accumulate funds in anticipation of future investment needs.[20] Tyers and Lu (2009) suggest that the high corporate savings rate also reflects the market power and extraordinary profits of a handful of state-owned firms that dominate key industries such as mining, petroleum refining, steel manufacturing, and transport and communications. Their situation contrasts with that of the textile, footwear, and processed agricultural products industries, where private firms dominate, entry is relatively free, and rates of return on capital (profitability) have been lower.

This diagnosis is not universally accepted.[21] If it is correct, however, potential solutions include passing state-owned enterprises' (SOE) dividend payments to the state on to consumers through a commensurate reduction in labor income taxes. Another solution involves using competition policy to encourage entry and reduce oligopoly rents. The government has embraced the practice of offsetting dividend receipts with reductions in labor taxes, although its dividend receipts remain limited. Entry (especially into heavy industry) sufficient to eliminate oligopoly profits is likely to take time, however.

Meanwhile, an alternative would be the imposition of price caps in sectors where market power is pervasive—a step in the direction of the undistorted equilibrium. It would reduce corporate savings, other things equal, but other things would *not* be equal in practice. The excessive markups associated with oligopoly power in China are concentrated in the sheltered sector. (This makes sense: exporters face the pressure of foreign competition.) Reducing the prices of the intermediate inputs they supply without reducing their quantity could end up making exports—of non-labor-intensive manufactures such as metals and motor vehicles—more competitive and could offset, in part, the reduction in national saving and in the current account surplus. In any case, all these policies run up against the constraint that the SOE sector is politically influential.

Finally, Green (2010) points to the contribution of government to national saving. The 2009–10 period was an exception; China rolled out a massive fiscal stimulus, the largest relative to GDP of any country, and the budget of the consolidated public sector swung into a deficit of roughly 3 percent of GDP. But this occurred against the backdrop of a steadily growing government budget surplus. Flow-of-funds data (arguably superior to the official budget figures in that they capture off-budget sources of revenue, including those from land sales) show that revenues of all levels of government as a share of national income rose by half between 1994 and 2007—from 16 percent to 24 percent—while spending failed to keep up. Green's data show that government saving, including revenue from land sales, contributed nearly half as much as either the household or corporate sectors to overall national saving.

Although the government's contribution to national saving could presumably be adjusted more quickly than the nongovernmental component, there are limits. Spending on infrastructure, among other things, would be difficult to ramp up further. The authorities are already making every effort to ramp up the rural health care system. They would like to fund three additional years of compulsory schooling, but training qualified teachers takes time. At the same time, the government could cut business taxes, on the underdeveloped service sector in particular. Such a tax cut would have the complementary effect of encouraging the reallocation of resources toward the production of nontraded goods, which would be helpful for global rebalancing.

The IMF sees the Chinese current account surplus as rising slightly, from 6.2 percent to 7.3 percent of GDP by 2013 and to 8 percent of GDP in 2015. Although China avoids an external surplus in excess of 10 percent of GDP (the 2007–08 average), only in that sense does it contribute to global rebalancing. Significant rebalancing would require it to do more. The analysis here suggests that this could be achieved only through a broad combination of policies.[22]

Other East Asian Countries

The recipe for moving Japan closer to current account balance is well known: ending deflation and restoring growth would (a) encourage investment by firms anticipating higher prices and profits and (b) encourage consumption by households anticipating higher incomes.

Reactions to the recent recession illustrate the point. In the 2009 downturn, the sizable increase in the fiscal deficit (discretionary fiscal measures were some 1.4 percent of GDP in 2009, and the total budget deficit increased to 4.9 percent of GDP) could have substantially reduced the current account surplus. That increased deficit, however, was offset by an increase in the household financial surplus of 2.8 percent of GDP and an increase in nonfinancial and financial corporations' financial surplus of another 2.8 percent of GDP as both households and firms cut back on their spending.[23]

The trend in household savings rates was downward in the past decade, reflecting a rising old-age dependency ratio and predictable life-cycle effects (Kawai and Takagi 2010). Most of the leverage for policy is thus likely to come from measures designed to stimulate corporate investment, not personal consumption. Getting spending going again is far from impossible, but it is something the authorities have been attempting to do, without noticeable success, for the better part of two decades. Given Japan's on-again, off-again fiscal stimulus and buildup of public debt, the scope for further fiscal measures is limited. Quantitative easing to push down the yen has never been particularly successful, for whatever reason.

By process of elimination, strong demand for Japanese capital goods and sophisticated intermediate inputs by China and other emerging East Asian countries holds out the most promise for encouraging corporate investment. To encourage this, Kawai and Takagi (2010) recommend currency appreciation in China and elsewhere in the region, together with active efforts to further liberalize intra-Asian trade.

Consistent with this view, Thorbecke (2010) finds that currency appreciation by non-China and non-Japan Asia would stimulate imports by developing Asian countries of both consumption and capital goods, from Japan and generally. Appreciation would likewise induce a significant reduction in exports to the United States.

Labor-intensive exports would be affected most dramatically—making it important that governments, when allowing their currencies to appreciate, take proactive measures to stimulate labor-intensive employment elsewhere, namely in the service sector.[24] Encouraging investment in this sector would both hold out the potential for employment-rich growth and be a step toward correcting the saving-investment imbalance that shows up as chronic current account surpluses in emerging Asia.

On the savings side, authors including Aziz and Lamberte (2010) recommend the same policy reforms as in China—building social safety nets and developing financial markets—although for countries such as Indonesia, the Philippines, and Thailand, they don't hold out hope for fast-enough progress to make a significant dent in imbalances.

In addition, the loss of exports by individual countries is less, but the overall contribution to reducing global imbalances is greater, when the countries of the region jointly appreciate their currencies (Thorbecke 2010). Moving together limits each individual Asian country's loss of competitiveness in the United States and other extra-Asian markets. In addition, joint appreciation would presumably be accompanied by measures to encourage consumption spending regionwide, opening up additional export opportunities within Asia.

The other constraint on rebalancing in emerging Asia—aside from concern with exports, employment, and overall economic growth—is reserve adequacy. Emerging Asian countries have run persistent current account deficits since 1997–98, partly in the desire to accumulate larger buffers of foreign exchange reserves, which they see as useful for insulating their economies from capital flow volatility. There is the distinct possibility that they will conclude from the experience of 2008–09 that still-larger reserve cushions are desirable. Supplements to national reserve holdings would therefore increase those countries' willingness to contribute to rebalancing.

The alternatives here include the following:

- Establishment of an effective, quick-disbursing, lightly conditioned facility at the IMF, together with the willingness of Asian governments to access it
- A network of currency swap lines and credits outside the IMF, as proposed by the government of the Republic of Korea in its capacity as Group of 20 (G-20) chair
- Regional reserve pooling arrangements, which could perhaps operate in conjunction with the IMF.

Of these three options, the third appears to be the most viable. Asian governments remain reluctant to approach the IMF, and the IMF's principal shareholders, for their part, would be reluctant to create a global system of currency swaps and credits that was tantamount to a shadow IMF. ASEAN+3 has made progress in strengthening and multilateralizing its Chiang Mai Initiative, which operates in conjunction with the IMF.[25] The implication for policy is that the participants now need to show a readiness to actually use the mechanism. The implication for the empirical work here is that reserve levels may be an important determinant of global imbalances, at least for certain countries and regions.

Oil-Exporting Nations

In the focus on China's external surpluses, it is sometimes forgotten that in 2008 the combined current account balance of the oil-exporting nations (as previously shown in figure 2.1) exceeded that of China and emerging East Asia. Of course, in 2009 the oil exporters' surpluses fell precipitously—from 1.08 percent to 0.34 percent of world GDP. This volatility in their current account balances is largely, but not wholly, driven by the volatility in petroleum prices.

Individual oil exporters can do little to mitigate the wide variation in their current account balances. Furthermore, it makes sense for some of these countries to save a large proportion of the oil revenue increases that are due to price increases (IMF 2008, box 6-1). Hence, substantial responsibility for these movements in current account balances devolves upon the consuming nations, including the United States and China. The former is the largest single importer of oil (2009 oil imports accounted for 86 percent of the total U.S. trade deficit), while the latter has contributed the largest increment to world oil imports in recent years. Small variations in demand conditions in these two countries, combined with relatively low price elasticities of supply and demand, explain a large share of the global imbalances in 2006–08.

The preceding discussion suggests that a concerted effort to reduce the pace of oil-demand increases in both the United States and China would moderate global imbalances. Increasing the relative price of oil would thus have a positive impact on efforts to rebalance. The United States, with its relatively low energy taxes, would be a prime candidate for progress here (Chinn 2005).

Empirics

This section offers a simple analytical and forecasting model of current account balances, building on the work of Chinn and Ito (2007). The analysis includes data for the crisis period, enabling an examination of whether the relationship between the current account and its proximate determinants changed around the time of the crisis.

These and earlier data are used to conduct in- and out-of-sample forecasting exercises. The analysis considers several familiar, not necessarily mutually exclusive, hypotheses and arguments that have been offered to explain global imbalances. These include the twin deficit hypothesis (Chinn 2005); the saving glut hypothesis (Greenspan 2005a, 2005b; Bernanke 2005; Clarida 2005); and the asset bubble-driven explanation of current account balances (Aizenman and Jinjarak 2009; Fratzscher and Straub 2009).

Following Chinn and Prasad (2003), Chinn and Ito (2007), and Ito and Chinn (2009), the authors estimate the following models:

Model 1

$$y_{i,t} = \alpha + \beta_1 BB_{i,t} + \beta_2 FD_{i,t} + X_{i,t}\Gamma + u_{i,t} \qquad (2.1)$$

Model 2

$$y_{i,t} = \alpha + \beta_1 BB_{i,t} + \beta_2 FD_{i,t} + \beta_3 LEGAL_i + \beta_3 KAOPEN_{i,t}$$
$$+ \beta_4 (FD_{i,t} \times LEGAL_{i,t}) + \beta_5 (LEGAL_{i,t} \times KAOPEN_{i,t})$$
$$+ \beta_6 (KAOPEN_{i,t} \times FD_{i,t}) + X_{i,t}\Gamma + u_{i,t} \qquad (2.2)$$

where

$y_{i,t}$ refers to three dependent variables: the current account balance, national saving, and investment, all expressed as a share of GDP;

FD is a measure of financial development, for which private credit creation (PCGDP) is usually used;

KAOPEN is the Chinn and Ito (2006) measure of financial openness;

LEGAL is a measure of legal or institutional development— the first principal component of law and order (LAO), bureaucratic quality (BQ), and anticorruption measures (*CORRUPT*);[26] and

$X_{i,t}$ is a vector of macroeconomic and policy control variables that include familiar determinants of current account balances such as net foreign assets as a ratio to GDP, relative income (to the United States), its quadratic term, relative dependency ratios on young and old populations, terms-of-trade (TOT) volatility output growth rates, trade openness (exports + imports/GDP), dummies for oil-exporting countries, and time fixed effects.

Panels of nonoverlapping five-year averages are used for all explanatory variables except when noted otherwise. All variables, except for net foreign assets to GDP, are converted into the deviations from their

GDP-weighted world mean before the calculation of five-year averages; net foreign asset ratios are sampled from the first year of each five-year panel as the initial conditions.[27] The data are extracted mostly from publicly available datasets such as the *World Development Indicators, International Financial Statistics*, and *World Economic Outlook* (for details, see annex 2.1).

In-Sample Results

The sample includes annual data for 23 industrial and 86 developing countries covering the four decades of 1970–2008.[28] The authors regress current account balances, national saving, and investment on the same set of regressors separately for industrial countries (IDC), less-developed countries (LDC), and emerging-market economies (EMG).[29]

Table 2.3 shows the results for model 1 (equation 6.1).

Note first that these results are consistent with the twin deficits hypothesis: budget surpluses and current account surpluses move together, other things equal. A coefficient of less than 1 suggests, however, that they move together less than proportionately.[30] Larger net foreign assets, which should generate a stronger income account, affect the current account balance positively, as anticipated. The relative income terms, which tend to be jointly if not always individually significant, show that higher-income countries generally have stronger current accounts (as if capital tends to flow from higher- to lower-income countries). Countries with higher dependency ratios (and, by the life-cycle hypothesis, slower savings rates) generally have weaker current accounts.[31] Oil-exporting countries have stronger current accounts, other things equal. All this is as expected.

The Caballero, Farhi, and Gourinchas (2008) hypothesis—that countries with more-developed financial markets should have weaker current accounts (capital flows from China, with its underdeveloped capital markets, to the United States, which has a comparative advantage in producing safe financial assets)—finds weak support in the full sample (leftmost column of table 2.3).[32] The pattern is the same, but the significance of the effect vanishes when disaggregating industrial and developing countries. This is perhaps not surprising in that the hypothesis in question emphasizes flows between industrial and developing countries, not among members of the two subgroups.

Table 2.3 Current Account Regression without Institutional Variables

	Current account			
	(1)	(2)	(3)	(4)
	Full	IDC	LDC	EMG
Government budget balance	0.283 [0.064]***	0.414 [0.086]***	0.28 [0.068]***	0.119 [0.065]*
Net foreign assets (initial)	0.039 [0.006]***	0.089 [0.014]***	0.029 [0.007]***	0.024 [0.013]*
Relative income	0.058 [0.015]***	0.023 [0.017]	0.097 [0.020]***	0.241 [0.092]***
Relative income squared	0.073 [0.019]***	−0.104 [0.082]	0.073 [0.018]***	0.161 [0.083]*
Dependency ratio (young)	−0.046 [0.015]***	0.012 [0.023]	−0.034 [0.017]**	−0.02 [0.018]
Dependency ratio (old)	−0.025 [0.009]***	0.013 [0.017]	−0.025 [0.011]**	−0.054 [0.019]***
Financial development (PCGDP)	−0.016 [0.011]	−0.025 [0.016]	0.013 [0.013]	−0.008 [0.016]
TOT volatility	0.007 [0.020]	−0.100 [0.053]*	−0.009 [0.022]	−0.003 [0.024]
Average GDP growth	−0.184 [0.121]	0.056 [0.173]	−0.209 [0.132]	0.028 [0.121]
Trade openness	−0.001 [0.006]	−0.013 [0.013]	−0.014 [0.008]*	−0.018 [0.010]*
Oil-exporting countries	0.034 [0.013]***	— —	0.033 [0.013]***	0.057 [0.016]***
Dummy for 2001–05	0.014 [0.011]	0.023 [0.010]**	0.018 [0.018]	0.04 [0.017]**
Dummy for 2006–08	0.007 [0.013]	0.010 [0.011]	0.016 [0.020]	0.023 [0.021]
Observations	670	180	490	256
Adjusted R-squared	0.45	0.50	0.47	0.42

Source: Authors' calculations.

Note: IDC = industrial countries. LDC = less-developed countires. EMG = emerging-market countries. PCGDP = ratio of private credit to GDP. TOT = terms of trade. — = not included. Time fixed effects are included in the estimation, but only those for the 2001–05 and 2006–08 periods are reported in the table.

Significance level: * = 10 percent, ** = 5 percent, *** = 1 percent.

Two dummy variables for the 2001–05 and 2006–08 subperiods look to the question of whether recent experience has been unusual. Emerging-market economies appear to have run unusually large surpluses in the first subperiod, consistent with the idea that they were fixated on minimizing financing vulnerabilities and accumulating reserves following the Asian crisis. Such behavior is not evident for emerging markets as a group in 2006–08, when the contribution of emerging markets to global imbalances was increasingly a China story.[33] Surprisingly, the industrial countries as a group ran larger surpluses in the same 2001–05 period than their other characteristics would lead one to expect. Evidently the United States was an outlier in this respect.[34]

Table 2.4 then reports estimates of the models for savings and investment separately.

A few results of note:

- Government budget deficits affect primarily national saving (in the same direction as government saving, contrary to Ricardian equivalence stories).
- Dependency ratios affect both savings and investment (as emphasized in Eichengreen and Fifer 2002).
- Financial development has a more consistent impact on investment than on saving (something that would not be obvious a priori).

Other variables that do not appear to have a significant impact on the current account balance in table 2.3—such as growth, trade openness, and terms-of-trade volatility—nonetheless affect both savings and investment significantly; they just affect them in the same direction.

Tables 2.5 and 2.6 add the institutional variables. (Here, only the results for the current account balance in table 2.5 are discussed.)

The principal result of interest is the coefficient on the interaction between capital account openness and financial development (together with the financial development effect discussed above). For the full sample, the results again support the Caballero, Farhi, and Gourinchas (2008) interpretation of global imbalances. Among emerging markets, those with better-developed financial markets and open capital accounts similarly have weaker current account balances, as if they were on the receiving end of inflows (or experience the least tendency for capital to flow out). Among the industrial countries, however, this pattern is no longer evident.

A number of alternative specifications yielded similar results. One of interest involved adding foreign reserves as a percentage of GDP, lagging one five-year period, as an additional explanatory variable.[35] Lagging

Table 2.4 National Saving and Investment Regression without Institutional Variables

	National Saving				Investment			
	(5) Full	(6) IDC	(7) LDC	(8) EMG	(9) Full	(10) IDC	(11) LDC	(12) EMG
Government budget balance	0.411 [0.111]***	0.582 [0.081]***	0.413 [0.113]***	0.246 [0.078]***	0.033 [0.035]	0.139 [0.060]**	0.028 [0.036]	0.026 [0.064]
Net foreign assets (initial)	0.024 [0.013]*	0.078 [0.011]***	0.015 [0.014]	0.053 [0.016]***	-0.006 [0.004]	-0.008 [0.007]	-0.005 [0.005]	0.014 [0.013]
Relative income	-0.007 [0.033]	0.003 [0.021]	0.025 [0.038]	-0.070 [0.096]	-0.043 [0.014]***	-0.042 [0.021]*	-0.043 [0.019]**	-0.268 [0.067]***
Relative income squared	0.048 [0.042]	-0.170 [0.093]*	0.065 [0.033]**	-0.174 [0.101]*	-0.009 [0.019]	-0.001 [0.093]	0.004 [0.019]	-0.316 [0.066]***
Dependency ratio (young)	-0.091 [0.018]***	-0.066 [0.023]***	-0.055 [0.020]***	-0.038 [0.019]**	-0.054 [0.012]***	-0.094 [0.022]***	-0.033 [0.014]**	-0.037 [0.018]**
Dependency ratio (old)	-0.030 [0.014]**	-0.042 [0.017]**	-0.010 [0.016]	-0.062 [0.018]***	-0.006 [0.009]	-0.046 [0.017]***	0.011 [0.010]	-0.007 [0.017]
Financial development (PCGDP)	0.031 [0.016]**	0.000 [0.012]	0.100 [0.026]***	0.031 [0.024]	0.033 [0.008]***	0.019 [0.007]***	0.061 [0.014]***	0.042 [0.016]***
TOT volatility	-0.009 [0.038]	0.243 [0.060]***	-0.058 [0.043]	-0.080 [0.033]**	0.026 [0.020]	0.335 [0.054]***	-0.002 [0.022]	-0.030 [0.030]

Table 2.4 (continued)

	National Saving				Investment			
	(5) Full	(6) IDC	(7) LDC	(8) EMG	(9) Full	(10) IDC	(11) LDC	(12) EMG
Average GDP growth	0.593 [0.173]***	0.193 [0.217]	0.547 [0.179]***	1.071 [0.16]***	0.908 [0.098]***	0.397 [0.302]	0.900 [0.101]***	1.134 [0.122]***
Trade openness	0.024 [0.007]***	0.029 [0.016]*	0.011 [0.009]	0.010 [0.011]	0.021 [0.005]***	0.029 [0.011]***	0.022 [0.007]***	0.027 [0.008]***
Oil-exporting countries	0.079 [0.018]***	—	0.088 [0.019]***	0.053 [0.015]***	0.046 [0.012]***	—	0.053 [0.011]***	0.017 [0.015]
Dummy for 2001–05	−0.015 [0.011]	−0.059 [0.011]***	0.047 [0.016]***	0.047 [0.019]**	−0.034 [0.014]**	−0.090 [0.019]***	0.019 [0.014]	−0.003 [0.018]
Dummy for 2006–08	0.007 [0.014]	−0.052 [0.012]***	0.082 [0.021]***	0.054 [0.026]**	−0.017 [0.014]	−0.070 [0.018]***	0.039 [0.015]**	0.019 [0.019]
Observations	670	180	490	256	670	180	490	256
Adjusted R-squared	0.44	0.61	0.47	0.55	0.32	0.43	0.37	0.49

Source: Authors' calculations.

Note: IDC = industrial countries. LDC = less-developed countries. EMG = emerging-market economies. PCGDP = ratio of private credit to GDP. TOT = terms of trade. — = not included.
 Time fixed effects are included in the estimation, but only those for the 2001–05 and 2006–08 periods are reported in the table.

Significance level: * = 10 percent, ** = 5 percent, *** = 1 percent.

Table 2.5 Current Account Regression with Institutional Variables

	Current account			
	(1) Full	(2) IDC	(3) LDC	(4) EMG
Government budget balance	0.295 [0.058]***	0.289 [0.086]***	0.278 [0.063]***	0.090 [0.055]*
Net foreign assets (initial)	0.037 [0.006]***	0.078 [0.008]***	0.028 [0.007]***	0.028 [0.012]**
Relative income	0.090 [0.018]***	0.018 [0.022]	0.135 [0.022]***	0.302 [0.096]***
Relative income squared	0.056 [0.018]***	0.020 [0.094]	0.048 [0.017]***	0.182 [0.085]**
Dependency ratio (young)	−0.033 [0.015]**	0.004 [0.025]	−0.029 [0.017]*	−0.030 [0.019]
Dependency ratio (old)	−0.018 [0.010]*	0.057 [0.021]***	−0.021 [0.011]**	−0.068 [0.020]***
Financial development (PCGDP)	−0.027 [0.014]*	−0.020 [0.010]*	0.002 [0.029]	−0.117 [0.038]***
Legal development (LEGAL)	−0.009 [0.005]*	0.015 [0.005]***	−0.015 [0.007]**	−0.019 [0.012]
PCGDP × LEGAL	−0.011 [0.008]	−0.014 [0.012]	−0.007 [0.008]	−0.033 [0.014]**
Financial openness (KAOPEN)	0.002 [0.005]	0.008 [0.004]*	−0.008 [0.008]	−0.008 [0.009]
KAOPEN × LEGAL	0.003 [0.001]***	0.012 [0.003]***	−0.001 [0.002]	0.003 [0.003]
KAOPEN × PCGDP	0.002 [0.007]	0.028 [0.010]***	0.003 [0.008]	−0.019 [0.010]*
TOT volatility	0.001 [0.023]	0.028 [0.047]	−0.010 [0.024]	0.025 [0.025]
Average GDP growth	−0.097 [0.091]	0.178 [0.178]	−0.092 [0.099]	0.067 [0.116]
Trade openness	−0.001 [0.006]	−0.001 [0.011]	−0.005 [0.010]	0.000 [0.012]
Oil-exporting countries	0.028 [0.013]**	— —	0.025 [0.012]**	0.045 [0.016]***
Dummy for 2001–05	0.025 [0.009]***	0.015 [0.009]*	0.034 [0.015]**	0.041 [0.017]**
Dummy for 2006–08	0.017 [0.011]	0.002 [0.010]	0.033 [0.018]*	0.021 [0.022]
Observations	620	174	446	249
Adjusted R-squared	0.49	0.63	0.52	0.45

Source: Authors' calculations.

Note: IDC = industrial countries. LDC = less-developed countries. EMG = emerging-market economies. PCGDP = ratio of private credit to GDP. LEGAL = legal development. KAOPEN = financial openness. TOT = terms of trade. — = not included. Time fixed effects are included in the estimation, but only those for the 2001–05 and 2006–08 periods are reported in the table.

Significance level: * = 10 percent, ** = 5 percent, *** = 1 percent.

Table 2.6 National Saving and Investment Regression with Institutional Variables

	National Saving				Investment			
	(5) Full	(6) IDC	(7) LDC	(8) EMG	(9) Full	(10) IDC	(11) LDC	(12) EMG
Government budget balance	0.430 [0.113]***	0.476 [0.087]***	0.417 [0.123]***	0.192 [0.071]***	0.032 [0.034]	0.304 [0.126]**	0.021 [0.033]	0.014 [0.061]
Net foreign assets (initial)	0.023 [0.014]	0.072 [0.008]***	0.019 [0.015]	0.057 [0.015]***	-0.007 [0.004]	-0.014 [0.010]	-0.002 [0.005]	0.013 [0.014]
Relative income	0.015 [0.034]	0.000 [0.027]	0.035 [0.043]	-0.017 [0.088]	-0.037 [0.004]	-0.006 [0.010]	-0.051 [0.021]**	-0.252 [0.076]***
Relative income squared	0.057 [0.034]*	-0.076 [0.116]	0.068 [0.029]**	-0.191 [0.092]**	0.002 [0.018]	-0.225 [0.032]	0.022 [0.017]	-0.326 [0.073]***
Dependency ratio (young)	-0.060 [0.018]***	-0.088 [0.025]***	-0.035 [0.022]	-0.058 [0.020]***	-0.050 [0.018]	-0.097 [0.026]***	-0.032 [0.015]**	-0.046 [0.018]**
Dependency ratio (old)	-0.017 [0.015]	-0.017 [0.021]	-0.004 [0.017]	-0.082 [0.020]***	-0.005 [0.009]	-0.058 [0.020]***	0.007 [0.010]	-0.013 [0.019]
Financial development (PCGDP)	0.020 [0.017]	0.017 [0.011]	0.080 [0.059]	-0.092 [0.053]*	0.037 [0.008]***	0.026 [0.012]**	0.078 [0.031]**	0.046 [0.043]
Legal development (LEGAL)	-0.012 [0.007]*	0.011 [0.006]*	-0.018 [0.012]	-0.037 [0.015]**	-0.002 [0.004]	-0.010 [0.006]*	0.008 [0.008]	-0.016 [0.014]
PCGDP × LEGAL	-0.021 [0.008]**	-0.028 [0.013]**	-0.015 [0.014]	-0.047 [0.018]**	0.000 [0.004]	-0.003 [0.012]	0.014 [0.010]	0.000 [0.015]
Financial openness (KAOPEN)	-0.004 [0.006]	-0.004 [0.005]	-0.012 [0.012]	-0.002 [0.010]	-0.011 [0.003]***	-0.010 [0.003]***	-0.015 [0.006]**	-0.006 [0.007]

	(1)	(2)	(3)	(4)	(5)	(6)	(7)	(8)
KAOPEN × LEGAL	-0.002	0.010	-0.006	0.003	-0.003	0.003	-0.005	-0.004
	[0.001]	[0.003]***	[0.004]	[0.004]	[0.001]***	[0.005]	[0.002]**	[0.003]
KAOPEN × PCGDP	0.008	0.009	0.014	-0.010	-0.001	-0.003	-0.002	0.003
	[0.009]	[0.011]	[0.014]	[0.014]	[0.005]	[0.011]	[0.008]	[0.012]
TOT volatility	-0.023	0.314	-0.051	-0.062	0.018	0.252	-0.003	-0.051
	[0.039]	[0.053]***	[0.045]	[0.035]*	[0.022]	[0.045]***	[0.025]	[0.031]*
Average GDP growth	0.692	0.417	0.689	1.118	0.951	0.380	0.940	1.139
	[0.166]***	[0.252]	[0.190]***	[0.168]***	[0.094]***	[0.268]	[0.097]***	[0.127]***
Trade openness	0.023	0.033	0.025	0.033	0.021	0.023	0.026	0.035
	[0.007]***	[0.016]**	[0.013]*	[0.012]***	[0.005]***	[0.012]*	[0.008]***	[0.009]***
Oil-exporting countries	0.078	—	0.086	0.032	0.049	—	0.059	0.010
	[0.018]***		[0.020]***	[0.017]*	[0.012]***		[0.011]***	[0.014]
Dummy for 2001–05	0.007	-0.053	0.064	0.049	-0.028	-0.080	0.013	-0.004
	[0.013]	[0.012]***	[0.017]***	[0.020]**	[0.014]*	[0.021]***	[0.014]	[0.018]
Dummy for 2006–08	0.029	-0.041	0.102	0.049	-0.009	-0.058	0.034	0.015
	[0.015]*	[0.012]***	[0.022]***	[0.026]*	[0.015]	[0.020]***	[0.016]**	[0.020]
Observations	620	174	446	249	620	174	446	249
Adjusted R-squared	0.46	0.63	0.49	0.57	0.36	0.46	0.40	0.50

Source: Authors' calculations.

Note: IDC = industrial countries. LDC = less-developed countries. EMG = emerging-market economies. FD = financial development. PCGDP = ratio of private credit to GDP. LEGAL = legal development. KAOPEN = financial openness. TOT = terms of trade. — = not included in the estimation, but only those for the 2001–05 and 2006–08 periods are reported in the table.

Significance level: * = 10 percent, ** = 5 percent, *** = 1 percent.

the reserves variable is designed to address the concern that the current account balance and contemporaneous reserves are simultaneously determined (that is, positive shocks to the current account will translate into positive shocks to reserves). Reserve-adequacy arguments suggest that, other things equal, larger reserves should mean less incentive for reserve accumulation and a weaker current account. For the industrial countries, the coefficient on this variable is negative and significant, as hypothesized. For emerging-market economies, it is insignificant. For developing countries, it is positive and significant, contrary to the hypothesis.[36]

Out-of-Sample Projections for Selected Countries

These estimated relationships now help to construct out-of-sample projections as a way of forecasting the prospects for global rebalancing. The forecasts of the independent variables cover 2011–15, with the estimates used to project values for the current account. The forecasts start with 2011, omitting the crisis years 2009–10, when behavior was unusual.[37] The assumptions and the data for the out-of-sample projections are explained in annex 2.2.

For the United States, the results suggest modest movement in the direction of rebalancing, as shown in figure 2.4.[38]

Figure 2.4 shows the same for the United Kingdom, whose deficit is projected to shrink over the 2011–15 period. However, the narrowing of current account deficits over the period is limited; substantial deficits remain, even in 2015.

The news for the surplus countries we consider—China, Germany, Japan, and Singapore—is even less reassuring. The forecasts suggest that their surpluses will remain stable or rise further, absent additional policy changes. One interpretation is that the circle will be squared by other countries that will run smaller surpluses and offset the United States' smaller deficits. A less reassuring interpretation is that the parts don't add up under current forecasts and that even partial rebalancing will require further policy changes. Either way, it seems clear that imbalances will persist.

Further exercises can be undertaken on the basis of these forecasts— for example, using data only through 2005 to see how the model does in tracking current accounts in 2006–08 (figure 2.5).

Figure 2.4 Out-of-Sample Current Account Predictions for Selected Countries, 2011–15

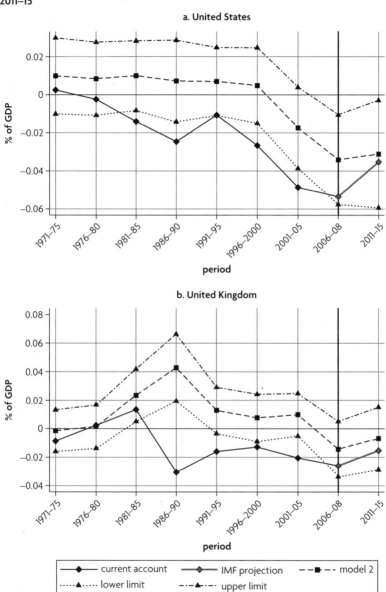

a. United States

b. United Kingdom

(continued next page)

Figure 2.4 (continued)

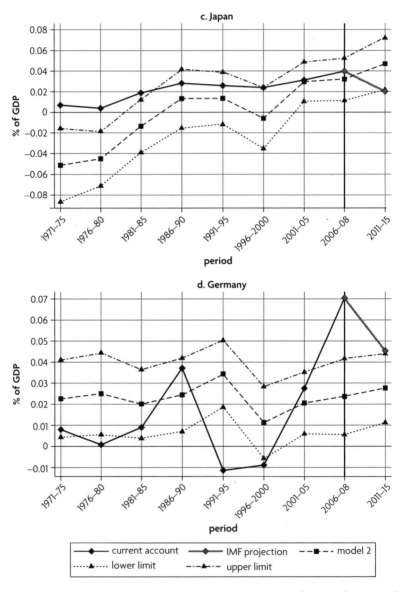

(continued next page)

Figure 2.4 (continued)

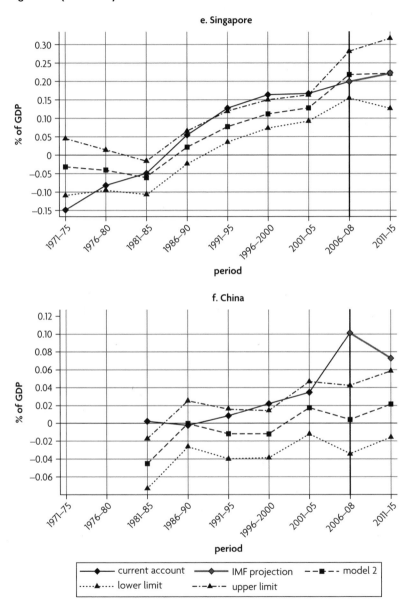

Source: IMF 2010a and authors' calculations.
Note: Predictions are based on data to 2008. Data for the financial crisis years, 2009–10, are excluded.

Figure 2.5 Out-of-Sample Current Account Predictions for Selected Countries, 2006–08 and 2011–15

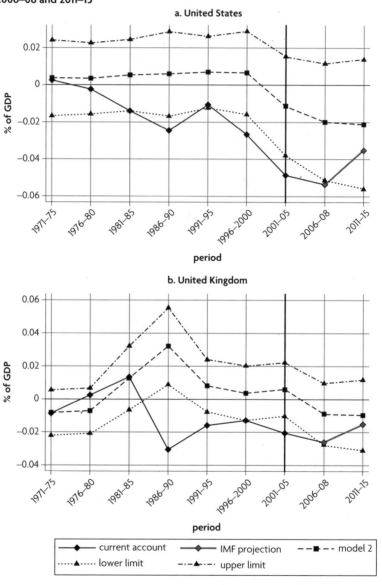

(continued next page)

Figure 2.5 (continued)

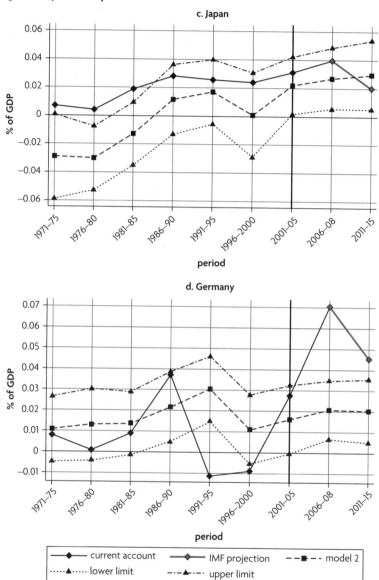

c. Japan

d. Germany

legend:
— current account   — IMF projection   – ■ – model 2
⋯▲⋯ lower limit   –⋅▲⋅– upper limit

(continued next page)

Figure 2.5 (continued)

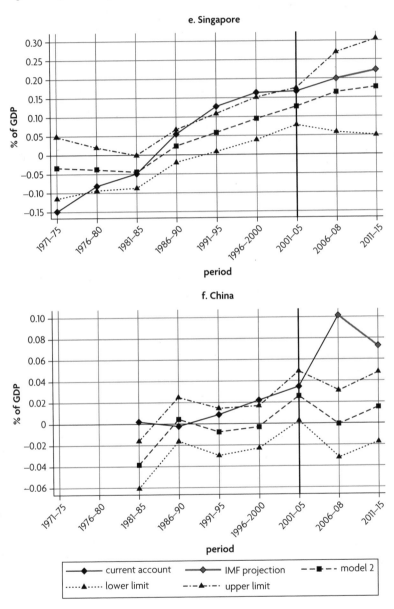

Source: IMF 2010a and authors' calculations.
Note: Predictions are based on data to 2005. Data for the financial crisis years, 2009–10, are excluded.

In the figure, the extent of imbalances of major current account deficit countries (United Kingdom and United States) or surplus countries (China and Germany) in the 2006–08 period is beyond what the model can predict using data up to 2005, signifying the pervasiveness of the global imbalances in the period. The 2011–15 forecasting also shows only modest rebalancing.

Both models persistently underpredict U.S. current account deficits, again suggesting that the United States is an outlier. In fact, when reestimating current account balances for the full sample, including the dummy for the United States, the coefficient on the country dummy is found to be significantly negative, with a magnitude of -0.031 (model 1) to -0.036 (model 2). This is consistent with the view that the United States has some special characteristic that allows it to run persistent current account deficits of some 3 percent of GDP: presumably its status as the issuer of the international vehicle currency (Gourinchas and Rey 2007).

United States: Alternative Scenarios

One of the big issues of macroeconomic management in coming years will be fiscal consolidation. The industrial countries will be required to reduce budget deficits without nipping the green shoots of recovery. How will global imbalances evolve under different fiscal scenarios?

Figure 2.6 presents different out-of-sample predictions for U.S. current account balances in the 2011–15 period depending on three different scenarios about its budget balances:

- *The baseline scenario,* based on the IMF (2010a) projection (see annex 2.2)
- *The optimistic scenario,* in which the average of the U.S. budget balances for the 2011–15 period is higher than the average based on the IMF projection (-6.5 percent of GDP) by 3 percentage points[39]
- *The pessimistic scenario,* in which the 2011–15 average is lower than the IMF projection by 3 percentage points.

Figure 2.6 shows that a 3 percentage point difference from the baseline scenario would change the predicted current account balance by half a percentage point, indicating that rebalancing cannot be accomplished through fiscal policy alone.

Figure 2.6 U.S. Current Account Projections under Three Scenarios

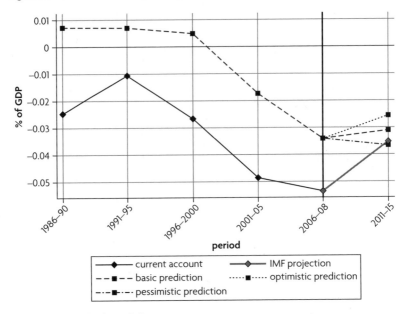

Source: IMF 2010a and authors' calculations.
Note: Data for the financial crisis years, 2009–10, are excluded.

China: Alternative Scenarios

Similarly, figure 2.7 presents alternative scenarios for financial development and capital account liberalization in China.

Panel A shows, for comparison, the same projection as shown previously in figure 2.4. Panel B shows the forecast if China's level of financial openness increases moderately—to the level of Thailand in 2008. In this case, the current account surplus falls significantly. Panels C and D show what happens when financial liberalization proceeds to the Brazilian and Mexican levels, respectively.[40] Again, this scenario leads to further declines in the current account surplus.

Figure 2.8 makes alternative assumptions about financial development.

Recall that financial development is measured by the average ratio of domestic credit to GDP, which fell, relative to the world average, between the 2001–05 and 2006–08 periods.[41] A modest assumption about Chinese financial development over the next five years is that this ratio returns to its 2001–05 levels. Placing this assumption with Mexican levels of financial openness, this is enough to eliminate China's surplus.

Figure 2.7 Chinese Current Account Projections under Liberalization of Financial Markets

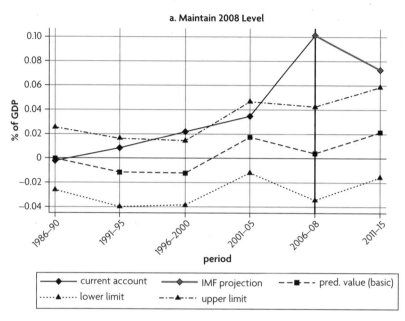

a. Maintain 2008 Level

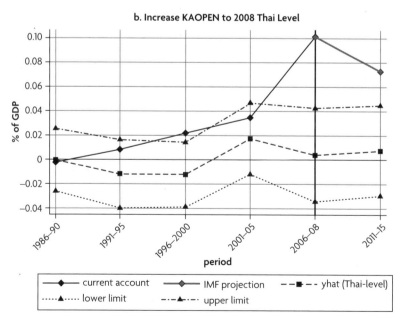

b. Increase KAOPEN to 2008 Thai Level

(continued next page)

Figure 2.7 (continued)

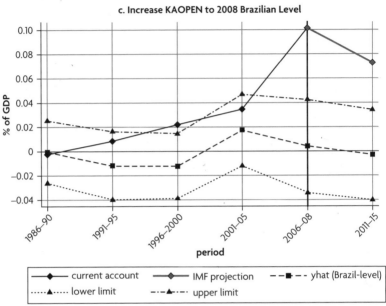

c. Increase KAOPEN to 2008 Brazilian Level

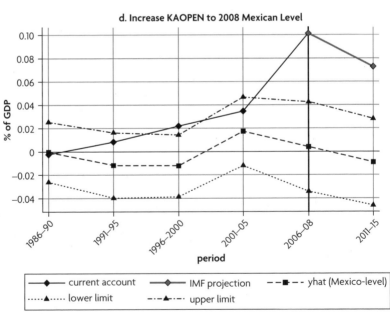

d. Increase KAOPEN to 2008 Mexican Level

Source: IMF 2010a and authors' calculations.
Note: KAOPEN = financial openness. Data for the financial crisis years, 2009–10, are excluded.

Figure 2.8 Chinese Current Account Projections under Liberalization and Development of Financial Markets

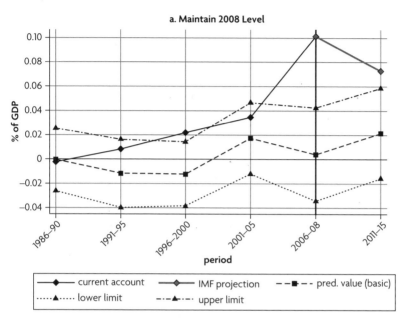

a. Maintain 2008 Level

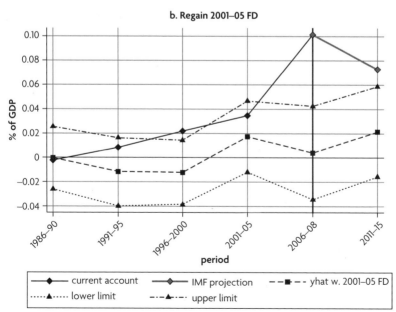

b. Regain 2001–05 FD

(continued next page)

Figure 2.8 (continued)

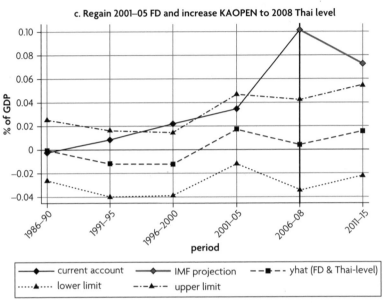

c. Regain 2001–05 FD and increase KAOPEN to 2008 Thai level

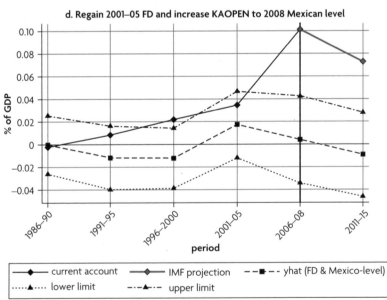

d. Regain 2001–05 FD and increase KAOPEN to 2008 Mexican level

Source: IMF 2010a and authors' calculations.
Note: FD = financial development. KAOPEN = financial openness. Data for the financial crisis years, 2009–10, are excluded.

As a caution, note that the model—based on average behavior in a cross-section of emerging markets—underpredicts the Chinese surplus in recent years. That the surplus *disappears* in 2015 under this scenario is at least as much an artifact of this underprediction as it is a consequence of the financial liberalization and development.

But the point remains: how quickly China narrows its surplus will be a function, in part, of how much progress it makes in financial liberalization and development. Furthermore, given that (a) the return of PCGDP to the 2001–05 level alone (panel B of figure 2.8) hardly changes the predicted current account level, and (b) the predicted level declines only when financial development is coupled with financial liberalization, one can surmise that financial liberalization would be more effective than financial development in reducing China's current account surplus.[42]

Living with Imbalances over the Transition

Large flows of capital across borders can both cause and be influenced by excessive risk taking and leverage. Had U.S. current account deficits resulted only in a consumption binge in the private and public sectors, the crisis of 2007–09 would have been more manageable. However, excessive capital flows induced a search for yield that made the financial sector extremely vulnerable to movements in asset prices. The lack of regulation, and heady optimism surrounding financial innovation, also pulled capital into the United States. This synergy means that it is futile to ascribe all the blame to global imbalances, but it would also be unwise to ignore the return of widening imbalances, exactly because none of the causes has thus far been addressed, either nationally or globally.

The out-of-sample forecasts presented above suggest that global imbalances are likely to wind down only very gradually. Intuitively, many of the policies that are their determinants, such as government budget balances, are themselves likely to adjust only gradually (discontinuous adjustments being painful and difficult). Even more obviously, there will be gradual adjustment of the structural determinants of current account balances—from relative per capita incomes to dependency ratios and levels of financial development. With time, these variables will tend to converge across countries, in turn creating a tendency for imbalances to shrink. But their movement is likely to be limited and hence to have limited impact in the short run.

The immediate task is thus to make the world safe for global imbalances. It is to prevent the continuing imbalances from derailing the maintenance and resumption of growth in the emerging and advanced economies, respectively. This objective points to the need for a concrete set of policy actions:

- *Redouble regulatory reform efforts.* To the extent that global imbalances contributed to financial excesses, it is important to accelerate regulatory reform to strengthen supervision and regulation while correcting incentive problems in financial markets. Analysts disagree about whether global imbalances were a central cause of the financial crisis, but there is no disagreement that those imbalances poured fuel on the flames. To say that crises like the recent one disrupt growth and should therefore be avoided is to understate the point. The authors do not subscribe to the idea that financial markets have learned their lesson and that—as the U.S. current account deficit widens again and more capital flows toward the United States—there is no danger that this capital will be used to finance dangerously speculative transactions. History tells us that financial market participants have short memories.
- *Coordinate financial reform internationally.* Individual countries are moving forward with their financial reform efforts. At this writing, the United States is putting the finishing touches on the regulations that must be issued to implement its financial reform bill, for example. But some aspects of financial reform will be effective only if coordinated internationally. Here much more needs to be done. It is uncertain whether the Basel Committee's negotiations on revising capital and liquidity ratios will be successfully completed in 2011, and there is talk of significant delay in phasing them in. This would be a mistake given the absence of progress on a global resolution regime for big financial conglomerates whose operations extend across borders. If imbalances persist and contribute to the recovery of leverage in financial markets to earlier levels, the threat to growth would be very real.
- *Apply regulation more countercyclically.* A lesson of the crisis is that regulators must do more to raise capital and liquidity requirements

when large amounts of foreign capital are flowing in and financing large current account imbalances. This is when banks, seeing their capitalization rising, will most aggressively expand their balance sheets. Once upon a time, the Bank of Spain was praised for having responded to these dynamics with countercyclical provisioning. We now know that its response, however admirable in principle, was inadequate in practice.

- *Monitor and limit foreign-currency-denominated borrowing.* Countries where the foreign finance associated with inflows is denominated in foreign currency should also be attentive to the mismatch problem. Hungary, which ran substantial current account deficits in the first half of the decade, now sees them causing serious problems for growth because the foreign finance for those deficits was in euros and Swiss francs; this created difficulties when the forint weakened against the two Western European currencies. The Hungarian authorities have now promulgated regulations limiting foreign-currency-denominated borrowing by the corporate and household sectors, but the horse has long since left the barn.

- *Redefine the central banks' role.* Similarly, central banks should now take greater account of imbalances and asset prices in the formulation of monetary policy. The old conventional wisdom was that imbalances were relevant to the decision of how to set policy rates only insofar as they had implications for the output gap and expected inflation. The new conventional wisdom, informed by the crisis, is that growth can be disrupted if external deficits are allowed to create systemic financial vulnerabilities or are apt to be compressed suddenly. Central banks need to think of themselves not only as inflation targeters but also as macroprudential supervisors, given that other supervisors are not always up to the task.[43] This redefined role is likely to mean using monetary policy to lean harder against the early signs of asset bubbles associated with persistent imbalances.

- *Adjust fiscal policy more proactively.* The new conventional wisdom is the same as the old conventional wisdom: as current account deficits widen and capital inflows rise, it is important for the fiscal authorities to tighten policy—again, to prevent a buildup of threats to financial stability and growth. This is a lesson that emerging markets in Asia and Latin America learned from their earlier crises. It would have been the appropriate response in the Baltics and in Southern Europe during the past decade. One concrete step toward making fiscal policy more proactive is to recognize that, for the advanced economies, it is urgent to run a fiscal policy that sets the cyclically adjusted budget balance near zero over the medium term. That calculation should include contingent liabilities as well; as resources become tighter, governments will be tempted to stimulate the economy by using guarantees for loans or for pensions.

- *Hasten correction of global imbalances.* The preceding analysis suggests that countries should redouble their efforts to speed the correction of global imbalances. Coordinated fiscal action is one obvious way of doing so; countries with large current account surpluses, such as China and Germany, can expand while those with large deficits and questionable prospects for financing them (particularly in Southern Europe) consolidate. If coordinated, these adjustments can help correct global imbalances while continuing to support global demand.[44] As these and related measures are taken, there will have to be adjustments in either relative inflation rates or exchange rates to clear markets, as discussed previously in the "Policy Challenges and Responses" section. Herein lies the case for more currency flexibility in China as a concomitant of other policies to speed the correction of imbalances.

- *Slow foreign exchange reserve accumulation.* The chronic surpluses of emerging markets also reflect the demand for still greater foreign exchange reserves as insurance against financial volatility—suggesting that the other policies suggested in this section to reduce volatility could also pay off in terms of correcting imbalances insofar as they also limit the appetite for reserves. In addition, the following steps would help to further moderate this appetite:

  o Regional reserve-pooling arrangements
  o Institutionalization of bilateral swap lines and credits
  o Creation of a quick-disbursing, lightly conditioned facility at the IMF that emerging markets would finally feel comfortable about accessing.

These options are addressed in the G-20 agenda for strengthening the international financial architecture. The success of these efforts is important, therefore, both to accelerate the correction of global imbalances and to make the world safe for growth in the meantime.

Annex 2.1 Data

Table 2A.1 lists the mnemonics for the variables used in the analysis, descriptions of those variables, and the source(s) from which the primary data for constructing those variables were taken.

Table 2A.1 Mnemonics for Variables in Analysis

Mnemonic	Variable description	Source
CAGDP	Ratio of current account to GDP	WDI, WEO
NSGDP	Ratio of national saving to GDP	WDI, WEO
KFGDP	Ratio of capital formation to GDP	WDI, WEO
GOVBGDP	Ratio of general government budget balance to GDP	WDI, IFS, WEO
NFAGDP	Ratio of stock of net foreign assets to GDP	LM
RELY	Relative per capita income, adjusted by PPP exchange rates, measured relative to the United States (range of 0 to 1)	PWT
RELDEPY	Youth dependency ratio, relative to mean across all countries (population under 15 / population between 15 and 65)	WDI
RELDEPO	Old dependency ratio, relative to mean across all countries (population over 65 / population between 15 and 65)	WDI
YGRAVG	Average real GDP growth	WDI
TOT	Terms of trade	WDI
OPEN	Openness indicator (ratio of exports plus imports of goods and nonfactor services to GDP)	WDI
PCGDP	Banking development (ratio of private credit to GDP)	WBFS
KAOPEN	Capital account openness	CI
BQ	Quality of bureaucracy	ICRG
LAO	Law and order	ICRG
CORRUPT	Corruption index	ICRG
LEGAL	General level of legal development (first principal component of BQ, LAO, and CORRUPT)	Authors' calculation
IR	Ratio of international reserves (excluding gold) to GDP	WDI

Source: Authors' compilation.

Note: PPP = purchasing power parity. CI = Chinn and Ito 2006 and updates. ICRG = International Country Risk Guide. IFS = IMF International Financial Statistics. LM = Lane and Milesi-Ferretti 2006. OECD = OECD Economic Outlook Database. PWT = Penn World Table 6.4. WBFS = World Bank Financial Structure Database. WDI = World Development Indicators. WEO = World Economic Outlook (IMF 2010a, 2010b).

Annex 2.2 Assumptions of Out-of-Sample Forecasting Exercise

Table 2A.2 Assumptions of Out-of-Sample Forecasting Variables

Variables	Assumptions
Government budget balance	*World Economic Outlook (WEO)* projections are used (IMF 2010a). In the *WEO*, the budget balance data and their projections are available only for 33 countries. However, the sum of output (in US$) for these countries accounts for 85–90 percent of total world output. Hence, the 33 countries' data are used to calculate the world-weighted average. The data are also used for U.S. projections. China's budget balance data are not available. We assumed the 2011–15 average of budget balances will be −2 percent, a reasonable assumption given information in other sources.
Net foreign assets (initial)	The level of net foreign assets is assumed to be unchanged as in 2004 (the last year for which data are available).
Relative income	The relative income series (originally based on Penn World Tables) is extrapolated using growth rates calculated from the *WEO*'s series of per capita income in international PPP.
Youth and old dependency ratios	Forecasts from the United Nations' World Population Prospects database are used.
Financial development (PCGDP)	This is a difficult variable to project. The global crisis must surely have made private credit creation smaller for many countries, but this may not be the case for some (for example, China). Also, GDP (the denominator for this variable) shrank for many countries, which can make the variable PCGDP relatively stable even for countries whose private credit also shrank. We use the average of the variable (though as deviations from the world-weighted averages) during the 2001–08 period. For China, we consider a range of alternative assumptions.
Legal development (LEGAL)	We assume no change.
Financial openness (KAOPEN)	For Germany, Japan, Korea, the United Kingdom, and United States, we assume the level of KAOPEN as of 2011–15 to be the same as in 2008. For China, we consider a range of alternative assumptions.
TOT volatility	We assume no change.
Average GDP growth	We use the data from the *World Economic Outlook* (IMF 2010a).
Trade openness	We assume no change.
Dummy for 2011–15	Because we have no estimated coefficient on the dummy for the 2011–15 period, we use the average of the time fixed effects for the other previous panels.

Source: Authors' compilation.
Note: TOT = terms of trade. PPP = purchasing power parity.

Notes

1. Don't say that you weren't warned (Eichengreen 2004).
2. That is, if something can't go on forever, it won't.
3. Given the small share of discretionary spending on the expenditure side, the combination will consist primarily of the first two components.
4. One can imagine, for example, that the additional debt bequeathed by the crisis will have to be serviced by levying higher taxes—including higher capital taxes, which will modestly discourage investment. Or one can imagine that long-term unemployment has adversely affected capital-labor complementarities.
5. However, it takes a few years for the full effect to be felt (Herve et al. 2010).
6. These observers may, of course, be underestimating the scope for expanding exports of services.
7. The downswing in the dollar began with the peak in February 22, 2002; the dollar has depreciated in real terms by 33 percent since then.
8. The dollar strengthened not just because of the weakness of the euro but also because some emerging-market economies such as China were reluctant to allow their currencies to appreciate against the dollar until the global implications of the crisis in Europe became clear.
9. Bertaut, Kamin, and Thomas (2009), projecting trends in the U.S. net international investment position, suggest that this process still has a considerable distance to run.
10. In the second half of the chapter, the authors present their own projections of the prospective widening of the U.S. current account deficit.
11. The United Kingdom, owing to its separate currency, may be able to follow a separate strategy—a topic further discussed below.
12. The acronym PIIGS refers to the five Euro Area nations that were considered weaker economically following the financial crisis: Portugal, Italy, Ireland, Greece, and Spain.
13. Of course, insofar as it was not net capital flows but gross capital flows (European banks taking risky positions in structured investment products associated with the growth of the subprime mortgage market in the United States being the flip side of U.S. purchases of European securities), neither can the Europeans and their investments be exonerated of all blame for the crisis.
14. IMF (2010b) reports no change in projected year-on-year growth rates in 2010 and a reduction of 0.2 percentage points in 2011.
15. This is the approach to which Greece has committed.
16. Again, the authors offer their own projections of the German current account balance in the second half of the chapter.
17. A more novel argument is that the sex imbalance encourages saving by single men as a way of signaling their attractiveness as marriage partners (Du and Wei 2010).
18. The view that gender imbalance contributes to Chinese saving similarly cautions against expecting much progress because the gender ratio similarly changes only slowly with time.

19. Since 2008, some state-owned enterprises have been required to make limited dividend payments to their state owners, but this only adds to government savings (as noted elsewhere).

20. See Herd, Hill, and Pigott (2010) for a status report on Chinese financial reform.

21. Ma and Yi (2010) question it on the grounds that market share and profits have been rising most rapidly not among state-owned firms but rather among smaller, private enterprises.

22. The authors' projections of the Chinese current account are in the second half of the chapter.

23. There was also a negative change in the income account owing to a lower return on foreign investments, so the shift in the current account was not simply the sum of the change in the net financial positions of the three sectors.

24. Note that these pieces do, in fact, fit together. Revaluation by emerging Asia against Japan and the other advanced economies implies an increase in exports by capital-abundant economies and a decline in those of their more labor-abundant counterparts.

25. The Association of Southeast Asian Nations (ASEAN) Plus Three, commonly abbreviated as ASEAN+3, coordinates cooperation between ASEAN and the three East Asian nations of China, Japan, and Korea. The Chiang Mai Initiative (CMI) established a multilateral currency swap among the ASEAN+3 countries to manage regional short-term liquidity issues after the 1997 Asian financial crisis. The CMI also facilitates other international financial arrangements, including ASEAN+3's work with the IMF.

26. *LAO*, *BQ*, and *CORRUPT* are extracted from the *International Country Risk Guide* database. Higher values of these variables indicate better conditions.

27. The variables for terms-of-trade volatility (TOT), trade openness (OPN), and legal development (LEGAL) are averaged for each country; that is, they are time-invariant.

28. The five-year panels are 1971–75, 1976–80, and so on. However, the last panel is composed of only three years: 2006–08.

29. The emerging-market economies are those that the International Financial Corporation classified as either emerging or frontier during 1980–1997, plus (a) Hong Kong SAR, China, and (b) Singapore.

30. These estimates are similar to those in Abbas et al. (2010), who find that the elasticity of the current account balance with respect to the fiscal balance is on the order of 0.2–0.3. Erceg, Guerrieri, and Gust (2005) also show simulation results that yield the coefficient of the budget balance to be around 0.2.

31. However, this result does not show up for the industrial countries.

32. The *p*-value is 15 percent.

33. This is confirmed by adding a dummy variable for China in the post-2005 period. Its coefficient is positive and significant at the 1 percent level, while the coefficient for emerging markets as a group in this subperiod continues to be zero.

34. This conclusion is confirmed by adding a dummy variable for the United States in the 2001–05 subperiod; its coefficient is negative, and adding it does not eliminate the significant positive coefficient for 2001–05 in the industrial-country column. Not surprisingly, when all countries are included (in the leftmost column), these period dummy variables are insignificant because, by definition, current accounts should sum to zero.

35. The results are not shown in the table.

36. These estimates are based on model 2 (see equation 6.2), including the institutional variables.

37. The forecasts are based on model 2 (including the institutional variables) and the separate estimates for industrial and emerging-market economies.

38. The confidence intervals for 2011–15 are those of predictions, not those of forecasting. The implicit assumption is that the economy of concern faces the exact conditions as assumed in annex 2.2. Once the uncertainty of the explanatory variables in the period is incorporated, the confidence intervals can surely widen.

39. Three percentage points are equivalent to 1.5 standard deviations in the distribution of U.S. budget balances in the 1969–2008 period.

40. The countries are ranked, by level of financial openness in 2008, as follows: Mexico (69.2 on the 100-point scale), Brazil (58.8), Thailand (40.3), and China (16.1). The average KAOPEN of the LDC group as of 2008 is 50.2, whereas that of the EMG group is 60.9.

41. Recall that in the empirical model all variables are normalized by the world average.

42. This conclusion relies upon the proxy of financial development—the ratio of private credit creation to GDP—accurately representing financial development. It would be preferable to use a broader measure of financial development such as the composite bond, equity, or bank indicators used in Ito and Chinn (2009), but the data are not yet available for that exercise.

43. And given that, when things go wrong, it is the central bank that will be forced to make them good.

44. Where the United States fits in this equation is not so clear. The desire to speed the correction of global imbalances suggests faster budget-deficit cutting. However, the need to support global demand and the still-low interest rates that suggest the existence of fiscal space suggest instead further fiscal stimulus to support global demand.

References

Abbas, S. M. Ali, Jacques Bouhga-Hagbe, Antonio Fatas, Paolo Mauro, and Ricardo Velloso. 2010. "Fiscal Policy and the Current Account." Working Paper 10/121, International Monetary Fund, Washington, DC.

Aizenman, Joshua, and Yothin Jinjarak. 2009. "Current Account Patterns and National Real Estate Markets." *Journal of Urban Economics* 66 (2): 75–89.

Aziz, Iwan, and Mario Lamberte. 2010. "ASEAN Imbalances and Rebalancing." Unpublished manuscript, Asian Development Bank Institute, Tokyo.

Bernanke, Ben. 2005. "The Global Savings Glut and the U.S. Current Account." Remarks at the Sandridge Lecture, Virginia Association of Economists, Richmond, VA, March 10.

Bertaut, Carol, Steve Kamin, and Charles Thomas. 2009. "How Long Can the Unsustainable U.S. Current Account Deficit Be Sustained?" *IMF Staff Papers* 56 (August): 596–632.

Caballero, Ricardo, Emmanuel Farhi, and Pierre-Olivier Gourinchas. 2008. "An Equilibrium Model of 'Global Imbalances' and Low Interest Rates." *American Economic Review* 98 (1): 358–93.

Carroll, Christopher, and Jiri Slacalek. 2009. "The American Consumer: Reforming or Just Resting?" Unpublished manuscript, Johns Hopkins University, Baltimore, and European Central Bank, Frankfurt am Main.

Chinn, Menzie. 2005. "Getting Serious about the Twin Deficits." Council Special Report 10, Council on Foreign Relations, New York.

Chinn, Menzie, and Hiro Ito. 2006. "What Matters for Financial Development? Capital Controls, Institutions, and Interactions." *Journal of Development Economics* 81 (1): 163–92.

———. 2007. "Current Account Balances, Financial Development and Institutions: Assaying the World 'Savings Glut.'" *Journal of International Money and Finance* 26 (4): 546–69.

Chinn, Menzie, and Eswar Prasad. 2003. "Medium-Term Determinants of Current Accounts in Industrial and Developing Countries: An Empirical Exploration." *Journal of International Economics* 59 (1): 47–76.

Clarida, Richard. 2005. "Japan, China and the U.S. Current Account Deficit." *Cato Journal* 25 (1): 111–14.

Darvas, Zsolt, and Jean Pisani-Ferry. 2010. "Future Development of Global Imbalances." Policy Note, Directorate General for Internal Policies, European Commission, Brussels.

Deutsche Bank. 2010. "China." *Emerging Markets Monthly,* June 1, 70–72.

Dooley, Michael, David Folkerts-Landau, and Peter Garber. 2003. "An Essay on the Revived Bretton Woods System." Working Paper 9971, National Bureau of Economic Research, Cambridge, MA.

Dooley, Michael, and Peter Garber. 2005. "Is It 1958 or 1968? Three Notes on the Revived Bretton Woods System." *Brookings Papers on Economic Activity* 2005 (1): 147–87.

Du, Qingyuan, and Shang-Jin Wei. 2010. "A Sexually Unbalanced Model of Current Account Imbalances." Working Paper 16000, National Bureau of Economic Research, Cambridge, MA.

Economist. 2010. "Nip and Tuck: Europe's Plans for Fiscal Austerity Are Not Quite the Threat to Recovery They Seem." June 10.

Eichengreen, Barry. 2004. "Global Imbalances and the Lessons of Bretton Woods." Working Paper 10497, National Bureau of Economic Research, Cambridge, MA.

Eichengreen, Barry, and Molly Fifer. 2002. "The Implications of Aging for the Balance of Payments between North and South." In *The Economics of Ageing Societies*, ed. Horst Siebert, 81–105. Tubingen, Germany: Mohr.

Eichengreen, Barry, and Gisela Rua. 2010. "Exchange Rates and Global Rebalancing." Unpublished manuscript, University of California, Berkeley.

Erceg, Christopher, Luca Guerrieri, and Christopher Gust. 2005. "Expansionary Fiscal Shocks and the Trade Deficit." International Finance Discussion Paper 825, Board of Governors of the Federal Reserve System, Washington, DC.

Fratzscher, Marcel, and Roland Straub. 2009. "Asset Prices and Current Account Fluctuations in G7 Countries." Working Paper 1014, European Central Bank, Frankfurt am Main.

Gourinchas, Pierre-Olivier, and Helene Rey. 2007. "From World Banker to World Venture Capitalist: U.S. Current Account Imbalances and the Exorbitant Privilege." In *G7 Current Account Imbalances: Sustainability and Adjustment*, ed. Richard Clarida, 11–66. Chicago: University of Chicago Press.

Green, Stephen. 2010. "China Can Reduce Its Surplus Savings." *Wall Street Journal*, January 24.

Greenspan, Alan. 2005a. "Mortgage Banking." Speech to the American Bankers Association Annual Convention, Palm Desert, CA, September 26.

———. 2005b. "Current Account." Keynote speech to the "Advancing Enterprise 2005" conference, sponsored by the U.K. Chancellor of the Exchequer, London, February 4.

Herd, Richard, Samuel Hill, and Charles Pigott. 2010. "China's Financial Sector Reforms." OECD Economics Department Working Paper 747, Organisation for Economic Co-operation and Development, Paris.

Herve, Karine, Nigel Pain, Pete Richardson, Frank Sedillot, and Pierre-Olivier Beffy. 2010. "The OECD's New Global Model." Economics Department Working Paper 768, Organisation for Economic Co-operation and Development, Paris.

IMF (International Monetary Fund). 2008. *World Economic Outlook* October 2008. Washington, DC: IMF.

———. 2010a. *World Economic Outlook* April 2010: *Rebalancing Growth*. Washington, DC: IMF.

———. 2010b. *World Economic Outlook Update*, July 2010. Washington, DC: IMF.

———. 2011. *World Economic Outlook Update*, April 2011. Washington, DC: IMF.

Ito, Hiro, and Menzie Chinn. 2009. "East Asia and Global Imbalances: Saving, Investment, and Financial Development." In *Financial Development in the Pacific Rim*, ed. Takatoshi Ito and Andrew Rose, 117–60. Chicago: University of Chicago Press.

Jaumotte, Florence, and Piyaporn Sodsriwiboon. 2010. "Current Account Imbalances in the Southern Euro Area." Working Paper 10/139, International Monetary Fund, Washington, DC.

Kawai, Masahiro, and Shinji Takagi. 2010. "Japan's Growth Rebalancing: What Can Japan Do?" Unpublished manuscript, Asian Development Bank Institute, Tokyo.

Kroeber, Arthur. 2010. "Economic Rebalancing: The End of Surplus Labor." *China Economic Quarterly* 14 (1): 35–46.

Lane, Philip, and Gian Maria Milesi-Ferretti. 2006. "The External Wealth of Nations, Mark II." Working Paper 06/09, International Monetary Fund, Washington, DC.

Ma, Guonan, and Wang Yi. 2010. "China's High Saving Rate: Myth and Reality." Working Paper 312, Bank for International Settlements, Basel, Switzerland.

Mody, Ashoka, and Franziska Ohnsorge. 2010. "After the Crisis: Low Consumption Growth but Narrower Global Imbalances." Working Paper 10/11, International Monetary Fund, Washington, DC.

Obstfeld, Maurice, and Kenneth Rogoff. 2007. "The Unsustainable U.S. Current Account Position Revisited." In *G7 Current Account Imbalances: Sustainability and Adjustment*, ed. Richard Clarida, 339–76. Chicago: University of Chicago Press.

———. 2009. "Global Imbalances and the Financial Crisis: Products of Common Causes." Paper presented to the "Asia Economic Policy Conference," sponsored by the Federal Reserve Bank of San Francisco's Center for Pacific Basin Studies, Santa Barbara, CA, October 19–20.

Prasad, Eswar. 2009. "Rebalancing Growth in Asia." Working Paper 15169, National Bureau of Economic Research, Cambridge, MA.

Roach, Stephen. 2009. *The Next Asia*. New York: Wiley.

Thorbecke, William. 2010. "Investigating the Effect of Exchange Rate Changes on Trans-Pacific Rebalancing." Unpublished manuscript, Asian Development Bank Institute, Tokyo.

Tyers, Rod, and Feng Lu. 2009. "Competition Policy, Corporate Saving and China's Current Account Surplus." Working Paper in Economics and Econometrics 495, Australian National University, Canberra.

3

Fiscal Policy and Growth: Overcoming the Constraints

Carlo Cottarelli and Michael Keen

This chapter discusses how fiscal policies—both the macro fiscal concerns of deficits and public debt and the micro fiscal detail of taxation and public spending—can be reconfigured to best support economic growth over the coming years, with a focus on advanced and emerging economies. It does so in light of the momentous developments in fiscal trends arising from the 2008–09 crisis. The crisis led to deterioration in the state of the fiscal accounts in virtually all countries, with consequences that, for most advanced economies and some emerging economies, will be felt for several years. Although these developments strongly color the short- and medium-term outlooks, the fiscal challenges are intensified still further by other trends in the fiscal outlook. This chapter aims to provide a coherent overview of both the macro challenges and the micro responses that might best address those challenges.

We are grateful to Bill Kline, Danny M. Leipziger, and Uri Dadush for helpful comments and suggestions. Raquel Gomez Sirera provided excellent research assistance. The views here are ours alone and should not be attributed to the International Monetary Fund, its executive board, or its management.

The broad context for this overview is provided in the next section, which sets out fiscal policy objectives and overarching trends. The main analysis follows in two parts:

- *The Macroeconomic Dimension* examines fiscal policy and, especially, the implications for growth of overall fiscal deficits and debt—ranging from the effect of fiscal risks on macroeconomic stability to the effects of high public debt on long-term growth and, conversely, the challenges of managing aggregate demand during periods of prolonged fiscal consolidation.
- *The Microeconomic Dimension* considers central issues and possibilities in designing and implementing revenue and spending measures that will answer the macroeconomic imperatives in a way most conducive to restoring strong, lasting growth. The fiscal policy response requires not only improving existing instruments but also deploying some new ones.

Fiscal Policy for Growth: Objectives and Challenges

Of course, economic growth is not the only dimension of economic performance that is, or should be, of interest. Distributional concerns matter (and are indeed closely linked with the political support for growth-oriented strategies), as do the quality of the environment and—as the crisis of 2008 reminds us—the stability of growth. Ultimately, it is some notion of individual and social well-being by which policy must be judged.

These indicators are important because fiscal policy can have quite varying effects on them. Measures that increase labor force participation, for instance, may increase output, have no impact on long-term growth, reduce the welfare of directly affected individuals, and raise some measures of overall social welfare. Moreover, although we now know quite a lot about how tax and spending measures affect individual behavior, we know much less about their impact on aggregate growth (Myles 2009a, 2009b). In the following analysis, although the primary concern is with sustained growth, the authors also have in mind effects on output levels and—albeit less overtly, given the focus of this book—on welfare and inequality.

The crisis has changed the fiscal outlook in all countries, most dramatically in many of the most advanced; the next section will amplify this. But the fiscal outlook also reflects deeper trends, posing further challenges for both broad macro strategy and micro implementation. Three of these challenges stand out: aging, climate change, and globalization.[1]

Conceptually, the most profound of these is the last. Aging creates fiscal pressures that are nothing new. Climate change is an externality problem that economists have known how to address, in broad terms, for decades—despite its horrendously complex features (IMF 2008). But globalization, although obviously beneficial in several respects, simultaneously increases the demands for social spending in the face of increased life uncertainties (Rodrik 1998) and increases the difficulty of meeting those demands. In a globalized economy, the increased mobility of capital, commodities, and people also means, to a large degree, increased mobility of national tax bases—hence greater difficulty of raising revenue and greater danger of beggar-thy-neighbor tax policies.

More fundamentally still, globalization changes how we think about fiscal instruments. When capital is mobile, for instance, the real burden of a source-based tax on capital income will fall not on capital owners but also on immobile factors, which may well include many low-paid workers. Faced with such a tax, capital will simply move abroad until the pretax rate of return has risen enough—as a consequence of lower prices of immobile factors—to restore the after-tax return to the level available elsewhere. Thus, we may have to learn to think of the corporate tax as largely a tax on labor, which emerging empirical evidence suggests is already the case.

The Macroeconomic Dimension: Trends, Outlooks, and Challenges

The 2008–09 economic crisis had different implications for advanced and emerging (indeed, also low-income) economies for two reasons: (a) they faced different initial fiscal conditions, and (b) the severity of the recession differed between them. Advanced economies fared much worse in both respects.

In a nutshell, advanced economies reached the crisis with arguably the worst fiscal outlook ever faced in the absence of a major war.

Meanwhile, the outlook in emerging economies, if not the *best* ever faced, was relatively strong, at least on average.

Contrasting Conditions

Let's start with the advanced economies. Their fiscal deficits in 2007, ahead of the crisis, were relatively contained because of some steady strengthening since 2003, as figure 3.1 shows.

Figure 3.1 General Government Balances in Group of Seven Economies, 1998–2007
% of GDP

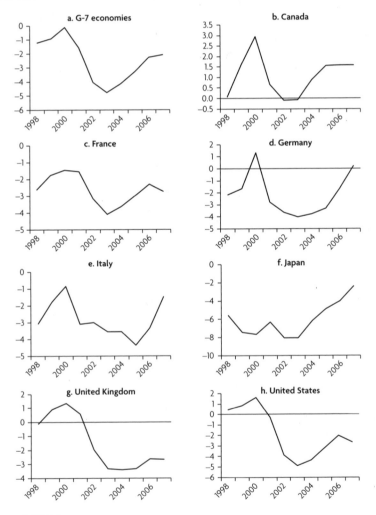

Source: IMF 2010d.

However, their overall fiscal position ahead of the crisis fell short of what had been a consistent policy goal for economies confronting weak demographic trends: to run surpluses, or at least balanced budgets, at times of strong economic growth.

Moreover—and something that did not attract much attention at that time—public debt had reached a level in 2007 never reached before except as a result of a major war. This was not true for all countries (for example, public debt was not high in Canada, particularly in net terms, or in the United Kingdom). But, as figure 3.2 shows, public debt reached a historical peak (leaving aside war-related debt surges) in the three largest advanced economies (Germany, Japan, and the United States) as well as in several other economies, including France and Italy.

In addition, these countries were facing major pressures from aging-related spending despite significant reforms. Although this is well known, some aspects of the problem are sometimes not fully understood. The focus, particularly in Europe, has traditionally been on pension spending, and indeed this is the area where most progress has been made. In the absence of reform to address the aging population (figure 3.3), pension spending would have increased by about 3 percentage points of gross domestic product (GDP) over precrisis levels by 2030 (figure 3.4). The pension reforms, however, are expected to contain the increase within 1 percentage point—a sizable increase but manageable and definitely not nearly as large as that projected for health care.

Health care spending pressures arise not only from aging but also from the projected cost increases related to Baumol effects and especially to the availability of better, but more expensive, medical products. Assuming that these non-aging-related factors continue to operate in the future as in the past—an assumption made, for example, in spending projections by the U.S. Congressional Budget Office (CBO 2009)—the projected average increase in health care spending over the next 20 years in the advanced countries would be on the order of 3.5 percentage points of GDP, somewhat larger in the United States (4.5 percentage points of GDP), but sizable also in Europe (3 percentage points).

The precrisis outlook for emerging economies was more favorable. First, years of strong growth and prudent macroeconomic policies had led to a sharp decline not only in fiscal deficits but especially in the debt-to-GDP ratio—essentially in all areas of the emerging-market

Figure 3.2　General Government Debt in Group of Seven Economies, 1950–2007
% of GDP

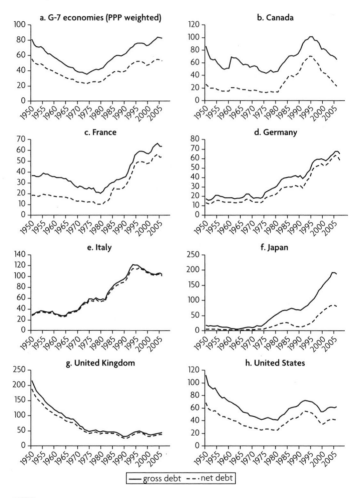

Source: HPDD.
Note: PPP = purchasing power parity.

world (figure 3.5)—and this decline was expected to continue over the medium term.[2]

Aging-related spending trends were also more favorable in emerging economies than in advanced countries, although demographic challenges do exist (as shown in figure 3.3). Given the less-generous welfare systems in emerging economies, spending increases are projected to be

Figure 3.3 Predicted Old-Age Dependency Ratio, 2009–50

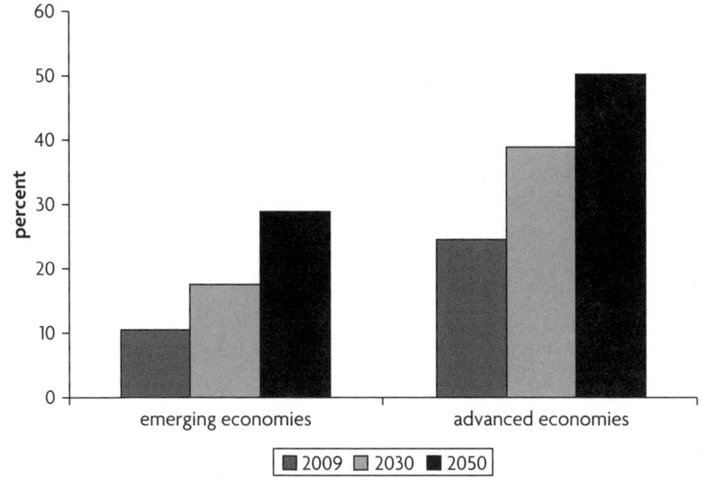

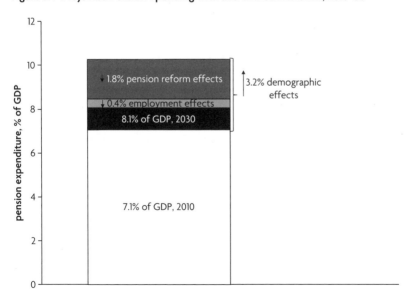

Source: UN 2009.
Note: The "old-age dependency ratio" is the proportion of the population aged 65 and older relative to those aged 15–64.

Figure 3.4 Projected Pension Spending with and without Reforms, 2010–30

Source: Authors.

Figure 3.5 General Government Debt in Emerging Economies, 1998–2007

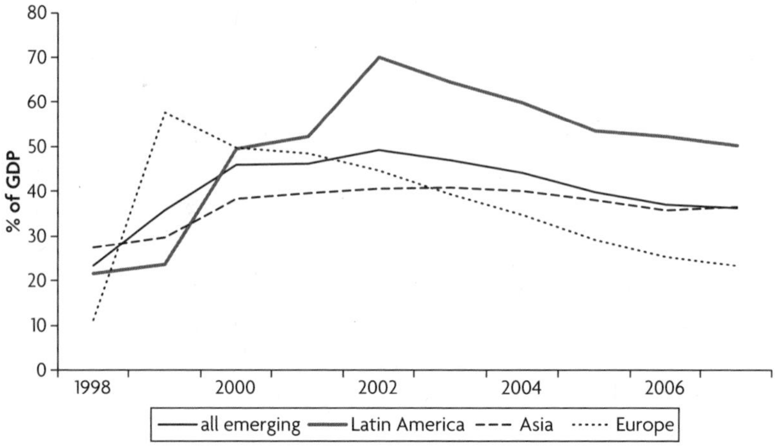

Source: IMF 2010d.

more contained, at least on average (by around 2.25 percentage points over the next two decades).

It is from these different starting points that the crisis hit the fiscal accounts of the world, with an intensity that reflected the intensity of the output shock across countries and the related policy responses (including through the automatic stabilizers). Deficit and debt increased in both country groups but much more in advanced countries, and most of the debt-ratio increases were related directly to the fall in GDP relative to the precrisis trend, as figure 3.6 illustrates.

The difference in the debt outlook is particularly striking over the medium term: debt in advanced countries is projected to continue to rise, albeit at a more contained pace than in 2009–10, while debt in emerging economies soon resumes a declining trend.[3] Over a longer horizon, deficits would start rising again, particularly in advanced countries, reflecting the demographic trends discussed above and leading to a debt spiral, as shown in figure 3.7.

One important caveat is in order, relating both to the nature of the shock to fiscal accounts and to its persistence. As figure 3.6 shows, even in the medium term, the fiscal deficit of both advanced and emerging economies is projected to remain weaker than in 2007. This persistent

Figure 3.6 General Government Balances and Debt in Advanced vs. Emerging Economies, 2007–15

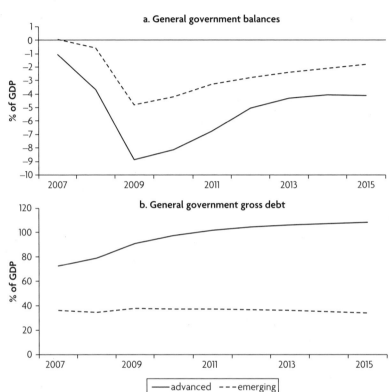

Source: IMF 2010d.

weakness reflects, in part, the higher debt levels and servicing needs as well as some permanent revenue loss relating to financial market cycles (revenues were probably above average in 2007).

Another important reason for this deficit hysteresis is the assumption that the crisis caused a long-lasting loss in output, which figure 3.8 illustrates. Whether this output decline is indeed the cause remains to be seen and depends, in part, on the policy decisions affecting growth discussed in this volume. Yet it now seems a reasonable assumption—one that finds support in earlier studies of financial crises' effect on potential output levels (IMF 2009b).

Figure 3.7 General Government Net Debt Projections for Advanced Economies, Projected to 2030

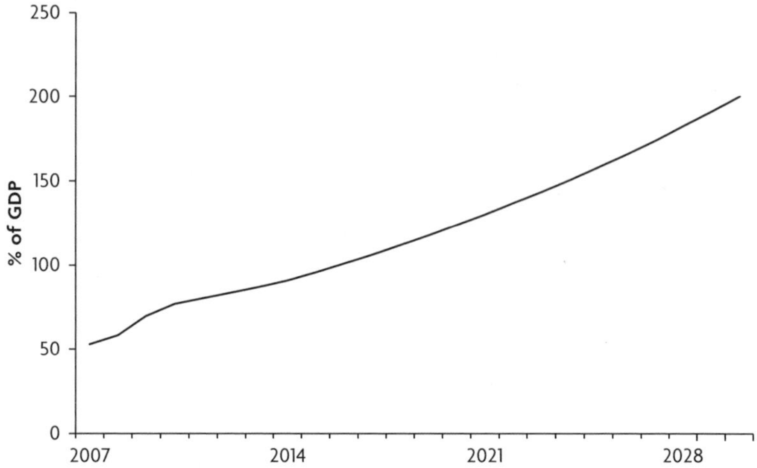

Source: IMF 2010b.

Effects of Deficits and Debt on Growth

The figures above illustrate how powerful the effects of growth could be on fiscal variables. What follows is the core concern of this chapter—the effect that fiscal variables can have on growth. Three dimensions should be explored:

- The implications of fiscal imbalances for macroeconomic stability and hence growth
- The implications of stable but high public debt for potential growth
- The effect of fiscal adjustment on growth.

Fiscal Imbalances and Growth. From a medium-term perspective, there is no doubt that the fiscal position of several economies in 2010 is unsustainable. Figure 3.9 plots the cyclically adjusted primary balances projected for 2010 against the projected general government debt ratio at the end of 2010, shown separately for advanced and emerging economies.

The slanted lines mark the relationship between primary balance and debt ratio at which the latter is stable. For advanced countries, the

Figure 3.8 Precrisis and Postcrisis Output in Advanced Economies, Projected to 2014

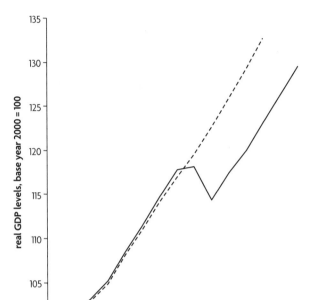

Source: IMF 2010d.
Note: WEO = World Economic Outlook.

relationship is positive because of the assumption of a positive interest-rate growth differential (at about 1 percent, the approximate average of the last two decades): the larger the debt ratio, the larger the required primary balance needed to stabilize it. The points below the lines indicate countries with insufficient primary balances that, if maintained, would lead to an explosion of their debt ratios. Most advanced countries were in that position in 2010.

Things are a bit more complicated for emerging economies. The equilibrium line slopes downward because of the assumption of a negative interest-rate growth differential, again in line with past long-term averages. Even so, many emerging economies have an insufficient primary balance, which would lead to an increase in the debt ratio.[4]

Figure 3.9 Actual and Debt-Stabilizing General Government Primary Balances, by Debt Ratio, 2010

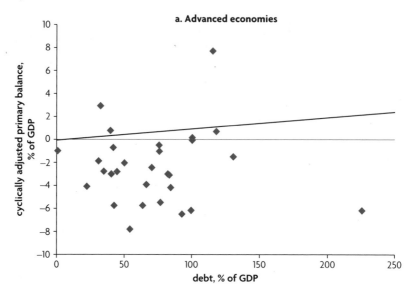

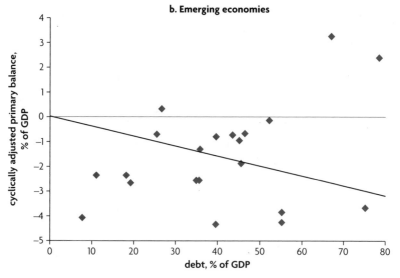

Source: IMF 2010d and IMF staff estimates.
Note: Slanted lines represent the equilibrium of primary balance (cyclically adjusted) and debt ratio at which the latter is stable.

What are the implications for growth? There is plenty of evidence that fiscal imbalances can lead to macroeconomic instability (Fatás and Mihov 2003) and that macroeconomic instability hampers growth, including potential growth (Ramey and Ramey 1995; Woo 2009). Dramatic developments in countries like Greece, Iceland, Ireland, and Portugal in 2009–10 provided a fresh reminder of the risks for macroeconomic stability and growth arising from fiscal imbalances. The transmission channel goes from a lack of confidence that the government will repay its debt to rising real interest rates, capital outflows, exchange rate pressures, and a surge of uncertainty—all of which undermine investment incentives. These effects manifest themselves more clearly in an overt debt crisis but are likely to be present in milder forms in precrisis situations.

Still unknown is how rapidly fiscal imbalances and, in particular, a rising public debt ratio are likely to have negative implications for growth via macroeconomic instability. For emerging economies, an often-quoted threshold beyond which the risk of a debt crisis increases rapidly is 40–50 percent (IMF 2003; Reinhart, Rogoff, and Savastano 2003). Even so, the predictive power of debt crisis models is usually low, particularly in terms of "false positives" (predicting crises that will never occur). For advanced economies, there is no clear statistical evidence in this area—and there could hardly be any, given the limited number (indeed, the absence) of major debt crises in advanced countries in past decades. This said, one can hardly expect an ever-increasing public debt ratio to be sustainable. Risk management principles require action to stabilize public debt before the need for action becomes self-evident.

Public Debt and Growth. Debt stabilization at some level is necessary to avoid macroeconomic instability. But at what level can a high public debt-to-GDP ratio become a drag on potential growth? There are no simple answers, but some general considerations are clear.

At an analytical level, higher public debt can hamper potential growth through its effect on investment in two ways. First, if foreigners hold debt, high debt involves higher payments made abroad to service external debt, thus subtracting resources for domestic investment. This external debt level is a key factor that may explain debt overhang problems in emerging economies.[5]

Second, high public debt—and the related deficits[6]—bring about higher interest rates, which discourage investment. Empirical work on the relationship between fiscal variables and interest rates does indicate that fiscal imbalances lead to higher real interest rates. A recent reassessment of this relationship shows that, for a panel of advanced and emerging markets, an increase of 1 percentage point in the debt-to-GDP ratio leads to an increase in government bond yields of 3–5 basis points (Baldacci and Kumar 2010). This means that, on average, the increase in the projected 2008–15 debt ratio for advanced countries (by about 35 percentage points of GDP, as figure 3.6 previously showed) could raise real interest rates by up to 1.75 percentage points—not a trivial amount. The precise magnitude of the impact also depends on initial fiscal, institutional, and structural conditions as well as spillovers from global financial markets.

The relationship between public debt and growth has also been assessed directly. Over the past two centuries, debt-to-GDP ratios above 90 percent have been associated with average growth of 1.7 percent, which is 2 percentage points lower than when the debt ratio is below 30 percent (Reinhart and Rogoff 2010).

One key difficulty in this area, however, is that of disentangling the effects of *growth on debt* from those of *debt on growth*. Maintaining strong fiscal accounts is clearly easier in a high-growth environment. Thus, one could argue that low public debt is not the *cause* of high growth but the *result* of high growth. Kumar and Woo (2010)[7] address this issue through proper econometric techniques, showing that, on average, a 10 percentage point increase in the initial debt-to-GDP ratio is associated with a slowdown in annual real per capita GDP growth of around 0.2 percentage points per year, with the impact being smaller in advanced economies (0.15 percentage points).

There is some evidence of nonlinearity, with only medium (30–90 percent of GDP) to high (above 90 percent) levels of debt having a significant negative effect on growth. This adverse effect largely reflects a slowdown in labor productivity growth, mainly because of reduced investment. At lower debt levels (below 30 percent), however, the effect on growth of higher public debt, while not significant, is positive. Based on these estimates, one can conclude that the projected 2008–15 debt ratio increase in advanced countries, if sustained, would lower potential growth by about 0.5 percent per year.

What are the implications of these findings for policies aimed at boosting potential growth over the medium term? The most important is that stabilizing public debt at the (significantly higher) postcrisis level would lead to a sizable decline in potential growth for advanced countries (and possibly for other countries through spillover effects). In other words, it will pay to bring public debt levels down.

Lowering debt ratios, however, will not be easy. Figure 3.10 reports the result of a simulation to identify the improvement in the cyclically

Figure 3.10 Scenarios for Primary Balance Adjustment and Debt in Advanced and Emerging Economies, 2007–30

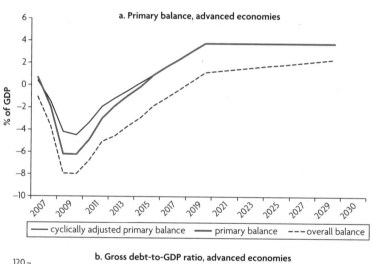

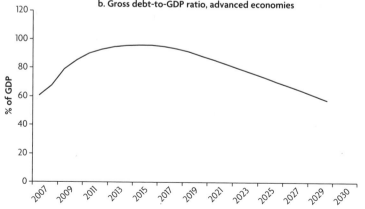

(continued next page)

Figure 3.10 (continued)

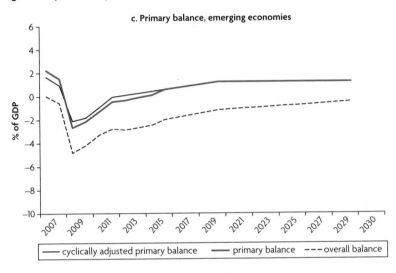

c. Primary balance, emerging economies

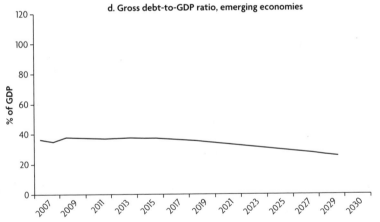

d. Gross debt-to-GDP ratio, emerging economies

Source: IMF 2010b.

adjusted primary balance needed to lower the average public debt ratio of advanced and emerging economies to less than 60 percent and 40 percent of GDP, respectively, by 2030.[8]

The adjustment is about 8.25 percentage points of GDP for advanced countries and 3 percentage points of GDP for emerging economies during 2011–20 (the primary balance would have to remain at this higher level for another decade to achieve the debt target). Some 1.5 percentage points of this adjustment would come from expiration of the temporary stimulus measures introduced in 2009–10. However, additional adjustment would be needed to simply offset the increase trend in aging-related spending expected over the next 20 years (previously illustrated in figures 3.3 and 3.4).

These are staggering figures that raise these questions: Is it possible to realize adjustments of this magnitude while sustaining the growth process? High public debt may be bad for potential growth in the long run, but is the fiscal adjustment needed to lower public debt consistent with maintaining adequate growth during the adjustment period?

Fiscal Adjustment and Growth. The effects of fiscal adjustment on growth have been thoroughly scrutinized, at least since the seminal paper by Giavazzi and Pagano (1990). One often-quoted result is that there is such a thing as growth-enhancing fiscal consolidation. Two (partially related) mechanisms may explain why fiscal consolidation (which per se should reduce aggregate demand and hence growth) may boost economic activity.

The first mechanism is the decline in interest rates that may accompany the fiscal consolidation process; this is, in some respect, the standard crowding-in effect that arises from the lower absorption of saving by the public sector. But effects are likely to be much stronger when the initial fiscal instability had caused uncertainty about inflation and depreciation rates, leading to a high risk premium on the holding of assets denominated in domestic currency.

The second, and related, mechanism involves reduced uncertainty about future economic developments (including the level of taxation) that accompanies fiscal consolidation and could boost private investment. A corollary of this mechanism is that the more credible the fiscal adjustment is, the more it should reduce uncertainty and hence have a benign effect on growth. This finding links the literature on the effect of fiscal adjustment on growth with that linking the composition of the fiscal adjustment to its "success," which is defined in terms of persistence of the fiscal adjustment. That is, to the extent that fiscal adjustment based on expenditure cuts (notably cuts in current spending) leads to a more durable and credible fiscal consolidation (see Alesina and Ardagna 2009 for recent results), such an adjustment will also be more beneficial for growth because it should be accompanied by a stronger recovery of private investment.

The prospect of a painless fiscal consolidation—painless for the economy as a whole, at least—is an attractive one for the years ahead, given the magnitude of the effort required. That said, in the present circumstances, some of the favorable processes described above will not operate. The main problem is that, at the start of the fiscal consolidation phase, nominal interest rates in almost all advanced countries (and in some emerging economies) are already historically low and are unlikely to decline as fiscal adjustment takes place. Of course, if fiscal consolidation occurs, central banks will not need to raise interest rates as much as in similar phases of exit from severe recessions, which will alleviate crowding in private investment. Nevertheless, the spectacular boost in private sector activity that has accompanied some fiscal consolidation episodes in the past is unlikely to materialize purely as a result of the fiscal adjustment.

Indeed, recent work by IMF staff members implies that caution is necessary in this area. In particular, the October 2010 *World Economic Outlook* finds that a fiscal consolidation of 1 percent of GDP typically reduces GDP by about 0.5 percent after two years and raises the unemployment rate by about 0.3 percentage points (IMF 2010d). Domestic demand—consumption and investment—falls by about 1 percent. Fiscal contractions that rely on spending cuts tend to have somewhat smaller contractionary effects than tax-based adjustments. Fiscal retrenchments in countries that face a higher perceived sovereign default risk tend to be less contractionary, but even these expansionary effects are unusual.

Altogether, given these prospects, the nature of the fiscal adjustment—whether it is focused on spending cuts or revenue increases, and, even more important, the nature of those spending cuts and revenue increases—will have paramount importance because the cuts or increases will affect economic incentives and efficiency. This effect is important not only because of the direct benefits of growth but also, notably, because policies that bring about even quite modest increases (or smaller reductions) in growth rates can lead to large reductions in the debt-to-GDP ratio and so ease the pain of fiscal adjustment.[9]

The Microeconomic Dimension: Taxing, Spending, and Growth

This brings the discussion to the all-important question of detail: how can spending and revenue measures best be designed not only to meet the challenges arising from fiscal consolidation but also to enhance output levels and growth?

This is a tough question, made even tougher by the wider trends flagged previously in the "Objectives and Challenges" section: beggar-thy-neighbor tax policies, for instance, may well become even more of a concern in the coming years because countries in trouble are not always overly concerned about the adverse impacts their policies have on others. Rhetoric on the growth effects of taxation and public spending, moreover, far outstrips available evidence. And any notion of "growth-friendly" tax or spending measures needs to be treated with particular care because the government's budgetary constraint means it makes little sense to speak of the growth impact of individual tax or spending measures. A research and development (R&D) subsidy may increase growth if paid for by an increase in the value added tax (VAT) rate, for instance, but not if it is financed by borrowing or cutting primary education.

The risk is of denigrating, as "anti-growth," measures that have a perfectly appropriate place within the wider fiscal scheme. Most tax measures, after all, impose distortionary costs that are a price paid for public expenditure—on infrastructure, education, and health, for example—and therefore are more obviously linked with growth and related objectives.

There are, nevertheless, ways ahead (to be shaped, of course, by country circumstances and preferences) that are clear, practicable, and responsive to both near-term imperatives and deeper trends. There are also mistakes to be avoided.

Spending Better: Taking the Dividends of Growth into Account

Instead of dwelling here on the appropriate balance between tax and spending measures (IMF 2010c provides principles, beyond those set out above, to guide that balance with some country specificity), the aim is to identify common themes and possibilities in the search for public spending and tax policies that can best support growth in the testing times ahead.

Welfare Reform. Welfare reform has quickly emerged as a central issue in framing fiscal adjustment in advanced countries (and the lessons they learn will be important in framing maturing social policies in emerging countries). Life would be easy if one could simply say, as some seem to think, that the welfare state in a given country is "too big" or "too small." But the issue is more complex than that, even leaving aside the distributional impact that is presumably the primary aim of social welfare spending.

The empirical evidence on the growth impact of aggregate social spending is mixed (Atkinson 1999). Indeed, theory suggests effects in both directions: The *risk sharing* implicit in social insurance and progressive taxation (taking from the lucky, giving to the unlucky) can spur growth by encouraging *risk taking* (in occupational choice, for instance). But individuals' expectations of future pension receipts exceeding their contributions and of guaranteed minimum income standards may harm growth by reducing private savings. What is needed is to look beyond broad generalizations on the impact of welfare spending to identify measures that will contain costs without jeopardizing efficiency or fairness.

Pressures on social spending are most intense in the areas of pensions and health care, which pose quite different challenges.

Pension Costs. Pension costs are driven by a few well-defined parameters, and restraining them is essentially a choice between increasing the retirement age, increasing contributions, and cutting benefits—or some combination thereof. These approaches will vary in their economic effects. Increasing the retirement age, for instance, is likely to boost current consumption because it implies higher lifetime incomes—which may have attractions for near-term macroeconomic management. Cutting benefits, however, will do the opposite by increasing private savings to replace the reduction in future receipts from the state—which may have attractions for longer-term growth.

One central fact that stands out, however, is that modest increases in the retirement age—especially modest relative to the increase in longevity since retirement ages were first set—can go a long way toward closing the gap. The IMF (2010a) estimates that increasing the age of receiving full benefits by two years over the next two decades[10] would be enough to stabilize pension spending at its 2010 level. Simulation results suggest, moreover, that this strategy also shows the greatest gains in long-term growth (Karam et al. 2010).

Other fiscal reforms to extend effective working lifetimes would be desirable for the same reason. In some cases, this may mean reforming entitlement rules for disability and sickness benefits as well as for pensions. Such rules were put in place deliberately to discourage participation by older workers, on the grounds—which both theory and evidence strongly suggest to be mistaken (Jousten et al. 2010)—that this prevents the employment of younger workers. Beyond that, evidence that the labor supply decisions of the near-retired are relatively sensitive to wage rates suggests another reform to delay retirement: reconfiguring income tax structures to have marginal tax rates that fall with age.

Health Care Costs. Increases in health care costs, on the other hand, arise less from the mechanics of demographic change than from the availability of increasingly expensive care. Therefore, options for easing fiscal pressures from this source are more complex than changing the parameters of an entitlement system. Cost containment is of the essence, and potential reform measures have emerged on both the supply side (including movement away from fee-for-service provision) and the demand side (increasing co-insurance rates and reducing benefits, for instance) (IMF 2010c).

Ultimately, a balance must be struck between (a) those basic services to be provided through, though not necessarily delivered by, the public sector (or at least services for which insurance is to be compulsory); and (b) those services to be left to voluntary insurance. Where that balance lies depends partly on efficiency considerations: compulsory coverage, for instance, can overcome market inefficiencies from adverse selection. But the balance depends even more on (a) social preferences as to the levels of health care credibly regarded as minimally acceptable and (b) the extent of implicit redistribution best achieved through health provision rather than income support.

Other Social Service Costs. Many economies, both advanced and emerging, provide other social insurance and support services (services to which many emerging-market countries aspire):

- In-work tax credits, transforming the income tax in some cases to a wage subsidy
- Unemployment assistance
- Contingent cash transfers
- Sickness and disability allowances
- Housing support.

Welfare Reform Mechanisms. The complexity of, and dissimilarities between, systems make generalization dangerous, but diverse experiences suggest common opportunities for improvement:

Targeting by means testing. A common response to pressures on social spending is to call for better targeting. All too often, however, "targeting" is taken as synonymous with means testing (that is, reducing the transfer paid at higher levels of income or assets), the difficulties of which are often overlooked. Meanwhile, other (perhaps more promising) types of targeting receive scant attention.

The difficulty with increased means testing is that it inescapably increases marginal effective income tax rates—reflecting the combined effects of taxation, social contributions, and the receipt or withdrawal of benefits—toward the lower income ranges, with consequent disincentives for work effort (and savings, too, if asset tests also apply). There is thus no avoiding the fundamental design question: how should marginal effective tax rates vary by income level? The answer depends on both equity considerations and on how taxation affects labor supply decisions.

Over the past few years, these responses have taught two things. First, a U-shaped pattern of marginal effective tax rates of the kind often observed in advanced countries is likely to be optimal, albeit with rates at lower income levels than those observed in, for instance, the United Kingdom (Brewer, Saez, and Shephard 2010). Second—and quite contrary to previous conventional wisdom—the sensitivity of participation decisions creates a case for subsidizing earnings at the very bottom, both on grounds of traditional efficiency and perhaps for other reasons not captured in standard models: for example, working may be socially valuable in itself. This reasoning points to schemes that (a) are generous to low earners (subsidizing even the lowest earners, as under the earned income tax credit pioneered in the United States) and (b) withdraw benefits fairly slowly, which means lower effective marginal rates at the bottom and higher rates further up the income ladder.

Targeting by tagging. Other forms of targeting include differentiation of individuals by observable characteristics correlated either with features of social relevance in themselves or with other features of direct interest, such as earning capacity or behavioral responses. Where the capacity to tax income is weak, as in many emerging economies, tagging of this kind is largely a necessity. And where the capacity to tax income is good, it still has a role. For example, providing support in kind to particular groups can improve the effectiveness of support by reducing the risk that the benefit will be too attractive to unintended recipients: disability support, for instance, can be provided in the form of home adaptations rather than cash. For the same reason, the public provision of basic education and health care may have merit not only in dealing with market failures but also as effective redistributional devices.

Tagging can also take the form of applying different tax schedules to groups that differ in some identifiable and relevant way. Although this is already quite common (child tax credits, for example), better recent understanding of how labor supply responses correlate with other attributes suggests that there may be scope for more differentiation of this kind.[11] One example is setting lower marginal tax rates for those nearing retirement. Another is the possibility of exploiting the likely greater responsiveness of women's participation decisions once their children reach school age. There are evidently equity issues to be faced in such strategies (for example, what kinds of tax differentiation will be seen as fair?), but the evidence suggests that the gains may be considerable. One estimate for the United Kingdom is that these approaches could increase the workforce by nearly 1 percent (Mirrlees et al. 2010).

Modernizing the contributory principle. Welfare reform also means looking carefully at the contributory principle (that contributions should carry benefits of broadly the same actuarial value) that has historically underpinned social insurance systems. Over the years, the link between contributions and benefits has become, almost everywhere, largely fictitious (partly because of the desire to pay benefits to the initial generation, partly because of the desire to support those with limited labor market attachment).

However, there are good arguments to strengthen the contributory principle—but in modernized form. One is that the disincentives of increasingly high contribution rates may be blunted to the extent that those paying them see them as providing some offsetting benefit, and so as a form of forced saving. Another argument favors contributions as a way of diminishing the distortions to labor mobility that can arise from mismatches in the timing of receiving and paying for benefits.

There seems to be no compelling evidence currently that behavioral responses to social contributions differ from those to explicit taxes, perhaps reflecting awareness that the link is weak. If so, the design contortions necessary to pay lip service to the contributory principle—for instance, caps on contributions by employers and special rates for the self-employed—risk resulting in marginal effective tax rates that can cause significant unintended distortions. One response to this would be simply to absorb social contributions within the income tax (which could also have administrative and compliance advantages). However, this response may give up too easily on the potential merits of a genuine contributory principle. One way to realize those merits could be to build systems of lifetime accounts (advocated, for instance, in Bovenberg, Hansen, and Sørensen 2008), into which individuals contribute while also being allowed withdrawals to provide their own consumption smoothing (in the face of such life events as unemployment, for example) that is a large part—70 percent or more in some countries—of current social spending.

Infrastructure and Innovation Expenditures. Theory leaves no doubt that output and growth can be increased by the public financing (though not necessarily the provision) of productivity-enhancing infrastructure that the private sector cannot be (or at least *is* not) relied upon to provide: water systems, highways, rail networks, fundamental R&D, legal systems, and the like. Empirically, the importance and nature of these effects remain subjects of contention. There is good reason to suppose, however, that public infrastructure spending has had strong positive effects on aggregate output, as Arslanalp et al. (2010) found based on unique data on cumulative stocks of public capital (though they also stress that this effect can come with a significant lag). Consistent with this finding is evidence that reallocation of public spending from "unproductive" to "productive" projects has been associated with faster growth in Organisation for Economic Co-operation and Development (OECD) countries (Gemmell, Kneller, and Sanz 2007).

Infrastructure. These generalities do not convey precisely which *types* of infrastructure spending are most conducive to growth. Some evidence from lower-income countries, for instance, found large gains from telephone network development (Canning 1999), but there is little research of similar directness for the higher-income countries.

The very specificity of the issues focuses attention on perhaps the most critical factor of all: the framework within which such spending decisions are made. The wide range of framework-related issues include

- realizing the scope for cost reduction (by, for example, improving procurement processes);
- addressing the corruption often associated with large infrastructure projects; and
- identifying and managing the fiscal risks associated with public-private partnerships (PPPs), as Antonio Estache discusses in chapter 4 of this volume.

What *is* clear is the importance of progress in the management of public infrastructure projects, including through realistic cost-benefit appraisal of significant projects and the assessment and disclosure of fiscal risks associated with PPPs. In some areas, user fees may have unrealized potential—one clear example being the potential value of congestion pricing in guiding highway development (as well as easing revenue pressures).

Climate Change. One area in which new infrastructure needs can be anticipated is climate change mitigation and adaptation. These needs must be addressed in country-specific ways: whether to strengthen sea defenses, to overcome network externality problems in the diffusion of low-carbon fuels, or to develop grids that incorporate small suppliers.

How large the net spending requirements may be remains uncertain (in some countries, some spending will be reduced, such as on winter fuel support for the vulnerable), but adaptation needs seem likely to require well under 1 percent of GDP in advanced economies for many years. In some emerging economies—more exposed to climate impacts and having less-developed social support systems—expenditures are likely to be substantially larger but still await reasonably firm quantification.

Innovation. In terms of innovation, too, the general principle is clear: public financing of fundamental R&D can play a worthwhile role, but its proper application is a matter of detail and process. Again, it is in the area of climate policy that the needs are most apparent. *The Stern Review* stressed that public support for basic energy research has fallen substantially since the 1980s and made a powerful case for increasing it (Stern 2007).

More generally, Philippe Aghion and Julia Cagé argue in chapter 5 of this volume that "clean" innovations need support to overcome factors tending to favor "dirty" innovations, notably the existing stock of physical and intellectual capital. More controversial, but worth particular mention, is the strong case for publicly financed research of geoengineering approaches to climate problems. The governance issues are horrendous (for example, who decides what the climate will be?), but prudence surely dictates exploration of options to deal with quick-onset catastrophic outcomes.

Subsidies and Tax Expenditures. The first rule of fiscal policy being to do no harm, subsidies (or equivalent measures, implemented as tax breaks) that serve no useful purpose ought to be eliminated. There is no shortage of candidates.

Petroleum Subsidies. Petroleum subsidies remain widespread in emerging-market and low-income countries, and taxes are low in many advanced ones. Outright subsidies are set to cost about US$250 billion (0.3 percent of world GDP) in 2010 (Coady et al. 2010) to little distributional purpose: the benefits accrue mainly to the better-off, and the poor can be better protected by other means (Coady et al. 2006).

Although G-20 members have committed themselves to eliminating fossil fuel subsides, many countries still have a considerable way to go toward establishing fuel taxes that reasonably reflect the externalities from fuel use, including not only—or even mainly—worsening global warming (discussed below) but also the cost of road infrastructure, local pollution, and congestion charges. Relative to a tax of US$0.30 per liter, the global revenue loss is about 1 percent of GDP, with around 80 percent of this arising in advanced and, especially, emerging economies.

Tax Breaks. Exemptions and special treatment pervade most tax systems. Mortgage interest breaks, where they remain, are only the paramount example. Such tax breaks forgo revenue, distort investment decisions, and undermine financial stability. They do not even encourage home ownership (the rationale sometimes offered), the evidence being that they simply induce owners to buy more expensive properties.

Each tax break sounds (to someone) like a good idea but is also potentially expensive and usually comes with unintended side effects. Education tax credits, for instance, may just lead to higher tuition fees. The recent bipartisan U.S. National Commission on Fiscal Responsibility and Reform shows how much can be saved—admittedly, in what is probably an extreme case—by scouring the tax code for myriad breaks and making a clean sweep of them.

Renewable Resource Subsidies. More contentiously, renewable resource subsidies are overdue for close examination. The implied costs of replacing carbon emissions are often well above common views of an appropriate carbon price. This is not to deny that (as Aghion and Cagé stress in chapter 5 of this volume) dealing with climate problems requires not only carbon pricing but also public support of innovation. But the missing link in current policies toward alternative energy sources seems to be less on the spending side—except perhaps in relation to some elements of R&D—than in establishing the stronger carbon pricing that will provide appropriate incentives for the private sector to develop alternative energies.

Taxing Smarter: In Search of Immobile Tax Bases

Theory, empirics, and changing circumstances all point to giving well-designed consumption taxes a central role in addressing fiscal challenges ahead:

- *Theory* because almost all analyses find consumption taxes to be the least growth-retarding form of taxation (Myles 2009b)
- *Empirics* because countries that rely more heavily on consumption taxes tend to grow faster (Kneller, Bleaney, and Gemmell 1999)[12]
- *Circumstances* because people tend to consume where they live, which—at least for goods[13]—is likely to remain less mobile than other factors.[14]

Value Added Taxes. Increased taxation on consumption may also go the right way in terms of redressing intergenerational inequities because (as some may feel is only appropriate, given the source of current fiscal challenges) the increase would fall most heavily on those spending out of accumulated assets, which is likely to mean a particularly strong impact on older groups (though the "retirement puzzle" of high saving by the elderly and any indexation of pension benefits will mitigate this effect).

The mainstay of almost all consumption tax systems—Saudi Arabia and the United States being the only G-20 members without one—is the VAT, some features of which are highlighted in table 3.1. And in almost all of these systems, there is clear room for improvement.

The first two data columns of table 3.1 show the standard VAT yield and rate in selected countries. The third column is especially important, reporting "C-efficiency": the ratio of VAT revenues to the product of consumption and the standard rate. Under a benchmark single-rate VAT, the C-efficiency would be 100 percent. In most cases, clearly, it is far from this. How this shortfall arises can be seen by decomposing it into elements that reflect imperfections of implementation (the "compliance gap") and of design (the "policy gap"). The two rightmost columns indicate the potential revenue gain from halving either of these gaps—that is, the often-sizable gains that can be realized without any change in the standard VAT rate.

Table 3.1 Key Features of the Value Added Tax in Selected Countries

	VAT revenue (% of GDP)	Standard VAT rate (%)	C-efficiency (%)	Compliance gap (%)	Policy gap (%)	Potential extra revenue (% of GDP)	
						From halving compliance gap	From halving policy gap
Advanced economies							
France	7.1	19.6	45	7	52	0.0	3.8
Germany	6.2	16.0	50	10	44	0.2	2.4
Italy	6.1	20.0	39	22	50	1.2	3.1
United Kingdom	6.5	17.5	43	13	50	0.5	3.3
Emerging economies							
Argentina	6.9	21.0	46	21	41	0.5	2.3
Hungary	7.4	20.0	49	23	37	0.8	2.2
Latvia	8.3	21.0	49	22	38	0.7	2.5
Lithuania	7.5	18.0	50	22	36	0.7	2.1
Mexico	3.7	15.0	33	18	60	0.1	2.8

Source: IMF 2010b.

Note: "C-efficiency" is the ratio of VAT revenue to the product of consumption and standard rate (equaling 100 percent under a benchmark single-rate VAT). The "compliance gap" is the portion of the C-efficiency ratio reflecting imperfect VAT implementation. The "policy gap" is the portion of the C-efficiency ratio reflecting imperfect VAT design.

In emerging economies, the scope for improved compliance is what tends to stands out. In the advanced economies, with older VATs, the problems are more marked on the policy side. Their key task is to rein back exemptions and multiple rates—especially zero rates on domestic consumption. In the United Kingdom, for instance, eliminating the extensive zero-rating of food and other items would raise about £23 billion. And the change need not have adverse distributional effects: even after compensating the losers, a net revenue gain of £11 billion remains (Crawford, Keen, and Smith 2010).

A broad-based sales tax is not, of course, a particularly progressive tax; viewed over individuals' full lifetimes (inheritances and bequests aside, so that all lifetime income and assets are spent), it is neutral. What matters for distributional concerns, however, is not the incidence of any tax viewed in isolation but the impact of all tax and spending instruments combined. Progressivity of this overall system must then be sought other than in the VAT. That means looking to the welfare system, as discussed previously. It also points toward shaping the income tax in light of equity objectives and perhaps also toward a greater role for the taxation of gifts and inheritances. Here the constraints imposed by tax base mobility, and the scope for addressing them through enhanced international cooperation, come quickly to the fore; these are taken up below.

Property Taxes. Buildings and land, in contrast, are the immobile tax base par excellence. The financial capital invested in them may be perfectly mobile, but the intrinsic value of their location and characteristics is not. Their value thus includes an element of rent that can, in principle, be taxed at up to 100 percent without causing distortion.

There is indeed evidence that property taxes are less damaging to growth than other types of taxation (Arnold 2008). Moreover, it seems likely that their impact is broadly progressive. With property tax revenue amounting to less than 1 percent of GDP in some countries and to more than 3 percent in the United Kingdom, the United States, and elsewhere, this too is an instrument ready for greater use.

"Green" Taxes. Addressing environmental issues—above all, climate change—provides one of the few areas in which there is scope for raising revenue in ways that will clearly enhance sustained, high-quality growth. Although environmental damage will build up relatively slowly, the slow-moving, stock nature of the externality at the heart of the climate problem calls for early action to mitigate it by reducing emissions, which now means both more aggressive carbon pricing and the adoption of credible plans for carbon pricing in the future.

Carbon Pricing. Whether implemented by taxation or by cap-and-trade schemes—the former being preferable[15]—carbon pricing can provide much-needed additional revenue. Quite how much depends on the level and path of carbon prices (views about which vary greatly) as well as on initial levels of fuel taxation and patterns of power generation (it being important to remember that gasoline is far from being the only source of carbon tax revenue; ultimately, coal is much more important).

The potential revenues in many advanced economies are substantial, though not transformational. Recent proposals for an emissions trading scheme in the United States, for example, could have raised about US$860 billion over 2011–19, or about 15 percent of the projected cumulative fiscal deficit. (The net revenue gain, of course, would have been smaller, though not eliminated, to the extent that poorer groups were compensated for the impact on final consumer prices). What is critical is that this potential revenue not be dissipated by awarding substantial rights free of charge, as has become all too common: the U.S. proposals, for instance, would have forgone nearly 80 percent of the potential revenue just mentioned. Free allocation does nothing to ease the impact on consumer prices, which will reflect the opportunity cost of holding permits (rather than the price actually paid), and compensating firms for the impact of the scheme would require giving away something on the order of 10 percent of rights.

Many emerging economies, of course, are reluctant to introduce carbon pricing, especially while leading advanced economies fail to do so. But for them the revenue potential may be even more significant, not only to the extent that their current carbon prices are low but also because they may be net sellers of emission rights or carbon offsets in an efficient global pricing scheme: India, for example, might receive inflows from this source of 1–4 percent of GDP between 2020 and 2060 (IMF 2008). For some, potential payments for avoided deforestation may be substantial if obstacles to the design of payment schemes (for instance, in defining the benchmark relative to which it is rewarded) are overcome.

Congestion Pricing. Other environmental taxes generally have little revenue potential—which is, to a large degree, as it should be: it is a mark of the success of the tax on plastic shopping bags in Ireland that the tax reduced use by 90 percent, but it raised almost nothing. One area in which worthwhile revenue *may* be gained, however, is in greater use of congestion pricing.

All the emerging evidence suggests that congestion externalities are by far the most important externality associated with motoring. And fuel taxation—undifferentiated by time and place of travel—is an imprecisely targeted instrument for dealing with it. More purposive use of congestion pricing (still in its early stages in most countries and not something that can be implemented overnight) can enable an unpacking of fuel excises into components related to carbon and other emissions and to congestion that can secure revenue and increase both narrowly defined productivity and the broader quality of life.

Capital Gains Taxes. Capital accumulation—in the sense of not only (indeed, probably decreasingly) tangible goods but also the development of future productive capacity generally—and the savings (public and private) that finance it are at the heart of economic growth. Central to the discussion of the role of fiscal policy in these areas is the question of whether the normal, risk-free return to capital should be taxed at all.

Some celebrated results find that, in the long run, capital gains should not be taxed (Chamley 1986; Judd 1985): even a small tax on interest implies an infinitely large distortion of future, relative to current, prices. Views differ, however, as to whether these results are "very general" (Myles 2009b) or "not robust" (Banks and Diamond 2010). This chapter's authors incline to the latter view. Not the least of the limitations is the assumption that the government can fully commit to future rates of capital income taxation. It seems more plausible to suppose that it cannot—given the temptation to tax what will then be an attractively inelastic tax base of accumulated capital. In sheer practical terms, too, the ease with which labor income can be made to appear as capital income implies a need for some tax on the latter.

This perspective does not mean that capital income should be taxed at the same rate as labor income, as under the traditional "comprehensive" income tax. The greater international mobility of capital as opposed to labor—combined with the principle of efficient taxation that more-elastic tax bases should be taxed at a lower rate—suggests that, absent international cooperation, the income that capital generates should be taxed less heavily. This is the heart of the case for the "dual income tax," pioneered in the Nordic countries and later attracting wider interest, which applies a progressive tax to labor income and a flat, low-rate tax on capital income (Cnossen 2000). This scheme does not necessarily reduce the progressivity of the overall tax system; in Sweden, for example, its adoption actually increased the revenue from capital income taxation (because the deductions for payments of capital income lost more revenue than was collected on receipts).[16]

Deciding whether capital income is, or is not, too heavily taxed requires recognition of country-specific characteristics and objectives. As a general proposition, the mobility of capital means that taxation of personal savings (based on the saver's residence) has an effect quite distinct from that of taxes on the income from underlying investments (which are typically taxed by the country in which the income arises, with additional tax sometimes payable where the investor resides). However, in an economy closed to capital movements, taxes on savings and investments would have the same impact. Therefore, these types of taxes must be considered separately—and on a country-specific basis.

Corporate Taxes. At the company level—at least for large firms—the impact of taxation on incentives to invest in a given country is characterized by the marginal effective corporate tax rate (MECTR), which is the difference between the after-tax return required on world markets and the before-tax return required to generate it. MECTRs vary hugely according to both the nature of the investment and the source of the firm's finance: they are often on the order of 25–35 percent for equity-financed investments but are strongly negative, often around -5 percent to -10 percent, for debt-financed instruments. (This variance occurs because interest expense is commonly deductible against corporate tax, but the return to equity is not—a point discussed further below.) The implication is that, at the margin, debt-financed investments are actually subsidized.

These variations in MECTRs can affect the cost of capital on the order of 100–200 basis points—very large amounts by the usual standards of monetary policies. The variations across investment types result in a misallocation of capital (including, in most cases, toward housing) that is a source of both output loss and (by impeding effective adjustment) growth.[17] Moreover—and an increasing focus of concern—the tax bias to debt finance clearly invites excess leverage.

These points make a strong case for unifying MECTRs at some common rate, and there are good reasons why that rate should be zero. That does not mean eliminating the taxation of capital income, which can be taxed at the personal level. It *does* mean converting the corporate tax into a tax on earnings in excess of a normal return—to a tax, that is, on rents. The appeal of this solution is that, absent the ability to shift rents across national jurisdictions (taken up below), it would be fully nondistorting.

One way to achieve such neutrality is by adopting an allowance for corporate equity (ACE) form of corporate tax, under which the interest deduction is maintained but an allowance also given for a notional return on equity. Several countries have, to varying degrees, already adopted the ACE or variants, and their experiences have been broadly positive (Klemm 2007). For a company using a mix of finance that initially implies an MECTR of 20 percent, movement to an ACE could add around 0.45 percentage points to the rate of its output growth.[18] This would not be permanent, and aggregate effects might be muted: as all firms expand investment, for instance, the price of capital goods might rise. But neither is it trivial.

Private Pension Taxes. The tax treatment of savings is complicated in almost all countries by a plethora of special arrangements for pensions and other privileged forms of saving, including housing. Although most forms of interest are taxable, private pension saving commonly receives special treatment that effectively exempts the risk-free return.

Such schemes have largely led to a reshuffling of savings between accounts rather than the creation of additional savings. Because most of them are capped, they have no impact on the marginal decisions of the wealthiest individuals, who typically account for a large share of personal savings. Consequently, there seems to be no easy, reliable, and cost-effective route to substantially encourage personal savings by special tax measures.

Other Tax Incentives. Two other tax measures often presented as pro-growth merit some (skeptical) comment:

- *Tax incentives for research and development,* which have proliferated in recent years, do increase R&D spending, often with an elasticity of more than 1 so that this increase exceeds the revenue forgone. Much less clear is whether this increased R&D yields significant social (as opposed to private) benefit. The main role of R&D tax incentives may be as an instrument of international tax competition.
- *Favorable tax treatment of small and medium-size enterprises,* including reduced corporate tax rates, sometimes rests on overstating their employment creation and innovativeness.[19] To the extent that such enterprises are relatively immobile internationally, efficiency considerations actually suggest that they be taxed more rather than less heavily. That may be a step too far, but the central argument for reduced small-business tax rates has a clear limitation: they face capital market constraints. Start-ups will typically have no taxable profits for some time, so taxation cannot be a major obstacle.

International Tax Competition—and Cooperation. The most marked instance of globalization at work in national tax design is the decline in headline rates of corporate taxation, which figure 3.11 illustrates.

No less striking is the resilience, also shown in figure 3.11, of corporate tax revenues preceding the crisis. One reason for this resilience was the high profitability of the financial sector, often accounting for 20 percent or more of taxable profits. However, one cannot count on similar levels of taxable profits returning soon. Nor is there any reason to suppose the reduction of rates to be over; the current constellation is underpinned by relatively high rates in both Japan and the United States, which are under substantial domestic pressures to reduce those rates.

The way to redress all this—converting the corporate tax back to one on capital (rather than, as previously explained in the "Objectives and

Figure 3.11 Corporate Income Tax Statutory Rates and Revenue in OECD Countries, 1985–2008

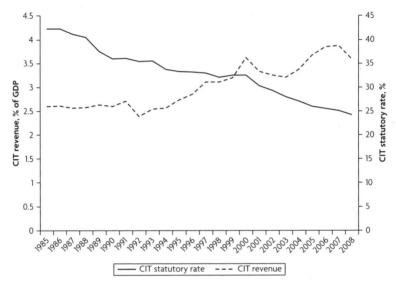

Source: IMF 2010c.
Note: OECD = Organisation for Economic Co-operation and Development. CIT = corporate income tax.

Challenges" section, one that falls largely on labor) and exploiting the greater inelasticity of the capital supply to the world as a whole rather than to any country in particular—is by international cooperation. But that is easier said than done. Coordination is much more attractive to some countries than to others. Small countries, in particular, have strong incentives to set low rates because what they can gain from the capital they attract from abroad (perhaps only on paper) far exceeds what they might lose on their domestic base. And the gain to those participating in agreements—perhaps regionally, as with attempts in the European Union—will be reduced by competition from those remaining outside those agreements. Technically, too, there are considerable challenges: effective tax coordination requires limiting not only the headline rate but also the base, and it may call for quite different ways of organizing international tax matters.

The crisis has produced some signs of increased willingness to cooperate on tax matters, including heightened pressure on tax havens to provide the information that would enable other countries to address citizen tax evasion more effectively. This is essentially administrative cooperation. What may ultimately be needed—and sooner rather than later if a further ratcheting of international tax competition is to be avoided—is heightened cooperation on policy matters.

On the spending side, too, international coordination can yield large gains. Part of the increase in consumption implied by increasing the retirement age, for instance, will show as increased imports, stimulating growth abroad (Karam et al. 2010). Such positive spillovers imply that countries will gain more if all act together—perhaps, as in this case, substantially.

Taxing the Financial Sector. The crisis has been a painful reminder that financial and banking crises can cause massive output losses and, as stressed earlier, permanent damage to growth. At the same time, there is strong evidence that a well-functioning financial system is conducive to growth. Treading the balance this calls for is primarily a matter of regulatory and supervisory policy, but tax policy may potentially have a much greater role than previously recognized in (a) facilitating supportive financial systems, (b) making crises both less likely to occur and less damaging when they do, and (c) raising some worthwhile revenue along the way.

The first task is to deal with two existing tax distortions that undermine financial stability:

- *Widespread, substantial tax advantages to debt over equity finance.* These advantages did not trigger the crisis, but there is strong evidence that they lead to higher corporate debt and—where mortgage interest deductibility remains—higher personal debt, thus increasing vulnerabilities and intensifying the effects of the crisis (IMF 2010a). A central merit of the ACE, proposed above, is that it would substantially eliminate the corporate-level debt bias. (Indeed, there is a case for going even further and applying a notional deduction not only to equity but also to debt.)
- *Commonplace exemption of financial services under the VAT.* Such exemption, which may well lead to the financial sector being larger than it otherwise would be, needs to be addressed. The best way to do this

would be by reforming the VAT itself, but there are alternatives, such as the financial activities tax (FAT) proposed by the IMF (2010a) and endorsed by the European Commission (2010).[20] The FAT would be a tax on the sum of wages and profits—in effect, a tax on value added implemented differently from the standard VAT. Many detailed design issues remain, but a FAT could ease a troubling distortion and raise quite large amounts of revenue: a 5 percent FAT in the United Kingdom, for instance, could raise about 0.3 percent of GDP.

Second, even under a perfectly reformed regulatory structure, failures will occur and cause potentially large social costs unless failing institutions are resolved swiftly and effectively. The costs of doing so are a cost of doing business responsibly and therefore should be paid by the institutions that benefit—preferably before the failure occurs (IMF 2010a). This solution calls for what the IMF calls a "financial stability contribution": a charge, linked to improved mechanisms for resolving systematically important institutions, that would cover at least the fiscal costs of direct interventions to prevent future failures and crises (IMF 2010a). Several European countries have begun to experiment with taxes of this kind.

Third, there may be a useful role for a corrective tax on systemically important financial institutions—perhaps a surtax on systemic institutions operating with particularly low capital ratios—to address the externalities associated with financial distress and failure (Keen 2011). The conventional approach is to address these externalities by regulatory means, but corrective taxation may in some circumstances have a useful supplementary role. For instance, taxation may deal more effectively than capital requirements with asymmetric information problems.

Taxing the Super-Rich. The fiscal treatment of higher earners and the extremely wealthy naturally attracts particular attention, with views differing sharply as to the extent to which, under tightened fiscal circumstances and in the face of increased income inequality in many countries, the wealthy should pay more than they now do. Any potential resolution requires a balance between (a) the equity considerations that, to many, suggest the rich should pay more; and (b) the potential disincentives that, to others, suggest they should not.

For super-high earners—the top 1 percent or so, whose importance has increased quite markedly in recent years—there is little evidence that taxation has especially strong effects on real behavior. Indeed, this seems broadly true in the higher reaches of income: for instance, the widely remarked revenue increase following the Russian Federation's adoption of a "flat tax" (which cut the top marginal rate from 30 percent to 13 percent) does not seem to have arisen from increased real activity (Ivanova, Keen, and Klemm 2005). Of potentially more concern in terms of the case for strongly progressive taxation are the avoidance and evasion opportunities of the rich, reflected in potentially high responsiveness of taxable income: for the top 1 percent or so of the U.S. income distribution, the long-run elasticity of taxable income with respect to unity minus the marginal tax rate is about 0.12–0.4 percent (Saez, Slemrod, and Giertz 2010).

Prominent among the tax reduction strategies favoring the richest are exploitation of the light taxation of capital gains relative to other forms of capital income and, in some cases at least, evasion by locating assets abroad. The former requires structural reform; the latter calls for enhanced international coordination, including—but ultimately perhaps going beyond—current initiatives focused on the exchange of information between tax authorities.

Reducing tax rates can help, but there is no free lunch. The signs are, for instance, that the Russian flat-tax reform in 2001 did improve compliance but not enough for the tax rate cut to pay for itself. Indeed, recent estimates of the tax-responsiveness of taxable income in both the United Kingdom and the United States suggest that current top marginal tax rates (including social contributions) are below levels that would maximize revenue (Brewer, Saez, and Shephard 2010; Saez, Slemrod, and Giertz 2010).[21]

Improving Compliance and Implementation. Effective implementation of tax and spending programs contributes directly to output and growth. Noncompliance leads to inefficiencies: for example, in-work benefits must reach all those entitled to them to have their maximum effect on work incentives. Implementation is also critical to sustaining the wider sense of fairness on which effective taxation ultimately rests, and here the crisis leaves the unwelcome legacy of reduced tax compliance. (Not paying taxes can be the cheapest source of finance for distressed businesses.) Such effects can be lasting.

Two of the many levels of administrative responses needed to improve compliance and implementation are especially important to establishing equitable and renewed growth (IMF 2010c):

- *Addressing aggressive tax planning.* Taxpayers continually push the boundaries of legality. Increased intelligence activities and disclosure requirements can help redress the balance, and general antiavoidance legislation—enabling tax authorities to see through the form of transactions to their substance—appears to have worked well, for instance, in Australia.

- *Strengthening international cooperation.* More effective international information exchange can reduce the risk that transactions will escape proper taxation. Administrative measures, however, are no substitute for addressing the fundamental policy problems posed by increasingly mobile tax bases. Information sharing does little to enhance revenue if tax rates are competed down to zero, for instance, and the most highly publicized forms of VAT fraud derive from the refunding on exports of tax levied on inputs for which there are now well-understood alternatives (as in Keen and Smith 2000, for instance).

Conclusions

The restoration of fiscal sustainability will place daunting constraints on public policies in the coming years, especially in advanced economies. Dealing with postcrisis macro fiscal imperatives—and doing so under the changing circumstances implied by deepening globalization, aging, and evolving climate concerns—will not be easy. But in this chapter the authors hope to have not merely spelled out the challenges but also to have given a sense of how to meet these challenges. Circumstances and options, of course, vary across countries in ways not fully addressed here, but the important common themes and possibilities have been presented.

Some elements of the needed response are clear:

- Announcing credible plans early to ensure fiscal sustainability where it is in jeopardy

- Exploiting more fully the potential of consumption and property taxes
- Swiftly implementing more aggressive carbon pricing (with no free allocation of rights)
- Taking more seriously long-standing tax biases toward debt finance.

Other elements, such as the appropriateness and design of new taxes on financial institutions, are only now being thought through and, to some degree, tested. Old instruments may have to be thought of in new ways: for instance, to recognize that corporate tax reform may have become, to a significant degree, a tax on labor. And new instruments (on financial institutions or on fossil fuels) will be resisted by powerful lobbies. But the difficulties, ultimately, are more political than they are technical. Tax exemptions and subsidies that serve little purpose but have political untouchability must be rethought.

Importantly, the gains from many aspects of fiscal reform discussed above (concerning pensions, business taxes, and climate change, for instance)—are likely to be substantially greater when countries act together. Realizing these gains requires thinking of international fiscal cooperation less as a loss of national sovereignty and more as a gain in policy effectiveness. Neither advanced nor emerging economies can afford to perpetuate or repeat the fiscal mistakes of the past.

Notes

1. One could add a fourth challenge: technological advancement. The ability to condition social benefits and tax payments on biometric characteristics and a mass of personal information, for instance, has profound implications for their potential design. But the associated challenges and opportunities lie mainly beyond the urgent near-term decisions that are of concern here.
2. A decline in debt ratios in low-income countries also reflected sizable debt relief.
3. This outlook assumes the implementation of announced policies, including the expiration (mostly in 2011) of the temporary stimulus measures introduced in 2009–10.
4. Note that the assumption of a negative differential implies that the debt ratio, for any given primary balance, would eventually stabilize because the larger the debt ratio, the lower the equilibrium primary balance. This said, a negative differential raises broader issues of dynamic inefficiency. It may persist over the medium term but is unlikely to last over the longer term. Indeed,

the differential—although remaining negative for the average of the emerging economies for several years—is positive in many emerging economies.

5. A variant of this story is that high public debt requires either higher primary surpluses or taxation to pay interest instead of to finance public investment or education. These explanations are valid but leave open the question of whether lowering public debt by running even higher primary surpluses has more favorable effects on private investment. After all, in net present value terms, the resources subtracted to productive investment are the same whether debt and interest payments are high or whether debt is lowered through surpluses.

6. In the long run, of course, a one-to-one relationship exists between a given *deficit*-to-GDP ratio and a *debt*-to-GDP ratio, for a certain nominal growth rate of GDP.

7. This paper looks at the effect of initial public debt on growth during the next five years. It also uses instrumental variables to control for any remaining simultaneity.

8. These thresholds are clearly indicative because it is difficult to identify empirically an optimal level of public debt. As noted above, econometric estimates imply that a negative impact of public debt on growth emerges at levels below 60 percent. This said, 60 percent—in addition to being the Maastricht Treaty threshold—was the median level of general government debt to GDP before the crisis in advanced economies. And empirical evidence suggests that 40 percent is a relevant threshold for emerging economies based on sovereign debt crises in these countries.

9. For example, if a country with an initial debt ratio of 100 percent of GDP manages to increase potential growth by 1 percent and saves the additional revenues (so that the effect on the debt-to-GDP ratio arises not only from higher GDP but also from lower debt), then after 10 years the debt ratio would fall by almost 30 percentage points.

10. This estimate is in addition to the increase in retirement age already envisaged by current legislation (which is one year for the average of the advanced countries).

11. See, for instance, Bastani, Blomquist, and Micheletto (2010), whose simulations suggest huge potential gains from age-relation in the income tax.

12. This rationale does not mean, it should be stressed, that growth could be increased by introducing a VAT and throwing away the proceeds. The claim is that the VAT appears to do less damage to growth than do alternative revenue raisers.

13. Services, of growing importance to consumption in many countries, pose a distinct set of challenges. Because services are readily provided across borders and not subject to interception in the same way that goods are, the effective taxation of services requires a distinct set of protocols.

14. The point is put neatly by Hines and Summers (2009, 125), who note that smaller economies rely more heavily on consumption taxes and that "globalization means that . . . all countries are becoming smaller."

15. The reasons for this preference are set out in IMF (2008), which also provides a fuller treatment of the issues raised here. Jones and Keen (2011) discuss the consequences of the crisis for these issues.

16. The distributional consequences of progressive capital income taxation are complex and can be counterintuitive. For instance, when different income classes face different marginal tax rates, borrowing by the rich from the poor (perhaps indirectly) can reduce the tax payable by the former by more than it increases the tax payable by the latter—benefiting, to some degree, both (Agell and Persson 1990).

17. Fullerton and Lyon (1988) put the consequent loss for the United States at 0.3 percent of GDP.

18. This assumes an elasticity of investment with respect to the user cost of capital of -0.75, a ratio of income to output of 10 percent, and a Cobb-Douglas technology with capital share of 0.3.

19. The argument in this paragraph draws on International Tax Dialogue (2007).

20. Keen, Krelove, and Norregaard (2010) consider the design of various forms of FAT in some detail.

21. Though international mobility is often cited as a particularly important constraint on the taxation of the highest-paid, Kleven, Landais, and Saez (2010) find that even for top-flight European footballers—presumably a particularly mobile group—revenue-maximizing tax rates (inclusive of social contributions and VAT) are above 75 percent.

References

Agell, Jonas, and Mats Persson. 1990. "Tax Arbitrage and the Redistributive Properties of Progressive Income Taxation." *Economics Letters* 34 (4): 357–61.

Alesina, Alberto F., and Silvia Ardagna. 2009. "Large Changes in Fiscal Policy: Taxes versus Spending." Working Paper 15438, National Bureau of Economic Research, Cambridge, MA.

Arslanalp, Serkan, Fabian Bornhorst, Sanjeev Gupta, and Elsa Sze. 2010. "Public Capital and Growth." Working Paper 10/175, International Monetary Fund, Washington, DC.

Arnold, Jens. 2008. "Do Tax Structures Affect Aggregate Economic Growth? Empirical Evidence from a Panel of OECD Countries." Economics Department Working Paper 643, Organisation for Economic Co-operation and Development, Paris.

Atkinson, Anthony B. 1999. *The Economic Consequences of Rolling Back the Welfare State.* Cambridge, MA: MIT Press.

Baldacci, Emanuele, and Mohan Kumar. 2010. "Fiscal Deficits, Public Debt, and Sovereign Bond Yields." Working Paper 10/184, International Monetary Fund, Washington, DC.

Banks, James, and Peter Diamond. 2010. "The Base for Direct Taxation." In *Dimensions of Tax Design: The Mirrlees Review*, ed. James Mirrlees et al., 548–648. New York: Oxford University Press.

Bastani, Spencer, Sören Blomquist, and Luca Micheletto. 2010. "The Welfare Gains of Age Related Optimal Income Taxation." Working Paper 3225, Center for Economic Studies and Ifo Institute for Economic Research, Munich.

Bovenberg, Lans A., Martin Ino Hansen, and Peter Birch Sørensen. 2008. "Individual Savings Accounts for Social Insurance: Rationale and Alternative Designs." *International Tax and Public Finance* 15 (1): 67–86.

Brewer, Mike, Emmanuel Saez, and Andrew Shephard. 2010. "Means-Testing and Tax Rates on Earnings." In *Dimensions of Tax Design: The Mirrlees Review*, ed. James Mirrlees et al., 90–173. New York: Oxford University Press.

Canning, David. 1999. "Infrastructure's Contribution to Aggregate Output." Policy Research Working Paper 2246, World Bank, Washington, DC.

CBO (Congressional Budget Office). 2009. "Cost Estimate for S. 1733, the Clean Energy Jobs and American Power Act, as ordered reported by the Senate Committee on Environment and Public Works on November 5, 2009." U.S. Government Printing Office, Washington, DC.

Chamley, Christophe. 1986. "Optimal Taxation of Capital Income in General Equilibrium with Infinite Lives." *Econometrica* 54 (3): 607–22.

Coady, David, Moataz El-Said, Robert Gillingham, Paulo Medas, and David Newhouse. 2006. "The Magnitude and Distribution of Fuel Subsidies: Evidence from Bolivia, Ghana, Jordan, Mali, and Sri Lanka." Working Paper 06/247, International Monetary Fund, Washington, DC.

Coady, David, Robert Gillingham, Rolando Ossowski, John Piotrowski, Shamsuddin Tareq, and Justin Tyson. 2010. "Petroleum Product Subsidies: Costly, Inequitable, and Rising." Staff Position Note 10/05, International Monetary Fund, Washington, DC.

Cnossen, Sijbren. 2000. "Taxing Capital Income in the Nordic Countries: A Model for the European Union?" In *Taxing Capital Income in the European Union: Issues and Options for Reform*, ed. Sijbren Cnossen, 180–213. New York: Oxford University Press.

Crawford, Ian, Michael Keen, and Stephen Smith. 2010. "Value-Added Tax and Excises." In *Dimensions of Tax Design: The Mirrlees Review*, ed. James Mirrlees et al., 275–362. New York: Oxford University Press.

EC (European Commission). 2010. "Communication from the Commission to the European Parliament, the Council, the European Economic and Social Committee and the Committee of the Regions: Taxation of the Financial Sector." COM (2010) 549/5 adopted October 7, EC, Brussels.

Fatás, Antonio, and Ilian Mihov. 2003. "The Case for Restricting Fiscal Policy Discretion." *Quarterly Journal of Economics* 118 (4): 1419–48.

Fullerton, Don, and Andrew B. Lyon. 1988. "Tax Neutrality and Intangible Capital." In *Tax Policy and the Economy, Vol. 2*, ed. Lawrence H. Summers, 63–88. Cambridge, MA: MIT Press.

Gemmell, Norman, Richard Kneller, and Ismael Sanz. 2007. "Tax Composition and Economic Growth in OECD Countries." Unpublished, University of Nottingham, Nottingham, U.K.

Giavazzi, Francesco, and Marco Pagano. 1990. "Can Severe Fiscal Contractions Be Expansionary? Tales of Two Small European Countries." In *NBER Macroeconomics Annual, Vol. 5*, 75–122. Cambridge, MA: National Bureau of Economic Research.

HPDD (Historical Public Debt Database). International Monetary Fund, Washington, DC. http://www.imf.org/external/datamapper/index.php?db=DEBT.

Hines, James R. Jr., and Lawrence H. Summers. 2009. "How Globalization Affects Tax Design." In *Tax Policy and the Economy, Vol. 23*, ed. Jeffrey R. Brown and James M. Poterba, 123–57. Chicago: University of Chicago Press.

IMF (International Monetary Fund). 2003. "Public Debt in Emerging Markets: Is It Too High?" In *World Economic Outlook, September 2003*, 113–52. Washington, DC: IMF.

———. 2008. "The Fiscal Implications of Climate Change." Paper of the Fiscal Affairs Department, IMF, Washington, DC. http://www.imf.org/external/np/pp/eng/2008/022208.pdf.

———. 2009a. "Debt Bias and Other Distortions: Crisis-Related Issues in Tax Policy." Paper of the Fiscal Affairs Department, IMF, Washington, DC. http://www.imf.org/external/np/pp/eng/2009/061209.pdf.

———. 2009b. "What Is the Damage? Medium-Term Output Dynamics after Financial Crises." In *World Economic Outlook, October 2009*, 121–51. Washington, DC: IMF.

———. 2010a. "A Fair and Substantial Contribution by the Financial Sector: Final Report for the G-20." Staff report, IMF, Washington, DC. http://www.imf.org/external/np/g20/pdf/062710b.pdf.

———. 2010b. "Fiscal Exit: From Strategy to Implementation." *Fiscal Monitor, November 2010*, World Economic and Financial Surveys, IMF, Washington, DC. http://www.imf.org/external/pubs/ft/fm/2010/02/fmindex.htm.

———. 2010c. "From Stimulus to Consolidation: Revenue and Expenditure Policies in Advanced and Emerging Economies." Paper by the Fiscal Affairs Department, IMF, Washington, DC. http://www.imf.org/external/np/pp/eng/2010/043010a.pdf.

———. 2010d. *World Economic Outlook October 2010: Recovery, Risk, and Rebalancing*. Washington, DC: IMF.

International Tax Dialogue. 2007. "Taxation of Small and Medium Enterprises." http://www.itdweb.org/smeconference/documents/plenary/PII%20Butler%20and%20Keen.pdf.

Ivanova, Anna, Michael Keen, and Alexander Klemm. 2005. "The Russian 'Flat Tax' Reform." *Economic Policy* 20 (43): 397–444.

Jones, Benjamin, and Michael Keen. 2011. "Climate Policy in Crisis and Recovery." *Journal of International Commerce, Economics and Policy* 2 (1): 103–19.

Jousten, Alain, Mathieu Lefèbvre, Sergio Perelman, and Pierre Pestieau. 2010. "The Effects of Early Retirement on Youth Unemployment: The Case of Belgium." In *Social Security Programs and Retirement around the World: The Relationship to Youth Employment*, ed. Jonathan Gruber and David A. Wise, 47–76. Chicago: University of Chicago Press in association with the National Bureau of Economic Research.

Judd, Kenneth. 1985. "Redistributive Taxation in a Simple Perfect Foresight Model." *Journal of Public Economics* 28 (1): 59–83.

Karam, Philippe, Dirk Muir, Joana Pereira, and Anita Tuladhar. 2010. "Macroeconomic Effects of Public Pension Reforms." Working Paper 10/297, International Monetary Fund, Washington, DC.

Keen, Michael. 2011. "Rethinking the Taxation of the Financial Sector." *CESifo Economic Studies* 57 (1): 1–24.

Keen, Michael, Russell Krelove, and John Norregaard. 2010. "The Financial Activities Tax." In *Financial Sector Taxation: The IMF's Report to the G-20 and Background Material*, ed. Stijn Claessens, Michael Keen, and Ceyla Pazarbasioglu, 118–43. Washington, DC: International Monetary Fund.

Keen, Michael, and Stephen Smith. 2000. "VIVAT, CVAT and All That: New Forms of VAT for Federal Systems." *Canadian Tax Journal* 48 (2): 409–24.

Klemm, Alexander. 2007. "Allowances for Corporate Equity in Practice." *CESifo Economic Studies* 53 (2): 229–62.

Kleven, Henrik, Camille Landais, and Emmanuel Saez. 2010. "Taxation and International Migration of Superstars: Evidence from the European Football Market." Working Paper 16545, National Bureau of Economic Research, Cambridge, MA.

Kneller, Richard, Michael F. Bleaney, and Norman Gemmell. 1999. "Fiscal Policy and Growth: Evidence for OECD Economies." *Journal of Public Economics* 74 (2): 171–90.

Kumar, Mohan, and Jaejoon Woo. 2010. "Public Debt and Growth." Working Paper 10/174, International Monetary Fund, Washington, DC.

Mirrlees, James, Timothy Besley, Richard Blundell, Stephen Bond, Robert Chote, Malcolm Gammie, Paul Johnson, Gareth Myles, and Jim Poterba. 2010. *Taxing by Design*. Oxford, U.K.: Oxford University Press in association with the Institute for Fiscal Studies.

Myles, Gareth D. 2009a. "Economic Growth and the Role of Taxation: Disaggregate Data." Economics Department Working Paper 715, Organisation for Economic Co-operation and Development, Paris.

————. 2009b. "Economic Growth and the Role of Taxation: Theory." Economics Department Working Paper 713, Organisation for Economic Co-operation and Development, Paris.

Ramey, Garey, and Valerie A. Ramey. 1995. "Cross-Country Evidence on the Link between Volatility and Growth." *American Economic Review* 85 (5): 1138–51.

Reinhart, Carmen M., and Kenneth Rogoff. 2010. "Growth in a Time of Debt." *American Economic Review* 100 (2): 573–78.

Reinhart, Carmen M., Kenneth Rogoff, and Miguel A. Savastano. 2003. "Debt Intolerance." *Brookings Papers on Economic Activity* 34 (1): 1–74.

Rodrik, Dani. 1998. "Why Do More Open Economies Have Bigger Governments?" *Journal of Political Economy* 106 (5): 997–1032.

Saez, Emmanuel, Joel Slemrod, and Seth Giertz. 2010. "The Elasticity of Taxable Income with Respect to Marginal Tax Rates: A Critical Review." Working Paper 15012, National Bureau of Economic Research, Cambridge, MA.

Stern, Nicholas. 2007. *The Economics of Climate Change: The Stern Review.* Cambridge, U.K.: Cambridge University Press.

UN (United Nations). 2009. *World Population Prospects, 2008 Revision.* New York: UN.

Woo, Jaejoon. 2009. "Why Do More Polarized Countries Run More Procyclical Fiscal Policy?" *Review of Economics and Statistics* 91 (4): 850–70.

Infrastructure Policy for Shared Growth Post-2008: More and Better, or Simply More Complex?

Antonio Estache

The policy reactions to the 2009 financial crisis around the world indicate that policy makers and their advisers had similarly internalized much of the macroeconomic research showing how and when infrastructure can help short- to long-term growth. International Monetary Fund (IMF) staff found that, right after the crisis, the Group of 20 (G-20) countries added to their expenditure measures an average annual allocation for infrastructure amounting to 0.4 percent of gross domestic product (GDP) (Freedman et al. 2009). Infrastructure represented roughly 20–30 percent of the average postcrisis fiscal stimulus package size among G-20 countries.

Short-Term Responses

Infrastructure thus dominated many countries' recovery packages, with outlays generally over a two- to three-year period (2009–11). For many

I am grateful to Danny M. Leipziger, Ada Izaguirre, Elena Arias, Daniel Benitez, Emmanuelle Auriol, Jose Carbajo, Gael Raballand, Richard Schlirf, and Tina Søreide for useful discussions. The chapter also benefited from partial funding from Growth and Sustainability Policies for Europe (GRASP), a collaborative project funded by the European Commission's Seventh Research Framework Programme. Any mistake or misinterpretation of facts is obviously my responsibility only.

developed economies, this additional allocation represented at least a 20 percent increase over previous average annual infrastructure expenditures. This effort was larger for richer countries than for others: for instance, in middle-income developing countries, the increase over recent trends was less than 10 percent on average.[1] Even if the variance of these additional commitments was large, short-term averages were high enough to show that the 2009 crisis renewed policy makers' faith in infrastructure spending.

To a large extent, it simply meant that Keynesian policies were formally back (at least for a while) and that projects anchored in public works were as popular as in Keynes's most famous book, *The General Theory of Employment, Interest and Money* (1936). An immediate outcome of the formal return of Keynesian policies was that infrastructure builders, investors, and operators could count on strong new fiscal commitments, at least in the few years following the crisis. This reliability is why the project finance business saw only a relatively modest drop in 2009.[2] Most countries had decided to use the infrastructure components of their fiscal packages to improve their transport capacity and increase the mobility of both people and goods. Some—such as Brazil, Japan, Portugal, and Spain—used the opportunity to address climate change concerns as part of their efforts to scale up investments in energy.[3] Many also focused on the need to close their information and communication technology (ICT) gap.

Longer-Term Changes

For the longer run, the crisis catalyzed some structural changes in the basic economics of the infrastructure sector—with some significant fiscal implications. The most apparent change is in the financing outlook. Private sources have lost much of their appetite to finance infrastructure projects because the crisis engendered an expectation of tougher regulation of the securitized and highly leveraged investments commonly used in infrastructure.

In 2009, infrastructure bond spreads reached their highest levels since 2001, averaging 300 basis points. This rise means that the relative importance of private financing will drop, not only because the public sector is spending more (an infrastructure-specific crowding out issue) but also because the private sector may become less willing to commit equity or borrow to build and operate infrastructures at historical return levels, given its sense that risks have become too high for ongoing returns.

Policy Implications

Overall, a clear policy challenge is the risk that increased public spending in the sector won't be enough to offset a drop in private spending, resulting in a net drop in total expenditures. This risk may be mitigated by an explicit effort to use public sector resources to leverage as much private financing as possible or to provide guarantees. But because decisions tend to be implemented slowly in the public sector in general, only time will tell how much of a problem this will be for the infrastructure sector.

A risk of crowding out is not the only policy challenge to result from postcrisis adjustments. The crisis is likely to amplify many incentive problems that preceded the crisis and remain unaddressed. Many of these issues arise from the large residual niches of technological and policy-driven limits to competition in infrastructure. Unfortunately, few of these policy concerns have made it into policy makers' speeches announcing the large commitments to infrastructure investment. Yet their resolution is likely to drive not only the distribution of the gains from revived public infrastructure investment but also the investment's long-term impact and sustainability. Discussions about the most desirable and politically sustainable solutions are also likely to revive passionate debates about the relative importance of the private and public sectors for infrastructure provision.

Chapter Overview

The main purpose of this chapter is to discuss these old and new policy challenges in some detail. It addresses the main issues associated with a scaling up of infrastructure in developed, transition, and developing economies. The emphasis is on the likely longer-term structural effects of crisis-driven changes on demand, supply, and financing of infrastructure transactions.

The discussion explicitly considers that infrastructure policy changes will not happen in a vacuum. Indeed, new policies will also have to deal with the need to adapt to the many long-term concerns associated with climate change and the growing desire to develop regional infrastructures to provide better growth opportunities for the smaller economies, especially the landlocked ones. These emerging issues also have strong regulatory implications because regulation determines risk sharing, which in turns drives the fiscal costs emanating from the sector.

The chapter is organized as follows:

- *Has Demand for Infrastructure Changed Postcrisis?* and *How Will the Supply of Infrastructure Change Postcrisis?* review the longer-term effects of the crisis on demand and supply, respectively.
- *How Much Will the Fiscal Cost of Infrastructure Change after the Crisis?* discusses the fiscal implications for infrastructure financing options in adjustment to the crisis.
- *Strengthening Traditional Government Roles in Infrastructure* reviews the main policy implications of these changes for key dimensions of the role of government in the sector.
- *Upcoming Challenges* discusses additional concerns about the design of infrastructure policies within the new global context.
- *Concluding Comments* summarizes some key questions that arise from the overall analysis.

Has Demand for Infrastructure Changed Postcrisis?

Less than 10 years ago, the academic discussions on the need for infrastructure focused largely on estimates of the infrastructure elasticity of growth or of productivity. At the time, no one seemed to use that research to have a good sense of how much infrastructure was really needed to support various growth scenarios.[4]

For developing countries, the focus changed during the first decade of the 2000s. In the past five years, every major international development agency has estimated infrastructure needs across regions according to the average development level of that region and its aspirations for growth.[5]

This section summarizes the most-quoted estimates of investment and associated operation and maintenance costs in the sector. It then discusses how the crisis is likely to have affected these figures.

How Much Infrastructure Is Needed?

Although precise figures are clearly country-specific, the order of magnitude of the global estimates gives a credible quantitative sense of the importance of infrastructure demand around the developing world. A rough averaging of the various estimates usually quoted suggests that many of the poorest developing countries need to invest more than 6–7 percent of their GDP in infrastructure, varying from about 5 percent on average in Latin America to up to three times as much in Africa and South Asia (Yepes 2007).[6] Depending on the size of the existing capital stock, an additional 50–150 percent of these amounts must be spent to operate and maintain the stocks. The orders of magnitude provided by research are summarized in table 4.1.

Developed countries, following the lead of developing countries, have also tried to assess their own needs. The Organisation for Economic Co-operation and Development (OECD 2006, 2007, 2008) has provided the most encompassing assessment of the global investment needs—in water, telecommunications, road, rail, and electricity—of a world growing at an average of 3 percent per year. OECD estimates that annual average global investment requirements, including those for developed and developing countries, are around 3–5 percent of world GDP.

Clearly the needs of the most-developed countries are relatively lower than those of developing countries because their capital stocks are already quite high. Yet they compete with developing countries in the international markets for funding—providing attractive risk-return

Table 4.1 Annual Infrastructure Investment Needs, Globally and by Developing Region, 2010–15
percentage of GDP

	Estimated infrastructure investment needed per year
World	3–5
Developing countries	6–8
Sub-Saharan Africa and South Asia	9–14
East Asia, Eastern Europe, and Middle East	6–8
Latin America	4–6

Sources: Author's compilation from ADB 2009; ADB, JBIC, and World Bank 2005; Fay and Morisson 2007; Foster and Briceño-Garmendia 2010; OECD 2006, 2007; Yepes 2007.

alternatives—and therefore can affect the appetite for private participation in infrastructure (PPI) in poorer and riskier countries.

How Much Should the Crisis Affect the Needs Estimates?

Did the crisis affect these estimations? Did it imply an upward or downward shift in the slope of the infrastructure demand function? Not really. To see that the crisis has not affected core demand for infrastructure, it is important not to be misled by two short-term facts: (a) effective demand for electricity and transport, for instance, dropped in 2008 and 2009, and (b) short-term effective supply increased in some infrastructure subsectors.

First, the drop in short-term demand says nothing about the trend. As suggested earlier, it would be a mistake to reestimate the trend of the needs based on data from 2008–09. The crisis has hurt current demand for infrastructure even if it had no impact on the long-term demand driven by the world's growth prospects. In most countries, the demand is simply temporarily slow, and it will recover as employment and income increase. The sense that infrastructure supply around the world is rationed continues to be validated by academic studies of infrastructure demand.[7] Private sector actors also validate this view. A survey of business executives in 69 countries, conducted by KPMG (2009a) in June–July 2009, showed that 79 percent are at least somewhat concerned that the current levels of infrastructure spending are not sufficient to sustain the long-term growth of their economies.

Second, it would also be a mistake to assume that the short-term increases in investment and some sectors reflect a response to an anticipated upward shift in long-term demand. In most countries, the increases simply represent an acceleration of planned supply, not a shift. France may have been the most explicit on this aspect: when it unveiled the details of a fiscal package worth €25.9 billion (around 1.5 percent of its GDP), about 40 percent corresponded to measures to speed up planned investment.

One major change in demand may take place, however, as discussed in more detail later: changes in demand will result from the new global concerns about climate change. The need to create jobs and to scale up and speed up the coverage of infrastructure has given an exceptional opportunity to meet the global demand for a greening of infrastructure and its use. Although demand management for energy, transport, and water aimed at reducing the environmental effects is likely to somewhat reduce consumption per capita, it is also likely that total demand over time will continue to grow as income levels, and the middle classes, grow with development.

Summing Up

Overall, the financial crisis has not significantly changed the basic demand drivers for infrastructure. The long-term elasticity of demand will continue to depend on the stage of development and the growth forecast, while the short-term elasticity will be driven by the short-term economic conditions.

The long-term needs have been relatively well known for a while. The world is quite familiar with the coverage gaps for water and energy in the poorest countries of the planet. The strongest impacts may simply have been not only the sector's increased visibility but also the increased realization that the significant additional investments needed to close infrastructure gaps would be fiercely competing with safety nets for fiscal space.

How Will the Supply of Infrastructure Change Postcrisis?

The stimulus packages designed to reverse the negative employment and growth effects of the crisis are obviously expected to have both short-term and longer-term impacts. This section discusses in some detail the short-, medium-, and long-term impacts of the crisis on the supply side of the infrastructure market. It then looks at the extent to which public procurement processes influence these effects as well as their sustainability.

Short-Term Impacts on Supply

The main and most obvious effect of the infrastructure component of stimulus packages is on jobs. Low-skill jobs can be created relatively easily during the construction phase of many infrastructure projects to allow some of the populations most exposed to the crisis to get an income and to spend.

A 2009 Canadian government survey documented significant infrastructure components in more than 30 OECD and upper-middle-income countries, illustrating the importance of infrastructure on the agenda in those countries (*CanadExport* 2009). A similar survey of 54 countries by the International Labour Organization (ILO 2009) covered many low-income countries and found that 87 percent of the countries had some infrastructure component. In fact, the proportion of stimulus on infrastructure spending averaged three times higher in developing and emerging economies than in developed economies (Khatiwada 2009). The ILO survey also showed that infrastructure was not only a major element of the recovery for many of the poorest countries but also particularly important to create jobs (ILO 2009).

Medium-Term Impacts on Supply

The medium-term effects of the stimulus packages on infrastructure supply concern not just labor-intensive infrastructure. As mentioned earlier, they also concern the timing of supply, particularly the opportunity to speed up delayed investment decisions in the sector. Indeed, as more resources become available to the sector, thanks to the stimulus packages, governments are likely to expand supply to levels closer to those needed to meet long-term demand. For some regions, this can produce a major supply effect.

Consider, for instance, the case of Sub-Saharan Africa. For the past decade or so, Sub-Saharan Africa has invested about 50 percent of what it needed to invest to sustain the high growth rates necessary to pull the 50 percent or so of Africans who live in poverty out of their unacceptable fate (Foster and Briceño-Garmendia 2010). It is difficult to believe that the significant volumes of aid resources mobilized by donors will not help to close this gap.

The need to speed up investment is not just in developing countries. The overwhelming domination of the transport sector as a beneficiary of stimulus packages in OECD countries attests to concern about logistic support to growth in these countries and the need to make decisions that had been postponed in the sector for too long. The Australian plan, for instance, expedited US$660 million in road funding (KPMG 2009b).

Longer-Term Impacts on Supply

A more subtle effect of the crisis—one that is just as important and clearly more lasting—is the transformation of infrastructure supply to address climate change concerns. Investment types and technologies are being adjusted to meet the demand for the greening of the sector and to meet the growing concern about anticipated natural disasters or their consequences.

China has allocated US$25 billion for infrastructure in the Wenchuan earthquake-affected area. The Republic of South Korea has allocated US$2.3 billion over four years to develop green technologies such as solar and wind generation, fuel cells, and carbon capture and storage. The United States has allocated US$19 billion specifically for flood control and sewage and water treatment.[8]

Influence of Public Procurement Processes on Crisis-Related Supply Effects

In the analysis of the supply effects of the crisis, the most complex aspect may be the evaluation of how quickly decisions can lead to short-term results on the ground. Indeed, implementation of decisions to expand or modernize strategic infrastructures is likely to take longer than casual observers may anticipate. Although many decisions have been made to spend more and spend faster, few governments, if any, have considered the need to address the processes that allow infrastructure supply to grow.

How do processes put the supply at risk? The first reason why the short-term effects may be slow to meet political and popular expectations relates to common procurement processes. These processes need to be factored in when assessing the impact of a fiscal stimulus largely anchored in infrastructure investments.

Even under accelerated procedures, procuring public works generally takes more than a year, and often twice as long, to implement from the time the decision to go ahead has been made. Specifying the terms of reference, organizing the auctions, assessing the bids, preparing the contracts, and negotiating these contracts are all essential steps typically needed before the works can start.

In the German debates on the composition of the public expenditures to be financed by the country's stimulus package, the infrastructure sector was, in fact, penalized because of these procurement issues. The German stimulus plan favored investment in education—to some extent because the German technocrats were quite aware of the slow procurement speed of large infrastructure projects and the risk it represented for the effectiveness of the recovery efforts. German concerns about the slow processes of public sector infrastructure activities were recently validated by a survey covering many more countries (KPMG 2010, 13). In that survey, 23 percent of the 455 senior public officials consulted in 69 countries around the world felt that governments were not able to meet commitments at the development or contract stage, and 30 percent of the respondents held the same view about the implementation stage.

Sustainability of Supply Effects

Slow or unreliable procurement practices are not the only cause of disagreement in the policy and academic communities over how much infrastructure support can help short-run growth recoveries. These disagreements have been fueled by differences in expectations associated with (a) the short-term job creation effects of infrastructure expenditures, and (b) the intensity and longer-run sustainability of those effects (ILO 2009).

The real issue is indeed the extent to which infrastructure projects do more than create short-term jobs. Political speeches tend to convey the implicit assumption that the effects on jobs will be sustained and will go beyond the short-term construction-phase jobs in the sector. In practice, the extent to which the jobs will last and multiply depends largely on the speed and the duration of the growth impact of the infrastructure stimulus.

Because infrastructures take quite a long time to build, short-term multipliers should be expected to be lower than longer-term ones (Spilimbergo, Symansky, and Schindler 2009). Most researchers do not distinguish between short- and longer-term effects and find an infrastructure multiplier in the range of 0.5 to 1.0 (see, for instance, Shanks and Barnes 2008). These conservative estimates give some reason not to be overly optimistic about the job-related effects of the policy. Stevans and Sessions (2010) suggest that this order of magnitude is fine in the short run but underestimate the longer-run effect. According to them, in the United States, the multiplier reaches 0.867 after a year but gets to 3.3 after two years when all secondary effects are properly accounted for. This happens because the real growth payoff comes after the construction phase, once the new assets can actually be used to meet demand.[9]

There is also some concern about the extent to which the job creation will be local rather than abroad. Expansions of infrastructure spending often imply some external leak from the basic short- and long-term multiplier effects, which are not picked up by macro models that do not account for some key sectoral dimensions. Indeed, for some infrastructures, many basic components are imported, meaning that some of the job-creation impact is abroad. For instance, for many countries, the rolling stock components of railway expansions are imported. This concern about subsidies to external jobs has been a reason why the domestic multipliers have not always been as high as hoped for.

Summing Up

In sum, the overall impact of the crisis on infrastructure supply must be unbundled into its short-, medium-, and long-term components as well as into the various expectations that increases in infrastructure investments must meet. When these various dimensions are considered, it seems reasonable to argue that the long-term effect is likely to be modest. Sooner or later, supply will have to meet demand for the growth effects to reach their potential. The short-term composition, however, may be influenced by a number of factors, and the associated risk of failing to meet expectations may lead politicians to favor other expenditure types over acceleration of infrastructure investments.

Globally, however, the indisputable beneficiaries of the crisis are the well-established infrastructure suppliers. Their sector has benefited from a major improvement in the general awareness of its importance, and this awareness has guaranteed short financing to the sector.

In addition, the crisis has provided an opportunity to address the increased concerns about more environmentally friendly infrastructure supply around the globe. If governments are serious about fighting climate change, the relatively large amounts they have committed to infrastructure to launch the recovery should be greener. In other words, they should require infrastructure to rely more on climate-friendly technologies. The size of such investment commitments is so large that the recovery plans could have created a tipping point for the greening of the sector.

How Much Will the Fiscal Cost
of Infrastructure Change Postcrisis?

Understanding the fiscal consequences of the crisis requires an assessment of the long-term impact of the crisis on the various financing options of the infrastructure sector. This is where the complexity of the crisis's impacts on the sector stands out. A fair assessment of these impacts requires a distinction between (a) the sources of cost recovery for investments and operations of the activity, and (b) the financing of the investments needed to deliver the infrastructure service.

This discussion can be quite sensitive because it must touch upon the highly controversial debate on the scope of the private sector's role in the delivery of infrastructure services. The way out of the controversy adopted here is to focus on the evidence on the size of observed private contribution in relation to the size of the needs.

The discussion of these issues starts with a review of the evidence on the scope for cost recovery to minimize the fiscal burden of subsidies in the sector. It then takes stock of the evidence on the scope for opportunities to cut the financing requirements, thanks to a larger role for the private sector. It concludes with a discussion of the importance of risks in the distribution of financing costs between the public and private sectors.

How Could Cost Be Recovered to Minimize the Fiscal Burden?

Regarding how costs should be recovered, the initial point—which unfortunately continues to be as relevant after the crisis as it had been for quite some time before the crisis—is that costs must be cut to minimize the financing requirements. In Africa, for instance (according to the recent diagnostic summarized by Foster and Briceño-Garmendia 2010), a more efficient use of infrastructure resources could cut these requirements by close to 20 percent of the total needs estimated. Almost 50 percent of that saving could be obtained by addressing operating inefficiencies through better road maintenance and greater efficiency at power utilities alone.

A formal review of regulatory decisions during tariff revisions under price-cap regimes suggests a similar scope for efficiency gains to be achieved across sectors in other regions, including the most-developed ones.[10] Making the most of the scope for cost savings is also a way to help the fiscal packages get a bigger bang for the buck. Lower unit costs mean that, for a given stimulus budget allocation for infrastructure, more infrastructure can be built or maintained, or more people can be subsidized if needed.

Ignoring for now the need to cut costs, and before trying to figure out who must pay and how much, it is useful to remember that any cost recovery can be targeted to only three main groups of actors: the users (who often pay for at least part of the cost of delivering the services they consume), current taxpayers (who finance subsidies through their tax payments), and future taxpayers (when current subsidies are financed through bonds or other forms of loans).[11]

Until the 1990s, current and future taxpayers had supported the bulk of the cost of operating and expanding infrastructure services because subsidies tended to be quite common in both developed and developing countries. Between the 1990s and the mid-2000s, the dominating philosophy changed. Most policy makers started to argue that users, through users' fees, should take on most of the cost of what they were using or consuming. Tax and loan financing were viewed as both inefficient and unfair instruments—inefficient because they were easily hidden inside budgets, and unfair because nonusers funded part of the bill.

After this new philosophy engendered some social unrest (for instance, the Bolivian rejections of private water operators enjoyed strong media coverage around the world), policy makers adopted strategies that started to rely again on taxpayers. By the mid-2000s, many policy makers became convinced again that relying on full cost recovery from users was politically unviable for basic infrastructures such as water and urban transport. This explains why subsidies and cross-subsidies progressively crawled back as the concern for affordability started to dominate the policy debates. Under the current political, social, and economic environment, there is no reason to believe that this new trend will be reversed again anytime soon. In other words, taxpayers are likely to again become the main source of cost recovery in this sector.

In the few years following the launch of the stimulus packages, initial evidence is already starting to validate that prediction. The fiscal packages will finance investments that will not all be recovered through

utilities tariffs and transport user charges. Even without the fiscal packages, the subsidies were already quite significant. For the energy sector,
annual energy subsidies around the world amount to about 1 percent of
world GDP (Bacon, Ley, and Kojima 2010). This corresponds to about a
third of the most conservative estimates of the annual electricity investment needs in developing countries.

Although governments are increasingly concerned about the distortions associated with these subsidies and their long-term fiscal costs, the
stimulus packages increased the fiscal space, and thus the scope, for such
subsidies (ILO 2009; Khatiwada 2009). Subsidies for railways, ports, and
airports will continue to be justified in terms of the positive regional
or national employment effects. Energy, urban, and transport subsidies
will continue to be justified by the concern to ensure affordable public
services, but they are significant nonetheless.

How Much Will the Private Sector Reduce
Fiscal Financing Requirements?

From a project finance perspective, the evidence points to a clear drop
in the average global level of new private commitments to infrastructure projects.[12] There is, however, a strong variance around the world.
DLA Piper and the European PPP Expertise Centre (EPEC) reported a
significant drop of such commitments in Europe as a result of the crisis,
with no obvious recovery in sight for 2010 (DLA Piper and EPEC 2009).
The average impact in developing countries has also been quite strong,
with a drop of 10 percent in 2008 commitments to new projects—albeit
with a partial recovery in 2009, according to preliminary figures (World
Bank and PPIAF 2010). Yet the distribution around that average drop
is huge. The 2009 recovery was largely driven by Brazil, China, India,
and Turkey, which have continued to benefit from large commitments,
particularly in the energy sector. Without those four countries, the 2009
average figure for developing countries would have revealed another
significant drop in commitments.

The 2009 situation may reflect a lag between decisions to slow investments and completion of signed commitments. Large infrastructure contracts take 18–24 months on average to get signed, so the full real impact
is likely to be observed only from 2011 on. Many of the contracts signed

in 2008 and 2009 were simply the end products of activities started earlier, suggesting that the current figures may still underestimate the full impact of the crisis.

This interpretation seems to be validated by the early figures for 2010: PPI projects reaching closure in developing countries fell by 25 percent in the first quarter of 2010 compared with the same quarter of 2009. It is also validated when looking at the recovery time after the most recent violent economic crises. It took three to four years after the 1997 East Asian and the 2001 Argentinean crises to get a sense of the full impact on the public-private partnership (PPP) market in developing economies, as seen in figure 4.1. Given that the 2008 crisis was more similar to the 1997 East Asian crisis in scope and degree of surprise, it would be reasonable to assume that the 2008 crisis is likely to generate an equivalent market response. The main difference is the strong Keynesian response to the current crisis, which should offset and reassure to a stronger extent.

The drop in the number of projects observed so far is quite consistent with the evidence available on the returns to equity and bonds in the two years that followed the crisis and the associated increases in the cost of capital expected for the sector. Observed returns on infrastructure equities reflect the short-term drop in demand and the uncertainty of the long-term financing options for the sector. Despite the strong public commitments, infrastructure funds in 2009 had returns 50 percent lower than the average market return.[13]

The stimulus plan did have an impact, however: Within the S&P Global Infrastructure Index, the transportation infrastructure sector led (up by about 41 percent)—driven by large toll-road companies that increased in value as the economic recovery led to improved traffic flow. Utilities trailed, with a return of 5.6 percent for 2009. Although returns are lower, the cost of bond financing has increased fast to internalize the new risks seen in the sector despite the strong public sector commitments. Indeed, the evolution of the prices on the bond market is quite consistent with the lower commitment levels. Few infrastructure bonds were placed in the market in 2008–09, and the costs of bonds and fees associated with PPPs have almost doubled, imposing a significant increase in the cost of capital in the sector.[14]

Figure 4.1 PPI Commitments to Infrastructure Projects in Developing Countries, by Implementation Status, 1990–2009

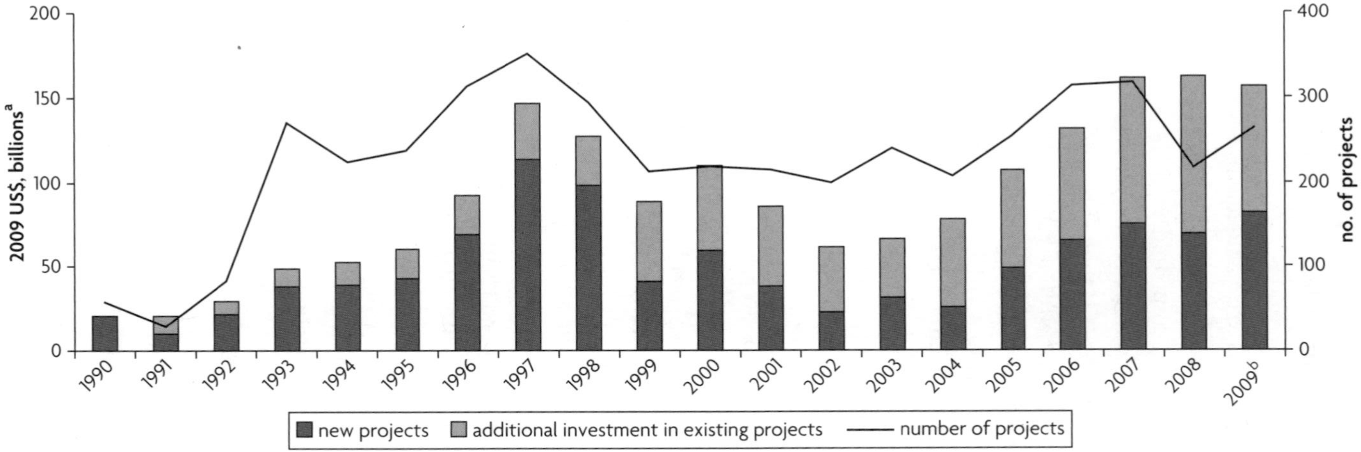

Legend: ■ new projects ■ additional investment in existing projects —— number of projects

Axes: no. of projects (0, 100, 200, 300, 400); 2009 US$, billions[a] (0, 50, 100, 150, 200); years 1990–2009.

Source: World Bank and PPIAF 2010; PPI Project Database.
Note: PPI = public-private investment.
a. Adjusted by U.S. Consumer Price Index.
b. Preliminary figures.

How Much Does the Fiscal Cost Depend on Risk Perceptions?

A recent article by Tenorio and Idzelis (2009), building on interviews of important players in the infrastructure finance world, reflected the increased anxiety with the discovery, through the crisis, that infrastructure assets are not immune to a downturn and, hence, cash flows are less predictable than assumed in many project finance designs.

Key actors such as pension funds seem to have discovered the demand side of infrastructure. The roughly 80 large global infrastructure funds have not been too successful in finding an estimated US$100 billion of commitments from financial institutions with large liquidities for the long run, such as pension funds and insurance companies.[15] This may explain why in the United States, rather than relying mainly on PPPs for large-scale infrastructures, tax-exempt bonds (often issued by local or state governments) are seen as more reliable financing tools.

It is thus not surprising to see operators more interested in bidding for public contracts than trying to convince the financial players of the sector's long-term prospects. The evidence is as robust for developing countries as it is for developed countries except for some of the major middle-income countries (DLA Piper and EPEC 2009). The collapsed bond and syndication markets have indeed taken their toll on financing for private foreign and domestic investments in infrastructure projects that require long-term commitments in risky environments. How long that impact will last is also likely to depend on international regulatory changes affecting asset risk management, its implementation, and its consequences for infrastructure assets.

Because the rationing of demand due to insufficient supply can be explained, in good part, by a financing gap, any reduction in the private financing of the sector will have to be addressed. If risk continues to be perceived as too high, the challenge for governments around the world will be to calm private investors' fears without stimulating the risk of either bubbles or cherry-picking, which cuts opportunities for cross-subsidies within countries and increases the public share of infrastructure financing costs. For developing countries, a reasonable target is to maintain at least the 20 percent share that private financing had contributed to the sector's needs in the decade before the crisis.

That might not be a bad target for developed countries as well. In the United Kingdom, where the value of PPP transactions had increased sharply in the 5–10 years before the crisis and which is generally seen as one of the greatest markets for PPPs, these transactions have accounted for only about 10–15 percent of all public sector capital investment since 1996 (Hall 2008).[16]

Until that target is met, it is likely that financial institutions' decreased appetite for risky investments will further fuel the short- to medium-run, and possibly longer-run, demand for public investment and subsidies. In a survey conducted by Siemens just a year before the crisis exploded, public loan financing was widely expected to remain the key financing instrument across Europe (Hall 2008). The upshot is that the public sector will likely continue to be the major source of financing for the sector—a trend that will be reinforced in the postcrisis world unless new ways of managing risks are introduced. Both regulation and guarantees (with their own fiscal costs) will probably be essential instruments in that effort, as discussed later.

Thus, the overall market for infrastructure project finance will survive the crisis, and the private sector will obviously continue to be an important minority source of financing for the continued need to increase or upgrade infrastructure. Yet it is unlikely that PPPs will represent the main way of financing infrastructure anytime soon, particularly in developing countries. Private financing has not been larger than 20 percent on average since PPPs took off in the late 1990s, and there is no evidence suggesting that it will be otherwise in the future once current relevant trends are accounted for.

How Can the Fiscal Consequences of Higher Risk Aversion Be Mitigated?

Private investors' increased concern about risk is likely to increase the pressure on government to finance infrastructure needs. Because governments are, at the same time, concerned about the sustainability of increased fiscal gaps, it is crucial to assess how to minimize the fiscal effects of risks taken by the public sector. The 2008 financial crisis is thus providing an opportunity, but it is also forcing the international community as well as individual countries to revisit the fundamentals of the PPP approach. There is no solution yet to this challenge, but the identification of the solution will have to start with a good degree of humility and realism.

This review of the lessons of experience must start with the growing evidence of the PPPs' failure to deliver on expectations, in particular for some infrastructure activities such as water and sanitation, urban transport systems, and to some extent, roads. Engel, Fischer, and Galetovic (2008), for instance, suggest that, from a fiscal viewpoint, PPPs did not really relieve budgetary pressures and release public funds. On the contrary, PPPs have often been used to circumvent budgetary oversight and add to government spending. Recognizing up front the real fiscal cost of the specific PPP instrument would already be a major achievement and help to minimize the risks of exacerbating fiscal problems.

The review also must build in the recognition that pervasive use of government guarantees to increase the volume of PPPs has not helped to promote growth as much as expected. The evidence reported in Engel, Fischer, and Galetovic (2008) also suggests that guarantees may have reduced the potential of PPPs' evaluation teams to filter out "white elephants," at least in developing countries. In practice, the guarantees often boil down to a redistribution of risk between the public and private sectors. Guarantees kick in as posttransaction cost increases get passed on to taxpayers rather than users. Engel, Fischer, and Galetovic (2008) summarize theoretical and empirical evidence on the fiscal costs of contract renegotiations in developing countries.

Hall (2008) provides indirect evidence suggesting that accounting practices may have helped redistribute the risk in Europe. His detailed synthesis of various European decisions suggests that the limits on government borrowing imposed by European Union, national, and IMF policies may have allowed PPP-related costs to be accounted for as non-government expenditures even if they were tax-financed (EC 2000).

Summing Up

The overall conclusion of this discussion of the recent evolution of infrastructure financing strategies is simple enough: the crisis may have revealed the importance of continuing to expect that the government, and hence the taxpayer, will be a major source of infrastructure financing.

The specific forms of intervention will include subsidies and guarantees, but these should ideally be recognized in ex ante budgets to reduce the risks of unexpected fiscal shocks. These budgets should also reflect the fact that public sector participation is also increasingly likely to take the form of an equity stake and that governments should get their fair share of return for risks taken to offset some of the expected fiscal costs of the sector. Proper budgeting is needed to ensure that the fiscal contribution is consistent with the fiscal ability of governments.

As Burger et al. (2009) suggest, governments' exposure to risk should be consistent with the broad definition of fiscal policy, including contingent liabilities, and should be adequately costed and budgeted. This has to be a condition for the sustained use of tax resources in the sector.

Additionally, governments will have to ensure that the financing process is fair, efficient, and fiscally sustainable—the three benchmarks against which public decisions about the state's role should be made in the postcrisis era. The need to look at these benchmarks jointly is not new for public economics academics, but it may be for some policy makers.

Strengthening the Traditional Government Roles in Infrastructure

Infrastructure is a major share of any economy. On average, it represents roughly 12–18 percent of GDP, depending on the country. What is remarkable, in the context of this chapter, is that the public sector already manages most infrastructure directly or indirectly, but many nongovernment actors have a stake in the policy decisions in the sector:

- *The media and macroeconomists* view the sector as fiscally important to soften the real social and growth consequences of the crisis through job creation.
- *Infrastructure construction or operations firms* see policy as affecting the demand for their services in the short run as the new infrastructure gets built and, in the longer run, as the larger new stock requires maintenance.
- *Development banks and agencies* that have infrastructure departments rely on the financial support of infrastructure projects to their core business.

Unfortunately, the focus of these interested parties also reflects their continual disdain for the microeconomic dysfunctions of the infrastructure sector. This section discusses the various policy areas on which reformers should focus as they try to manage the fiscal dimensions of the sector. It covers efficiency and equity concerns as well as public sector management of key responsibilities with high fiscal costs, such as procurement, risk management, and sector planning.

The Forest behind the Fiscal Trees

In a postcrisis world, just as there is a lot of talk about how to improve the regulation of the financial sector, there should be a lot of talk—and eventually a lot of action—about how to improve the regulation of the infrastructure sector. Appropriate regulation may be the sector's biggest challenge, and the discussion must go well beyond debate about the sector's fiscal importance.

There should also be an interest in assessing the drivers of the policy decisions on how to use public resources. These decisions have to ensure that public investments in the infrastructure needs of growth are not associated with unanticipated increases in fiscal costs. From the perspective of infrastructure policy, stimulating jobs and income will be sustainable only if these microeconomic policy diagnostics are conducted properly. This is not to deny that the elements everyone focuses on during a crisis are essential, but such crisis management focuses on the short-term, temporary role of government; it says nothing about the more fundamental concerns that should define the medium- to long-run policy agenda.

The real infrastructure policy challenges come from what no budget will show: a serious assessment of the extent to which the short-term policy decisions address the long-term needs of the sector. None of the decisions seriously discusses the risks of financing many small "white elephants" with the excuse of increasing growth and jobs. Even less in times of urgency than in regular times do regulators show proper concern for how much rent the construction firms, bankers, and operators will capture on the backs of the taxpayers and the users.

Such structural concerns do not seem to interest the opinion makers of the world. The only indicators of poor public sector management that attract media attention seem to be dramatic corruption cases, accidents, and abusive prices. The serious incentive problems that lead to these actions have not been on the agenda so far. Yet they can have huge fiscal costs to be covered by today's and tomorrow's taxpayers. The post-crisis deficit concerns may provide a good opportunity to start addressing them.

Where should the discussion start? The obvious answer is with an assessment of the opportunity the crisis may provide to improve regulation in the sector. From an efficiency point of view, it is essential to get a sense of how effective regulatory incentives have been to push operators to invest in much-needed low-cost coverage in some parts of the world and to innovate and modernize in others. From an equity point of view, it is important to get a sense of how fairly operators, users, and taxpayers are treated and whether the expanded role of government in financing the sector makes a difference.

Strengthening the Efficiency Outcomes of Infrastructure Regulation

For many countries, regulation had been the main weakness of the infrastructure sector before the crisis, just as it had been the weak spot of the financial sector. Countries relying on self-regulation of infrastructure services had traditionally been exposed to political interference with optimal regulatory decisions. The goal of increasing regulators' independence boiled down, in many countries, to simply creating a separate institution in charge of regulation without succeeding in eliminating political interference in the sectors. This is as true in OECD countries as it is in developing economies.

When regulators are competent and independent enough, there is evidence of a positive impact on outputs, quality, or prices from the institutional unbundling of policy making and regulation in most infrastructure sectors. Unfortunately, regulators seldom have the necessary independence, particularly to manage crises when they arise. An extreme example is the almost total suppression of Argentinean regulators' independence immediately after the 2001 crisis, which resulted in a suspension of many contractual commitments to operators. Similar, albeit less extreme, interferences have also been observed in Europe, and it is hard to ignore the common U.S. practice of seating political appointees on the boards of state-level regulatory agencies (see, for instance, Gilardi 2002 and Johanssen 2003).

Unhappiness with the management of regular or extraordinary tariff setting processes around the world has been increasingly well documented by researchers interested in understanding the sources of regulatory failures. Since 2000, this has allowed the literature on the independence of regulation to go beyond the normative debates that discuss the choice on regulatory institutions as a binary one: with or without independence. As nicely summarized by Andres, Guasch, and Azumendi (2008), the literature on the regulatory agencies has identified these desirable attributes:

• Management autonomy and independence from political authorities
• Mechanisms for accountability, both to other branches of government and to the public
• Transparency of both rule- and decision-making procedures.

Few countries, whether developed or developing, score well on all three dimensions.

A review of this evidence in the new context defined by the 2008 crisis leads to an alarming message: infrastructure regulation, just like financial regulation, has not been systematically conducted in the simultaneous interest of the main stakeholders (users, operators, and taxpayers). When regulators were created as part of a privatization strategy, the evidence suggests, any weakness of regulation has tended to benefit the private operators. All the empirical studies looking at the actual impact of regulation suggest that if operators were losing money, they would pull out or close the business. With the exception of the odd experience of Enron, there are no obvious cases of bankruptcy in telecoms, energy, or water services around the world. In a few cases, large operators have pulled out of a country—as in Mali or Senegal, for instance. Regulation is still an outstanding challenge in infrastructure as it is in finance.

Strengthening the Fairness of Infrastructure Regulation

The incidence of imperfect regulation is also quite obvious. The winners have not changed from the evidence shown five years ago: investors and operators have done quite well (Estache 2006). For instance, infrastructure stocks and funds outperformed their respective market averages for the past 10 to 12 years, roughly since the liberalization of the sector started to be implemented.

Peng and Newell (2007) studied the total returns for the listed Australian infrastructure funds and companies from 1995 to 2006. As seen in table 4.2, infrastructure funds outperformed all other investments.

A similar assessment conducted just before the crisis by RREEF, a Deutsche Bank research branch, confirmed the Australian conclusions, showing that infrastructure funds in the United States and Europe outperformed many other assets, although not all of them (Mansour and Nadji 2007).

The high infrastructure returns to date should be strong evidence that regulation has not significantly hurt rents in the sector. The institutional changes in the management of regulation (associated with the restructuring of these sectors to open capital to the private sector) were designed to attract capital. The best way to attract capital is to promise high rents. Moreover, any time a large utility or major transport company has been in trouble, it has been supported by its government through subsidies or tariff increases. The "too big to fail" argument so intensely discussed in the context of financial institutions seems to apply just as well to negotiation strategies in regulatory decisions concerning the infrastructure sector.

The losers of the weak regulation of financial and infrastructure services remain the same: taxpayers and users. Nothing new under the sun. The main change may be an increase in the share of the total financing

Table 4.2 Precrisis Risk-Adjusted Infrastructure Performance in Australia, 1995Q3–2006Q2

	Average annual return (percent)	Annual volatility (annualized standard deviation of quarterly returns)
Composite infrastructure	22.4	0.16
Toll roads	25.7	0.24
Airports	8.1	0.31
Utilities	21.9	0.16
Stocks	12.9	0.11
Bonds	7.2	0.04

Sources: Author's compilation, based on Peng and Newell 2007.

burden to be absorbed by taxpayers because the crisis is giving govern-ments an opportunity to finance subsidies demanded by producers to deliver services at relatively low average tariffs. As unemployment rises and financing costs increase with perceived risk levels, populations are unlikely to be able to maintain current consumptions without some form of subsidy.

Increasing the Transparency of the Fiscal Cost

Why should effective regulation be more important after the crisis than it was before, from a fiscal point of view? Lack of transparency and accountability for unjustified high costs was a source of inefficiency and unfairness before the crisis and will continue to cause just as much inef-ficiency and unfairness after the crisis. The big difference is likely to be the *size* of inefficiency's fiscal cost. More spending in the sector at a given level of subsidy due to excessive costs simply means higher fiscal costs.

If excessive operating and capital costs continue to be tolerated through weak regulatory assessments and decisions, the fiscal costs to the sectors are likely to increase. Thus, the tolerance for high costs is not just inefficient; it is also unfair to taxpayers. Monitoring costs and cut-ting them where they are unjustified would mean less need to subsidize consumption. Better regulation would not only reduce unit costs but would also increase the share of production costs that can be absorbed by the final users and reduce the share that has to be passed on to the taxpayers.

The significant increase of the fiscal share of infrastructure spending in the postcrisis era should afford an opportunity to take a good look at the extent to which weak regulatory capacity leads to the high costs and profit margins in the sector. This effort should include a look at the distribution of the cost recovery efforts among economic agents. Infra-structure projects tend to have high price tags. This seems reasonable to uninformed observers because infrastructure projects tend to be large and costly. It turns out, however, that a lot of research in the past few years has shown that this price tag tended to be excessive.[17]

Reforming Procurement to Cut Costs

In many countries, the problem of high infrastructure costs starts at the procurement stage. Despite huge progress in the theoretical assessment of procurement design, in most countries, many projects continue to be awarded and monitored under rules that do not meet the standards of transparency and accountability expected to prevail when the amounts involved provide a strong incentive for wrongdoing.

The problem is serious and does not apply only to developing countries. Significant infrastructure-related corruption cases have made it into media coverage and, hence, public opinion in various European countries—for instance, in Germany (where the Siemens case shows how major companies from countries with strong governance traditions may become involved in corruption in developing countries to win contracts) or in Spain (where many infrastructure projects have been used to illegally finance political parties).

For the past five years, all major aid actors have finally been willing to seriously open their eyes to various forms of corruption that infect the infrastructure sector. Yet the policy actions tend to focus more on normative headline messages than on the crucial technical dimensions that should improve governance and accountability in the sector. The parallel with the failures of regulation, governance, and accountability in the financial sector is hard to miss.

Restoring Planning in a Sector with Long-Lived Assets

From a strategic viewpoint, it is also important to consider the dynamics of the sector's financing needs. Even if costs are kept under control, governments should anticipate future subsidy requirements associated with increased service availability. (Coverage increases faster simply because public funding can be used more to invest, and less to subsidize, current consumption.) As larger shares of the population get access to many basic services—the coverage rate increasing much faster than income as a result of the stimulus packages and improved regulation—the demand for consumption subsidies may increase as well.

From a fiscal management viewpoint, it is thus useful to point to the revenue consequences of successful regulation. If cost savings are larger than revenue increases based on increased consumption, the tax base will shrink, fueling the fiscal deficit. It is indeed important to keep in mind that finance ministers face a strong dilemma. Because the sector is such a large share of the economy, it is a useful tax handle. Cutting costs in the sector boils down to cutting revenue from the sector. In Belgium, for instance, water, electricity, gas, and ICT are subject to a value added tax of 21 percent. Assume (realistically) that costs could be cut by 10 percent. If demand does not increase with the cost cut—and demand is unlikely to increase because environmental concerns are leading to improved demand management to cut consumption—given that the sum of these activities represents about 10 percent of GDP, the reduction in cost implies a revenue loss of about 0.5 percent of GDP. This order of magnitude may be the most intuitive explanation for the poor commitment of governments around the world to serious regulation.

The political economy perspective also points to the need to anticipate the continuation and possible increase of demand for fiscal contributions to the sector. Because populations view most infrastructure services as entitlements—the public service obligations of governments—and because infrastructure services are regularly presented as key drivers of countries' investment climate, it is unlikely that users will be asked to take on part of the burden of financing the sector commonly imposed on taxpayers. Political stability and competitiveness are the benefits expected from a shift of the financing burden from users to taxpayers, so the prospect of shifting such costs to users is at least as unlikely postcrisis as it was before the crisis.

Becoming Honest about Risk Assessments and Their Fiscal Effects

Increased commercialization, including a larger role for PPPs, will simply increase the burden on taxpayers unless regulation anticipates and manages the risks of higher fiscal costs. These additional fiscal liabilities can come from an increased risk of cream skimming by the private sector, an overgenerous system of guarantees, or lax performance incentives in regulatory designs.

Risks from Cream Skimming. The main risk for taxpayers is allowing infrastructure ministries to unbundle projects or sectors to increase the PPP opportunities. Cream skimming arises because the packages proposed to potential private partners are put together to reduce the number of obligations that represent risks of high cost with low opportunities for full cost recovery. This strategy is in contrast to traditional modes of financing of the sector—in which, for instance, high-cost rural areas are subsidized by low-cost urban areas. Unbundling urban and rural infrastructure obligations has often resulted in the private sector taking over the high-profit urban obligations and the public sector keeping the low-profit rural obligations, thus eliminating the intrasectoral cross-subsidies and requiring direct subsidies when full cost recovery in rural areas is politically and socially impossible.[18]

News summaries of conferences and interviews with investors are in many ways more revealing than the more technical, complex papers that look at the trade-offs between cross-subsidies and cream skimming in the sector.[19] They show that the concern about postcrisis risk levels are leading potential private sources of financing to expect more-focused, less-risky projects, increasing the likelihood of cream skimming. In other words, the concerns about risks—including the increased concerns about demand risk in basic services—are resulting in more selective investments of equity in the sector.

As long as the bond market continues to have cold feet in the sector as well—and this is likely as long as the financial system has not reduced the uncertainty of prospects for exotic instruments—the projects and activities packaged for PPP will have to be particularly attractive. Any source of uncertain costs to be addressed as part of service obligations commonly imposed as part of PPPs is likely to reduce the attractiveness of PPPs. Reducing service obligations for the private sector implies the end of common forms of intrasectoral cross-subsidies. Experience shows that when this happens, the taxpayers end up being the residual source of financing.

Risks from Increased Guarantees. Taxpayers may also be exposed to an increased burden as a result of increased guarantees aimed at attracting the private sector. In January 2009, for example, the U.K. government introduced a guarantee program to stimulate the demand for asset-backed securities. The guarantees were made available four months later.

The interesting aspect is that the program has not been that successful so far. The lack of success is revealing in terms of how major banks value these guarantees. The guarantees were apparently not enough or too costly to stimulate the market for infrastructure securities in the United Kingdom (DLA Piper and EPEC 2009). For the program to work, the fiscal allocation to the programs would have to increase.

The taxpayers' cost has to increase to cut costs for investors and increase the protection of their investments.

Effects of Risk Allocation Renegotiation. Another effort to attract the private sector that could unexpectedly affect the fiscal sector stems from a progressive shift toward regulatory options that reduce the share of risks assigned to operators. In developing countries, Guasch's (2004) assessment of renegotiation experiences already pointed in that direction. It showed that one of the most common occurrences associated with renegotiation is the pass-through of cost increases to users or taxpayers through increased subsidies. This is what is meant in practice by a progressive switch from price-cap to cost-plus regulatory regimes, which reduces operators' sense of risk by reducing the share of the costs they must absorb.

Whether the cost is actually passed on to the users or to taxpayers is irrelevant to the operators, but it should not be irrelevant from a fiscal point of view. The Latin American experience of the 1990s showed that the initial fiscal gains achieved through privatization had only a limited tenure because renegotiation often ended up increasing subsidies to absorb part or all of the underestimated costs in the initial regulatory contracts (Campos et al. 2003).

Risks from Inadequate Public Processes. Increased fiscal risks do not stem only from poorly regulated efforts to attract private sector partners in the financing of infrastructure needs. Fiscal costs and risks also flow from the sizable market of infrastructure projects directly under public sector supervision. In the United Kingdom, the National Audit Office reported that 35 percent of the projects undertaken by ministries and agencies using the conventional procurement approach were completed at a cost exceeding the bid price (U.K. National Audit Office 2009).

In developing countries, despite growing private finance, official development assistance still plays an important role in infrastructure development. However, a growing volume of research shows that the official financial resources are used inefficiently, particularly as a result of insufficient competition in the public procurement systems. Estache and Iimi (2008) argue that the design of procurement packages, especially lot size, can be blamed for at least 8 percent of excess costs.

Summing Up

It is essential to recognize that the role of government in infrastructure should not boil down to simply spending more and figuring out how to get the private sector involved in cofinancing infrastructure expenditures. Governments also need to be able to pick, price, and monitor their projects well. They need to deliver as fair and efficient regulators. The real challenge for the future is the need to achieve a more balanced approach to supporting the implementation of governments' various responsibilities in the sector.

Many governments and international agencies tend to underfund the efforts to improve public procurement and delivery of the services that are not of interest to the private sector. For instance, infrastructure PPP promotion benefits from an extraordinary allocation of administrative financial resources in all major development agencies as well as earmarked resources for technical assistance in the preparation of transactions.[20] The evidence suggests that PPPs tend to work better when they are monitored by regulatory agencies that enjoy enough independence from political interference and possess enough technical ability. When PPPs are not an option, for whatever reason, public enterprises have to deliver the services as effectively as a well-regulated private operator would—including learning to live without blind subsidies or earmarked resources. Of course, traditional loan financing is still an important component of the portfolio of development agencies, but many of these traditional loans command less preparation and supervision resources than they did 10 years ago and certainly fewer resources for promoting PPPs.

It seems reasonable to wonder whether infrastructure service users would be at least somewhat better off today if similar resources had been allocated to seriously assess the opportunities to improve public sector management of the infrastructure sector components that are of no interest to private investors?[21] The failure to support institutions in the sector strikes an obvious parallel with the mismanagement of securitization in the banking and housing sectors.

The policy work in the sector needs to go beyond largely superficial discussions on the ground of the efficiency, equity, and financial cost of poor sector governance. Obviously, getting the investment going is essential, in particular when service coverage is so low. However, ignoring the specificity of governance weaknesses in governments and banks in general—and in bilateral and multilateral development agencies, in the case of developing countries—should no longer be acceptable. We now have enough understanding of, and evidence on, how much these weaknesses drive the excessive costs, distortions, delays, and the inadequate renegotiations that have been observed in the sector to be able to better tailor policies, particularly economic regulation, to the specific needs of any country.[22]

Upcoming Challenges

Like any other sector, infrastructure subsectors are subject to the unpredictability of fiscal allocations over the medium-to-long run. In addition, two main developing events are likely to pose new challenges to policy makers in the sector and shape their strategic options: The first is the central role of infrastructure in the emerging phenomena of adaptation and mitigation efforts to address climate change. The second is the central role of infrastructure in regional integration efforts around the world.

The Greening of Infrastructure

That infrastructure investments and policies are central to the implementation of any policy to deal with climate change risks and other major environmental challenges is relatively well internalized conceptually, but much less so in practice. Addressing the need to coordinate infrastructure and environmental policies implies an effort to coordinate economic and environmental policies, regulations, and institutions.

Policy Coordination. From a policy perspective, the desire for green infrastructure has already forced intense debates on the optimal technological choices for transport and energy production. Significant subsidies have indeed been allocated to infrastructure to stimulate its transformation into an environmentally friendly sector. The fiscal costs of the transformation efforts demonstrate the difficulty of coming up with rational, coordinated policies. In the European context, for instance, the costs per ton of reductions in emissions achieved through public support of biofuels could purchase more than six tons of carbon dioxide equivalent offsets on the European Climate Exchange (Kutas, Lindberg, and Steenblik 2007). As the pressures to restore fiscal balances mount, these are the types of incoherent policies to be addressed by more careful policy coordination.

The greening of infrastructure will also increase the relative importance of demand management in the policy agenda of infrastructure ministers. Demand management may end up being a crucial transitional instrument because it is likely to take quite a long time to adapt or discard existing infrastructure assets (Strand 2010). It is also likely that prices will play a central role in this effort. Unfortunately, prices can have undesirable consequences that should not be ignored, particularly in view of the sector's political sensitivity. Holland and Mansur (2006), for instance, showed that the introduction of time-varying prices in three U.S. states would have desirable environmental benefits, albeit with a wide dispersion of effects across customer types.

Regulatory Coordination. The discussion of prices as mechanisms to coordinate environmental and infrastructure policies also illustrates the need to better coordinate the regulation of those sectors. As infrastructure regulatory reform is implemented to address the important failures mentioned earlier, it should increase the awareness of public and private operators as well as their customers about the growing environmental concerns.

> Tomain (2009, 951) summarized the regulatory reform agenda perfectly in the context of the electricity sector: "Where the old model encouraged consumption, the new model must encourage conservation. Where the old model fostered economic inefficiency, the new model must foster the efficient use of electricity. Where the old model was content with capital-intensive, centralized power production, the new model must promote distributed, small-scale power production. Where the old model was satisfied with burning dirty fossil fuels, the new model must expand the development, production, and consumption of alternative and renewable resources. Much of these gains can be realized through a renegotiated regulatory compact."

A few countries are ahead of the game on this front. Pollitt (2008) provided early insights on U.K. reform needs, making a strong case for changes in U.K. regulatory processes simply because the country has strong economic energy regulators to build on. For other countries, however, Pollitt suggests that other institutions may be more effective to reform long-term policy goals concerning energy and emissions. He argues that competition and effective regulation of the residual monopoly powers could, and should, be a central element of all models in the sector in view of the positive outcomes achieved when competition and regulation have worked well.

Institutional Coordination. Pollitt's diagnostic points to the importance of defining the institutional framework needed to implement and enforce this new regulation. The traditional models usually divide the infrastructural and environmental responsibilities among multiple independent public bodies. For example, in most developed and developing countries, the incentive for firms to invest in network expansion when needed is usually the mandate of sector-specific economic regulators. The environmental risks such as toxic emissions and environmental damage are left to environmental agencies. Thus, at least two agencies, both arms of the state, are expected to generate a coordinated framework of monitoring and sometimes enforcement to push the providers of key public services to deliver socially conscious outputs.

The consequence of this separation is that multiple agencies, each with a limited scope of responsibilities, cannot internalize all the concerns that their rulings should include. Where industry-specific regulators limit the abuses of residual monopolies in the sectors, until now, they have seldom been required to take into account long-term concerns relevant to the climate change debate such as innovation and environmental protection. Their main focus tends to be more about higher quantity for a lower price.

Similarly, the environmental agencies have little concern about the need to expand service coverage where needed. In fact, in some cases, they prefer less coverage when service expansions are directly related to environmental damage. Their main focus tends to be on quality, not quantity, and possibly a higher price to influence demand through the price mechanism and not just regulatory standards. The specific mandates of these uncoordinated independent regulators continue to be at the source of the risks of incoherence in public policy.

The empirical evidence on these risks is modest but reasonably robust. The efforts to deal with acid rain in the United States were a source of conflict between state economic regulators (such as public utility commissions) and state environmental regulators (Baron 1985). Fullerton, McDermott, and Caulkins (1997) modeled the effects of cost-plus regulation on the costs of sulfur dioxide compliance by electric utilities under the U.S. Clean Air Act[23] (tradable emissions permits) and validated the concerns of high costs associated with the lack of coordination. The models show that allowance-trading incentives combined with traditional cost-plus treatment of spending on abatement can substantially increase the social cost of compliance.

Similar conflicts were identified elsewhere more than 10 years ago. For instance, a study of electricity generation in England and Wales showed similar coordination problems (Acutt and Elliott 1999). The lack of cooperation is thus a major risk to the success of climate change policies that involve economic and environmental regulators.

Regionalization of Large Infrastructure Projects

The second major upcoming challenge that governments must address is the increased demand for regional economic integration. Regional integration has been on the agenda of the European Commission for quite some time now, but it has also been important in every developing region. It has been on Africa's political agenda since independence, for instance. And more than 50 years later, although progress has been achieved, it is still on the agenda.

Infrastructure is now at the center of the integration debate as well. The European Commission has specific sources of funding for large cross-national projects. All the regional development banks have similarly earmarked sources of funding for multicountry projects.

The African Union even created a special institution, the New Partnership for Africa's Development (NEPAD), with a mandate to promote integration initiatives across infrastructure sectors. In a nutshell, NEPAD's (2002) action plans to accelerate and achieve regional integration include the following:

- *Trade-related policies* to facilitate transport of goods and services, including efforts to (a) standardize documents for cross-border transactions and clearance of cargo, vehicles, and people within each community; (b) complete free trade areas and customs unions; and

(c) harmonize trade and industrial policies (that is, tariff and non-tariff barriers to integration) to promote manufacturing
- *Infrastructure investment plans* that focus largely on high-profile transport corridors, regional power pools, and ICT backbones
- *Governance reforms* that focus on PPP-equivalent policies, particularly those that (a) encourage the private sector in the financing of intraregional trade and cross-border investment; and (b) design and implement processes and institutions to increase transparency and accountability of decision making processes, including the independence of the judiciary and regulatory functions needed to stimulate investment in cross-border infrastructure projects.

As for the European efforts to achieve regional coordination through the creation of regional markets for all goods and services (including transport and energy, for instance), the main lesson is that the challenge is not just about investment in interconnected transport or energy networks. It is also about the coordination of policies, including infrastructure regulation. This coordination may have to deal with a wide range of institutional and economic differences across countries, such as differences in access to finance and in various populations' ability to pay.

The politics of coordination are obviously essential, and their failures can result in insufficient coordination. The risks associated with this underinvestment in coordination reflect the risks associated, in contract theory models, with hold-up problems from governments' limited commitment abilities. Underinvestment in electricity transmission, for example, may result in (a) underinvestment in energy generation in Country A in spite of its strong potential comparative advantages, and (b) overinvestment in Country B due to concern about inability to import energy from Country A.

An additional challenge associated with regional integration stems from the fact that independent national regulators often have been set up with national policies in mind, with little attention paid to international coordination issues. These issues are handled ex post in complex political contexts. For countries still working on the implementation of the regional integration of infrastructure networks, Auriol and Biancini (2009) show the significant gains to be achieved from the definition of national regulatory mandates that *anticipate* the possible need to coordinate regulation internationally. For countries with established national agencies under restricted regulatory mandates, they also suggest ways in which such mandates can be coordinated ex post under various transitional rules to achieve efficient outcomes.

The regional integration challenge is, however, not only about efficiency. It is also about equity—the extent to which the gains from integration will be distributed fairly across countries. Experience from trade integration efforts shows that specific redistribution mechanisms are needed, at least during the transition period in which the growth payoffs of integration can be distributed unevenly across producers or regions. In electricity, for instance, this redistribution can be achieved through national tariff rebalancing once energy markets have become more integrated.

Summing Up

Even assuming policy makers' awareness of the nexus between infrastructure and environmental-regional integration, the complexity of the associated regulatory and institutional issues have not yet been fully internalized in the policy discussions. Yet these discussions are essential, not only to the efficiency and fiscal consequences of coordination efforts but also to their equity consequences. As soon as equity costs become excessive, experience also shows that the political viability of attempted policy changes is threatened.

Concluding Comments

The initial enthusiasm for the return of infrastructure in macroeconomists' stabilization toolkit somewhat hides the important upcoming challenges mentioned earlier. It may also have pushed policy makers to underestimate, at least initially, the complexity of the environment in which the policy has been decided and the importance of some longer-term fiscal and policy consequences of their stimulus plans.

Can Infrastructure Be Saved in a Debt-Constrained Period? The complexity of the environment stems from the impact of a continued deficit on the countries' debt stocks. By mid-spring 2010—to a large extent as a result of the Greek crisis—OECD countries' debt stocks returned to the forefront of the policy debate. This return, in turn, has demanded efforts to control deficits. Subsequently, the temptation to review the commitments to scale up infrastructure expenses is strong. As it had been 30 years ago, infrastructure is an easy target for quick, high-impact expenditure cuts.

The odds—and risks—of a repeat of history are high. The new Cameron-Clegg British government may have been the first to reverse commitments to the sector made less than a year earlier, but others are likely to follow. In the past, infrastructure was excessively cut as part of structural adjustments to reduce structural fiscal deficits. It took a generation to recover from that mistake. The initial indications are that policy makers around the world are trying to avoid a repeat of history, including in Europe and in the United States, where the debt stocks have become the most unsustainable.

Can the Private Sector Assume More of the Cost? The complexity of the environment in which infrastructure policy is now conducted also stems from a recurring tendency to underestimate the much longer-term, recurrent expenditure commitments associated with infrastructure investment. Increasing infrastructure stocks implies increasing the commitments to sustain operational and maintenance expenditures at levels that will avoid the deterioration of the assets. Because most of the stimulus plans are based on two- to three-year horizons, it is likely that these longer-term consequences have been ignored. In an environment in which debt stocks are defining the longer-term deficits, there should be a concern that a trade-off between long-term asset quality and medium-term fiscal viability will emerge if maintenance is cut to restore medium-term fiscal balance.

The natural solution to this issue is to rely more on the private sector, which has fewer reasons to cut recurrent expenditures. Yet this option has always been limited in the past and may actually be even more limited for the foreseeable future, depending on how the financial sector evolves.

In the best-case scenario, given its relative importance, the private sector may bear some, but clearly not all, of the fiscal responsibility for infrastructure. However, it will never pay for subsidies unless they are cross-subsidies—that is, built into a project portfolio or the design of the allowed tariff structure. All of this simply means that the public sector will continue to be the main actor in infrastructure for the foreseeable future.

Can Governments Address the Political Challenges? Ultimately, the drivers of infrastructure challenges have not changed much with the crisis. Uncertainty has increased for now and, hence, complexity as well. Whether high infrastructure investments stay on the agenda in an increasingly constrained fiscal environment is not the real issue. The real issue, if cuts are needed, is whether such decisions will undergo some analytical rigor that accounts for real bottlenecks and for opportunities to cut costs without changing physical commitments. This challenge will be driven by governments' ability to address the many institutional weaknesses they have demonstrated in the sector.

Improved project selection, improved costing, improved regulation, improved coordination within the sector and across sectors, and improved monitoring of outcomes are easy goals to set. Their implementation boils down to political will to deal with the governance problems of the sector. And political will has not been a defining characteristic of the sector in the past—neither in developing countries nor in developed countries.

Notes

1. There are some outliers. China, for instance, expects to add 10–13 percent of its expenditures to scale up its infrastructure.
2. According to Blanc-Brude, Jensen, and Arnaud (2010), project finance dropped by only 9 percent in 2009—a small impact compared with the 42 percent one-year drop that followed the 2001 crisis.
3. The crisis did not have quick positive impacts on the sector. As business activities and household income dropped in Organisation for Economic Co-operation and Development (OECD) countries, so did the countries' consumption of electricity and transport services, thus reducing the financing of longer-term service expansions based on user fees.
4. For a recent survey, see Estache and Fay (2010).
5. See, for instance, World Bank (2005) and Fay and Yepes (2003), who provided the initial estimates on behalf of the World Bank. Similar estimates have been produced more recently by the New Partnership for Africa's Development (NEPAD 2002) and Kandiero (2009) for the African Development Bank;

Fay and Morisson (2007) for the World Bank and the Inter-American Development Bank; and the Asian Development Bank (ADB 2009) for its own estimate updates. See also the Commission on Growth and Development's Growth Report (CGD 2008) on the case for infrastructure investment.

6. Note that the data concerning investment needs appear to be sensitive to the method. For Africa, for instance, the bottom-up approach that the Africa Infrastructure Country Diagnostic (AICD) followed for water and energy, summarized by Foster and Briceño-Garmendia (2010), suggests that the top-down approaches based on macroeconometric estimates such as Yepes (2007) tend to underestimate the needs. But these differences in methods are sometimes credited with differences in estimates that are not totally correct. The AICD coverage of infrastructure included ports, irrigation, and electricity transition and distribution—areas the Africa Commission omitted in its own estimates of Africa's infrastructure. The differences in coverage explained a lot more than the differences in methods about the varying needs estimates.

7 See Straub (2008) for a global view of the evidence on the links between infrastructure and development.

8. These are just three examples among the many that can be identified in the details of the stimulus around the world. *CanadExport* (2009) and ILO (2009) are two useful sources for more details.

9. That the supply effects of increased government investment in the sector are uncertain because of the time it takes to build that investment is not a new concept. The original idea can be credited to Hayek (1941), and its most elegant analytical presentation can probably be attributed to Kydland and Prescott (1982). All of these illustrious authors already warned that the structure and time of a good's production is a possible source of business-cycle persistence underestimated by models that ignore the importance of these timing dimensions.

10. Recent good sources of such reviews include Walter et al. (2009) for water and Haney and Pollitt (2009) for electricity.

11. For developing countries, foreign taxpayers could be a source of funding because international aid is an additional source of funding of loans and grants.

12. History will obviously tell us, but for existing regulated infrastructure, there has been no evidence of major increases in the costs of capital. In the United Kingdom or Australia, where tariff revisions were under way when the crisis hit, the crisis was seen as a temporary shift in risks that should not affect the cost of capital for the full revision period and, hence, should not influence the average allowed revenue and tariffs.

13. Indeed, the S&P 500 Utilities Index/S&P Global Infrastructure Index showed a 25.2 percent return, while the global equity market returned 37.76 percent (measured by the S&P Global BMI Index).

14. Blanc-Brude, Jensen, and Arnaud (2010) offer a useful and well-documented analysis of the impact of the crisis on debt financing in the sector.

15. Most private infrastructure funds are sponsored by large financial institutions through their investment banking units.

16. From 2001 to 2007, the United Kingdom signed 501 PPP deals, while Spain and Germany (which were second and third in the number of projects) had signed 38 and 34 deals, respectively (DLA Piper and EPEC 2009).

17. See, for instance, the collection of papers by Premius, Flyvbjerg, and Van Wee (2008) and also Walter et al. (2009) for water and Haney and Pollitt (2009) for electricity.

18. Seldom does the tax revenue from the taxation of PPP profits cover rural subsidy needs.

19. See Tenorio and Idzelis (2009) for how the concerns about risks are leading investors to push for careful cherry-picking in project finance. See Estache and Wren-Lewis (2009) for an overview of the academic research showing, among other things, how sectoral unbundling can result in the end of intrasectoral cross-subsidies and the increased total demand for tax financing.

20. PPIAF (the Private-Public Infrastructure Advisory Facility) has financed, over the years, an important number of studies and support to PPP transactions. In fiscal 2009, it had a budget of about US$19 million.

21. See Gomez-Ibañez (2007) for a review of progress on public sector management of infrastructure in the past 25 years or so.

22. See Benitez, Estache, and Søreide (2010) for a longer discussion of governance challenges in the sector.

23. See http://www.epa.gov/air/caa/.

References

Acutt, Melinda, and Caroline Elliott. 1999. "Regulatory Conflict? Environmental and Economic Regulation of Electricity Generation." Working Paper 40.99, Fondazione Eni Enrico Mattei, Milan.

ADB (Asian Development Bank). 2009. *Infrastructure for a Seamless Asia*. Manila: ADB Institute.

ADB, JBIC (Japan Bank for International Cooperation), and World Bank. 2005. *Connecting East Asia: A New Framework for Infrastructure*. Washington, DC: World Bank.

Andres, Luis, J. Luis Guasch, and Sebastian Azumendi. 2008. "Regulatory Governance and Sector Performance: Methodology and Evaluation for Electricity Distribution in Latin America." Policy Research Working Paper 4494, World Bank, Washington, DC.

Auriol, Emmanuelle, and Sara Biancini. 2009. "Economic Integration and Investment Incentives in Regulated Industries." Discussion Paper 7296, Centre for Economic Policy Research, London.

Bacon, Robert, Eduardo Ley, and Masami Kojima. 2010. "Subsidies in the Energy Sector: Measurement, Impact, and Design." Background paper for the World Bank Group Energy Strategy, World Bank, Washington, DC.

Baron, David P. 1985. "Noncooperative Regulation of a Nonlocalized Externality." *The RAND Journal of Economics* 16 (4): 553–68.

Benitez, Daniel, Antonio Estache, and Tina Søreide. 2010. "Dealing with Politics for Money and Power in Infrastructure." Policy Research Working Paper 5455, World Bank, Washington, DC.

Blanc-Brude, Frederic, Olivia Jensen, and Camille Arnaud. 2010. *Infrastructure Project Finance Benchmarking Report (1995–2009)*. Shanghai: Infrastructure Economics.

Burger, Philippe, Justin Tyson, Izabella Karpowicz, and Maria Delgado Coelho. 2009. "The Effects of the Financial Crisis on Public-Private Partnerships." Working Paper 09/144, International Monetary Fund, Washington, DC.

Campos, Javier, Antonio Estache, Noelia Martin, and Lourdes Trujillo. 2003. "Macroeconomic Effects of Private Sector Participation in Infrastructure." In *The Limits of Stabilization*, ed. William Easterly and Luis Servén, 139–70. Stanford, CA: Stanford University Press.

CanadExport. 2009. "Worldwide Inventory of Infrastructure Spending Plans." January 21. Canadian Trade Commissioner Service, Foreign Affairs and International Trade Canada. http://www.international.gc.ca/canadexport/articles/90121h.aspx?view=d.

CGD (Commission for Growth and Development). 2008. "The Growth Report: Strategies for Sustained Growth and Inclusive Development." CGD, Washington, DC.

DLA Piper and EPEC (European PPP Expertise Centre). 2009. "European PPP Report 2009." Annual report, DLA Piper, London.

EC (European Commission). 2000. "Commission Interpretative Communication on Concessions under Community Law." 2000/C 121/02, EC, Brussels.

Engel, Eduardo, Ronald Fischer, and Alexander Galetovic. 2008. "The Basic Public Finance of Public-Private Partnerships." Discussion Paper 1618, Cowles Foundation for Research in Economics, Yale University, New Haven, CT.

Estache, Antonio. 2006. "PPI Partnerships vs. PPI Divorces in Infrastructure." *Review of Industrial Organization* 29 (1): 3–26.

Estache, Antonio, and Marianne Fay. 2010. "Current Debates on Infrastructure Policy." In *Globalization and Growth: Implications for a Post-Crisis World*, ed. Michael Spence and Danny Leipiziger, 151–93. Washington, DC: Commission on Growth and Development.

Estache, Antonio, and Atsushi Iimi. 2008. "Procurement Efficiency for Infrastructure Development and Financial Needs Reassessed." Working Paper 2008-022, ECARES (European Center for Advanced Research in Economics and Statistics), Brussels.

Estache, Antonio, and Liam Wren-Lewis. 2009. "Towards a Theory of Regulation for Developing Countries: Following Jean-Jacques Laffont's Lead." *Journal of Economic Literature* 47 (3): 729–70.

Fay, Marianne, and Mary Morisson. 2007. *Infrastructure in Latin America and the Caribbean: Recent Developments and Key Challenges.* Washington, DC: World Bank.

Fay, Marianne, and Tito Yepes. 2003. "Investing in Infrastructure: What Is Needed from 2000 to 2010?" Policy Research Working Paper 3102, World Bank, Washington, DC.

Foster, Vivien, and Cecilia Briceño-Garmendia, eds. 2010. *Africa's Infrastructure: A Time for Transformation,* Africa Development Forum Series. Paris and Washington, DC: Agence Française de Développement and World Bank.

Freedman, Charles, Michael Kumhof, Douglas Laxton, and Jaewoo Lee. 2009. "The Case for Global Fiscal Stimulus." Staff Position Note 09/03, International Monetary Fund, Washington, DC.

Fullerton, Don, Shaun P. McDermott, and Jonathan P. Caulkins. 1997. "Sulfur Dioxide Compliance of a Regulated Utility." *Journal of Environmental Economics and Management* 34: 32–53.

Gilardi, Fabrizio. 2002. "Policy Credibility and Delegation to Independent Regulatory Agencies: A Comparative Empirical Analysis." *Journal of European Public Policy* 9 (6): 873–93.

Gómez-Ibáñez, José A. 2007. "Alternatives to Infrastructure Privatization Revisited: Public Enterprise Reform from the 1960s to the 1980s." Policy Research Working Paper 4391, World Bank, Washington, DC.

Guasch, J. Luis. 2004. *Granting and Renegotiating Infrastructure Concessions: Doing It Right.* Washington, DC: World Bank.

Hall, David. 2008. "PPPs in Europe: A Critical Appraisal." Paper presented at the 10th International Conference of the Association for Studies in Public Economics, St. Petersburg, Russian Federation, October 31–November 1.

Haney, Aoife Brophy, and Michael G. Pollitt. 2009. "Efficiency Analysis of Energy Networks: An International Survey of Regulators." *Energy Policy* 37 (12): 5814–30.

Hayek, F. A. 1941. *The Pure Theory of Capital.* London: Routledge & Kegan.

Holland, Stephen, and Erin Mansur. 2006 . "The Short-Run Effects of Time-Varying Prices in Competitive Electricity Markets." *The Energy Journal* 27 (4): 127–56.

ILO (International Labour Organization). 2009. "Protecting People, Promoting Jobs: A Survey of Country Employment and Social Protection Responses to the Global Economic Crisis." Report to the G-20 Leader's Summit, Pittsburgh, September 24–25.

Johannsen, Katja Sander. 2003. "Regulatory Independence in Theory and Practice: A Survey of Independent Energy Regulators in Eight European Countries." Research paper, Danish Institute of Governmental Research (AKF Forlaget), Copenhagen.

Kandiero, Tonia. 2009. "Infrastructure Investment in Africa." Development Research Brief 10, African Development Bank, Tunis.

Keynes, John Maynard. 1936. *The General Theory of Employment, Interest and Money*. Basingstoke, Hampshire, U.K.: Palgrave Macmillan.

Khatiwada, Sameer. 2009. "Stimulus Packages to Counter Global Economic Crisis: A Review." Discussion Paper 96/2009, International Institute for Labour Studies, International Labour Organization, Geneva.

KPMG. 2009a. "The Changing Face of Infrastructure: Frontline Views from Private Sector Infrastructure Providers." Research report commissioned by KPMG International in conjunction with the Economist Intelligence Unit, KPMG, New York.

———. 2009b. "Financing Australian PPP Projects in the Global Financial Crisis." Research paper, KPMG, Sydney.

———. 2010. "The Changing Face of Infrastructure: Public Sector Perspectives." Research report commissioned by KPMG International in conjunction with the Economist Intelligence Unit, KPMG, New York.

Kutas, Geraldine, Carina Lindberg, and Ronald Steenblik. 2007. "Biofuels—At What Cost? Government Support for Ethanol and Biodiesel in the European Union." Report for the Global Subsidies Initiative of the International Institute for Sustainable Development, Geneva.

Kydland, Finn E., and Edward C. Prescott. 1982. "Time to Build and Aggregate Fluctuations." *Econometrica* 50 (6): 1345–70.

Mansour, Asieh, and Hope Nadji. 2007. "Performance Characteristics of Infrastructure Investments." Report of RREEF Research, Deutsche Bank Group, San Francisco.

NEPAD (New Partnership for Africa's Development). 2002. "Short-Term Action Plan for Infrastructure." Program document, NEPAD, Johannesburg.

OECD (Organisation for Economic Co-operation and Development). 2006. *Infrastructure to 2030: Telecom, Land Transport, Water and Electricity*. Paris: OECD.

———. 2007. *Infrastructure to 2030 (Volume 2): Mapping Policy for Electricity, Water and Transport*. Paris: OECD.

———. 2008. "Infrastructure to 2030." *Policy Brief* (January), OECD, Paris.

Peng, Hsu Wen, and Graeme Newell. 2007. "The Significance of Infrastructure in Investment Portfolios." Paper presented at the 13th Annual Conference of the Pacific Rim Real Estate Society, Fremantle, Australia, January 21–24.

Pollitt, Michael G. 2008. "The Future of Electricity (and Gas) Regulation in a Low-Carbon Policy World." Special issue, *The Energy Journal* 29 (S2): 63–94.

PPI (Private Participation in Infrastructure) Project Database. World Bank and PPIAF (Public-Private Infrastructure Advisory Facility), Washington, DC. http://ppi.worldbank.org.

Priemus, Hugo, Bent Flyvbjerg, and Bert van Wee, eds. 2008. *Decision-Making on Mega-Projects: Cost-Benefit Analysis, Planning and Innovation*. Cheltenham, U.K., and Northampton, MA: Edward Elgar.

Shanks, Sid, and Paula Barnes. 2008. "Econometric Modelling of Infrastructure and Australia's Productivity." Internal Research Memorandum 08-01, Australia Productivity Commission, Melbourne.

Spilimbergo, Antonio, Steve Symansky, and Martin Schindler. 2009. "Fiscal Multipliers." Staff Position Note 09/11, International Monetary Fund, Washington, DC.

Stevans, Lonnie K., and David N. Sessions. 2010. "Calculating and Interpreting Multipliers in the Presence of Non-stationary Time Series: The Case of U.S. Federal Infrastructure Spending." *American Journal of Social and Management Sciences* 1 (1): 24–38.

Strand, Jon. 2010. "Inertia in Infrastructure Development: Some Analytical Aspects and Reasons for Inefficient Infrastructure Choices." Policy Research Working Paper 5295, World Bank, Washington, DC.

Straub, Stéphane. 2008. "Infrastructure and Development: A Critical Appraisal of the Macro-Level Literature." Policy Research Working Paper 4590, World Bank, Washington, DC.

Tenorio, Vyvyan, and Christine Idzelis. 2009. "Can Private Equity Play the Infrastructure Game?" *The Deal,* April 3. http://www.thedeal.com/newsweekly/features/can-private-equity-play-the-infrastructure-game.php.

Tomain, Joseph P. 2009. "'Steel in the Ground': Greening the Grid with the Utility." *Environmental Law* 39 (4): 931–76.

U.K. National Audit Office. 2009. "Performance of PFI Construction." Report of the Private Finance Practice, National Audit Office, London.

Walter, Matthias, Astrid Cullmann, Christian von Hirschhausen, Robert Wand, and Michael Zschille. 2009. "Quo Vadis Efficiency Analysis of Water Distribution? A Comparative Literature Review." *Utilities Policy* 17 (3–4): 225–32.

World Bank. 2005. *Global Monitoring Report 2005: Millennium Development Goals; From Consensus to Momentum.* Washington, DC: World Bank.

World Bank and PPIAF (Public-Private Infrastructure Advisory Facility). 2010. "New Private Infrastructure Activity in Developing Countries Recovered Selectively in the Third Quarter of 2009." PPI Data Update Note 35, World Bank and PPIAF, Washington, DC.

Yepes, Tito. 2007. "Investment Needs for Infrastructure: 2007 Update." Unpublished report, World Bank, Washington, DC.

Part 2
The Way Forward

Rethinking Growth and the State

Philippe Aghion and Julia Cagé

Government intervention is often perceived as a constraint on market forces and thereby on economic growth. In particular, over the past three decades, increasing awareness that product and labor market liberalization enhances growth has led scholars and policy makers to also recommend a reduction in the role and size of governments. True, the recent global financial crisis showed the importance of the state as a regulator for the financial system. Indeed, when financial institutions are "too big to fail," the state may have to intervene to preserve the stability of the whole system.[1]

In the United States and other industrialized countries, fluctuations in current opinion show that doubts remain as to whether government intervention should go beyond this regulatory role. At the same time, there is the striking example of Scandinavian countries, where governments remain big and yet markets have been liberalized and the rates of innovation and productivity growth have increased over the past two decades. In this chapter, the authors argue that it is not so much the size of the state that is at stake but rather its main functions and efficiency. To foster economic growth in our countries, we need not so much a reduced state but a "suitable" and noncorrupt state.

More specifically, this chapter points to two main growth-enhancing functions of governments in addition to regulating financial systems: as investors in the knowledge economy and as guarantors of the social contract.

State as Investor in the Knowledge Economy

A primary role of the state is as an investor in the growth process. This section explains why government can help foster growth by intervening through education policy, market liberalization, macroeconomic stabilization, and environmental (and more generally, sectoral) policy.

Education Policy

A primary area for growth-enhancing government intervention is higher education. To the extent that education investments involve knowledge spillovers and therefore are not fully appropriated by private agents, a laissez-faire economy will tend to generate too few of these investments, which, in turn, provides a justification for government intervention.

A difficult issue concerns the governance of that intervention: how can one make sure that government funds will be appropriately used? For example, regarding higher education, Aghion et al. (2009) argue that the closer a region is to the technological frontier, the more growth-enhancing the research education funding is, and the higher the growth externalities generated by that funding. But the same study also shows that the more autonomous the universities and the more competitive the overall university system (in particular, the more funding relies on competitive grants), the more effective the higher-education investments are. Figure 5.1 shows, for example, a positive correlation between European universities' Shanghai rankings (of university output) and the autonomy index.[2]

Market Liberalization

Liberalization of trade or entry involves winners and losers (Aghion and Howitt 2009). In particular, increased trade and entry tend to foster productivity growth in firms and sectors that are closer to the technological frontier and inhibit productivity growth in firms or sectors that are further away from the frontier. In the former case, firms innovate to escape the increase in competition. In the latter case, the increased trade

Figure 5.1 Relation between University Output and Autonomy in Selected European Countries

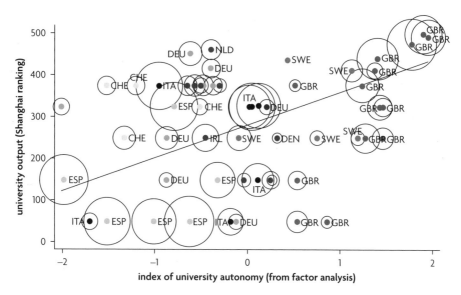

Source: Aghion et al. 2009.
Note: coefficient = 78.5. p value < 0.001.

or entry discourages innovation because laggard firms know they have little chance to win against potential entrants.

This unequalizing effect of liberalization, together with constraints that limit the scope for capital and labor reallocation from laggard sectors to leading sectors under laissez-faire, suggests a role for government as an investor in reallocation. Here, government investment may typically include subsidies to train workers who wish to relocate to more-advanced sectors, which, in turn, would help speed up the growth of those sectors following trade or product market liberalization. In other words, acknowledging the virtues of market liberalization does not mean reducing the role for government intervention but rather redirecting government toward policies that complement the liberalization and thereby help it become even more growth-enhancing.

Macroeconomic Stabilization

Macroeconomic volatility tends to be detrimental to innovation and growth in more credit-constrained firms or countries (Aghion et al.

2005). The underlying intuition is that growth-enhancing investments (in skills, research and development [R&D], and structural capital) need to be maintained over the long run. However, maintaining such investments over the business cycle may be hard, particularly for firms that face credit constraints that prevent them from investing more than a fixed multiple of their current cash flows.

Hence, a potential role for government intervention is to partly circumvent credit market imperfections and thereby help firms to maintain their growth-enhancing investments over the cycle. More countercyclical fiscal policies—policies that increase public deficits in recessions and reduce them in booms—are thus more growth-enhancing in countries or sectors that are more credit-constrained (Aghion and Marinescu 2008; Aghion, Hemous, and Kharroubi 2009).

Although this argument provides some justification for stimulus packages during recessions, that justification—which emphasizes long-run growth effects, working primarily through the supply side of the economy—is quite distinct from the argument based on the Keynesian multiplier, which emphasizes short-run demand effects.

Climate-Change Policy

A laissez-faire economy may also tend to innovate in the wrong direction—that is, toward innovation favoring more-carbon-emitting industries and products. Thus, Aghion, Dechezlepretre, et al. (2010) explore a cross-country panel data set of patents in the automotive industry. They distinguish between "dirty innovations," which affect combustion engines, and clean innovations such as those in electric cars. Then they show that the larger the stock of past dirty innovations by a given entrepreneur, the dirtier the current innovations by the same entrepreneur. This correlation, together with the fact that most automotive innovations have been dirty so far, implies that in the absence of government intervention, economies would generate too many dirty innovations. Hence, government intervention has a role to "redirect technical change" toward clean innovations (Aghion, Dechezleprete, et al. 2010).

Assuming this "path dependence" in the direction of innovation, Acemoglu et al. (2009) show that the optimal policy to fight climate change should combine a carbon tax with direct subsidies for clean innovations. More specifically, they develop an endogenous growth model whereby a consumption good can be produced using either a clean or a dirty input. Only the production of dirty inputs harms the environment. The environment, in turn, affects consumer utility. Inputs are produced with labor and machines, and innovation can improve the efficiency of production of either clean or dirty machines. Innovation results from the work of scientists who try to improve either the quality of dirty machines or the quality of clean machines. An important assumption is the "building on the shoulders of giants" effect, namely that technological advances in one sector make future advances in that sector more effective (Acemoglu et al. 2009).

Innovators direct their efforts to the sector where the expected profits from innovation are the highest. Thus, under laissez-faire, when the dirty technology enjoys an initial installed-base advantage, given the "building on the shoulders of giants" effect, the innovation machine will work in favor of the dirty technology. The clean technology may never take off unless the government intervenes. What Acemoglu et al. (2009) show is that the laissez-faire equilibrium will typically lead to environmental disaster, where environmental quality falls below the level at which it can be regenerated and therefore utility collapses. Where the dirty technology is based on exhaustible resources, this may help to prevent such a disaster because the dirty technology is eventually priced out of the market. But even in this case, the innovation machine left on its own works suboptimally, favoring the dirty technology for too long.

A critical parameter for the effectiveness of policy intervention is the extent to which dirty and clean technology are substitutable. In particular, when they are sufficiently close substitutes, a temporary policy involving both a tax on dirty input production (a carbon tax) and a subsidy for clean research activities will be sufficient to avoid an environmental disaster and, thus, to guarantee long-run growth sustainability. Indeed, by redirecting technical change toward clean innovation, such a policy will make clean technologies catch up and eventually leapfrog dirty technologies, at which point—by virtue of the "building on the shoulders of giants" effect (which now plays in the right direction)—private firms will spontaneously choose to innovate in clean machines.

Thus, the optimal policy is targeted—directed toward clean production and innovation—but it also relies on a complementarity of roles between the government and the private sector. Delaying such directed intervention leads not only to further deterioration of the environment but also to strengthening the lead of the dirty-innovation machine, making the dirty technologies more productive and further widening the productivity gap between dirty and clean technologies. This widened gap, in turn, requires a longer period for clean technologies to catch up and replace the dirty ones. Because this catching-up period is characterized by slower growth, the cost of delaying intervention, in terms of forgone growth, will be higher. In other words, delaying action is costly, as shown in table 5.1.

Two-Instrument Policy. Not surprisingly, the shorter the delay and the higher the discount rate (the lower the value put on the future), the lower the cost will be. This is because the gains from delaying intervention are realized at the start in the form of higher consumption although the loss occurs in the future through more environmental degradation and lower future consumption.

Moreover, because there are two basic problems to deal with—the environmental one and the innovational one—using two instruments proves to be better than using one. The optimal policy involves using (a) a carbon price to deal with the environmental externality and, at the same time, (b) direct subsidies for clean R&D (or a profit tax on dirty technologies) to deal with the knowledge externality.

One-Instrument Policy. Of course, one could always argue that a carbon price on its own could deal with both the environmental and the

Table 5.1 Welfare Costs of Delayed Intervention as a Function of the Elasticity of Substitution and the Discount Rate

percentage reduction in consumption relative to immediate intervention

Elasticity of substitution	10		3	
Discount rate	0.001	0.015	0.001	0.015
Delay = 10 years	8.75	1.87	2.71	0.05
Delay = 20 years	14.02	1.92	4.79	0.12
Delay = 30 years	17.65	1.99	6.88	0.23

Source: Acemoglu et al. 2009.

knowledge externalities simultaneously (that is, discouraging the use of dirty technologies also discourages innovation in dirty technologies). However, relying on the carbon price alone leads to excessive reduction in consumption in the short run. And because the two-instrument policy reduces the short-run cost in terms of forgone short-run consumption, it reinforces the case for immediate implementation, even for values of the discount rate under which standard models would suggest delaying implementation. In fact, the Acemoglu et al. (2009) model allows one to calibrate the cost of using only the carbon price instead of a combination of a carbon price and a clean-R&D subsidy. This cost can be expressed as the amount of "lost" consumption in each period, expressed as a percentage of the level of consumption that would result from the optimal policy, which involves using both instrument types. Using a discount rate of 1 percent, this cost in terms of lost consumption amounts to 1.33 percent.

An alternative way of showing the higher cost when using only one instrument (that is, the carbon price) rather than a combination of carbon pricing and the more industrial-policy-like subsidies is to express how high the optimal carbon price would have to be when used as a singleton relative to its optimal level when used in combination. Simulating this scenario in the model of Acemoglu et al. (2009) reveals that the carbon price would have to be about 15 times higher during the first five years and 12 times higher over the following five years. The intuition behind the initial high differential is that the early period is particularly critical to inducing the catch-up by clean technologies.

By the same token, using only the subsidy instrument, while keeping the carbon-price instrument inactive, would imply that subsidies would have to be on average 115 percent higher in the first 10 years compared with their level when used in combination with a carbon price. In other words, here also the state has an important role to play to deter innovation in the wrong direction, which can be costly in terms of welfare.

Industrial Policy

Industrial policies had been implemented after World War II in a number a countries to promote infant industries and protect local traditional activities from competition against products from more-advanced foreign countries. Thus, several Latin American countries advocated import substitution policies whereby local industries would more fully benefit from domestic demand. East Asian countries such as Japan or the Republic of Korea, rather than advocate import substitution policies, would favor export promotion, which, in turn, would be achieved partly through tariffs and nontariff barriers and partly through maintenance of undervalued exchange rates. And in Europe, France engaged in so-called Colbertist policies of targeted subsidies to industries or to "national champions."

For at least two or three decades after World War II, these policies remained fairly noncontroversial because the countries implementing them were growing at relatively fast rates. However, the slowdown in Latin America as of the 1970s, and then in Japan as of the late 1990s, contributed to growing skepticism about the role of industrial policy in the process of development. Increasingly since the early 1980s, industrial policy has raised serious doubts among academics and policy advisers in international financial institutions. In particular, it was criticized for allowing governments to pick winners and losers in a discretionary fashion and consequently for increasing the scope for capture of governments by local vested interests.

Instead, policy makers and growth and development economists now advocate nontargeted policies aimed at improving the "investment climate": the liberalization of product and labor markets, a legal and enforcement framework that protects (private) property rights, and macroeconomic stabilization. This new set of growth recommendations came to be known as the "Washington consensus" because it was primarily advocated by the International Monetary Fund, the World Bank, and the U.S. Department of the Treasury, all based in Washington, DC.

However, the authors believe that industrial policy should not be systematically opposed to competition policy. In particular, current work argues that targeted subsidies could be used to induce several firms to operate in the same sector instead of escaping competition through excessive horizontal differentiation (Aghion, Dewatripont, et al. 2010). This approach, in turn, may enhance innovation for two main reasons. First, it helps maintain a higher equilibrium degree of competition (that is, by reducing horizontal differentiation), which then induces firms to innovate vertically to escape competition. Second, it favors technological progress because firms operating in the same sector are more likely to benefit from knowledge spillovers or communication among them.

Of course, much depends upon the design of industrial policy. Such policy should target sectors, not particular firms (or "national champions"). This, in turn, suggests a need for new empirical studies in which productivity growth, patenting, or other measures of innovativeness and entrepreneurship would be regressed over some measures of sectoral intervention and interacted with the degree of competition in the sector and with the extent to which intervention in each sector is not concentrated on one single firm but rather distributed over a larger number of firms. Thus, using Chinese firm-level panel data, Aghion, Dewatripont, et al. (2010) show that sectoral subsidies tend to enhance total factor productivity (TFP), TFP growth, and new product creation—more so if they are implemented in sectors that are already more competitive and also distributed in each sector over a more dispersed set of firms.

The State and the Social Contract

Beyond the state's role as investor in the knowledge economy, one of its main roles is as guarantor of the social contract—an economic and social pact on which all citizens and their government agree. This pact has to allow the state to control the public deficit in a postcrisis context while maintaining social peace and avoiding strikes and social protests. Indeed, the current economic context can be characterized by a weakening of public finances, a tightening of credit constraints, and a need to correct global imbalances.

Although government debts increased greatly during and after the crisis, it now appears necessary to reduce public deficits while investing in growth at the same time. But such a reduction effort won't be easy, and to be accepted by everybody, it will have to be fairly shared to maintain a peaceful social climate. This result supposes that the state (a) invests in trust, (b) promotes redistributive policies while reducing deficits, and (c) fights corruption.

Investing in Trust—a Necessity

To understand why the state needs to invest in trust, remember the following statement by Nobel Prize-winning economist Kenneth Arrow in

1972: "Virtually every commercial transaction has within itself an element of trust, certainly any transaction conducted over a period of time. It can be plausibly argued that much of the economic backwardness in the world can be explained by the lack of mutual confidence."

Recent literature has studied the positive correlations between trust and various economic outcomes: financial development, entrepreneurship, and economic exchanges (Guiso, Sapienza, and Zingales 2004, 2006, 2009, respectively). Trust is also closely linked to institutions (Aghion, Dechezlepretre, et al. 2010; Aghion, Dewatripont, et al. 2010; Algan and Cahuc 2009; Bloom, Sadun, and Van Reenen 2009; Tabellini 2010). This chapter emphasizes that trust is particularly important for economic growth and innovation.

Trust, Innovation, and Growth. Various studies have shown that, on the firm level, trust and a good social climate are related to growth and innovation. For example, there is a strong empirical correlation between trust and economic growth (Knack and Keefer 1997; La Porta et al. 1997; Tabellini 2010).

More important for this discussion, trust is not only correlated with growth but is also an essential and causal factor of growth. For example, Algan and Cahuc (2010), focusing on the inherited component of trust and its time variation, have shown a causal effect of trust on economic growth. Figure 5.2 shows a scatterplot of the changes in income per capita between 1935 and 2000 against the changes in inherited trust between the same periods, relative to Sweden. It appears clearly that there is a strong positive correlation: the higher the increase in inherited trust, the higher the increase in income per capita.

Moreover, the impact of inherited trust is economically sizable: income per capita in 2000 would have been increased by an estimated 546 percent in Africa if the level of inherited trust had been the same as in Sweden (Algan and Cahuc 2010). This effect is strong not only for developing countries but also for more developed ones.

How Can the State Increase Trust? Trust thus appears to be a crucial factor for innovation and economic growth. This raises the following question: how can the state increase trust? Indeed, if growth depends on inherited trust and if no policies can increase trust, the state would

Figure 5.2 Relation between Changes in Inherited Trust and Per Capita Income, 1935–2000

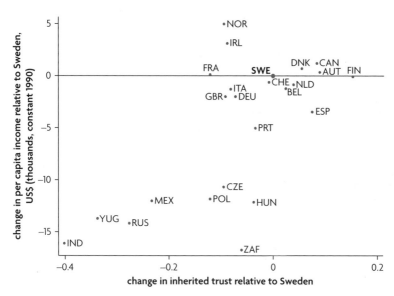

Source: Algan and Cahuc 2010.
Note: $R^2 = 0.43$.

seem to be useless. On the contrary, much can be done to increase citizens' trust in the state (a point to be readdressed below concerning corruption), as well as among each other, and to improve the social climate in the firms. If the social capital literature is today a mature and influential subfield in economics, few studies explore the mechanisms through which social capital accumulates (a recent exception being Jacob and Tyrell 2010). Future research on this crucial topic seems of first importance.

Limit Regulation. One important way the state can increase trust is to refrain from overregulation, in the sense that it does not have to substitute itself for social actors (which is the case, for example, in France where trust is low compared with other European countries and the United States [Algan and Cahuc 2007; Ehrenberg 2010]).

On the contrary, the state has to favor the emergence of social actors and collective negotiations with labor unions. Indeed, in a cross-section of countries, government regulation is strongly negatively correlated with measures of trust, and not only does distrust increase the demand for regulation but regulation also influences trust (Aghion, Algan, et al. 2010). Figure 5.3 illustrates the strong positive correlation between the regulation of entry (as measured by the number of steps to open a business) and a country's level of distrust.

Catalyze Social Relationships. This is not to say that the state has no role to play; for example, in Scandinavian countries, where trust is high, the state plays a central role. However, rather than substituting itself for social partners, the state has to be the catalyst of social relationships to increase trust between employers and employees. Hence, it has to favor the emergence of mass unions in all firms that are not yet unionized (see, for example, Cahuc and Zylberberg

Figure 5.3 Relation between Distrust and Extent of Entry Regulation

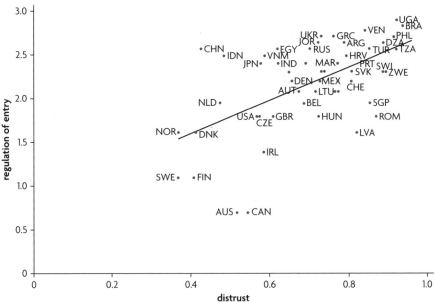

Source: Aghion, Algan, et al. 2010.
Note: R^2 = 0.32. Regulation of entry is measured by the (ln) number of procedures to open a firm. Distrust is normalized between 0 and 1.

2009). It also has to gain unions' agreement before implementing important reforms.

Encourage Decentralization. Finally, the state should not be too centralized. (France suffers so much from distrust in part because of its high degree of hierarchical centralization, especially as to state decision making [Algan and Cahuc 2007].)

On the contrary, the state has to encourage decentralization policies and give more power to local governments, which can take advantage of their better knowledge of local issues. In a sense, one can apply the conclusions of Acemoglu et al. (2007)—about the decentralization of the firm—to the state: if firms closer to the technological frontier are more likely to choose decentralization, the same may be true for developed countries. Indeed, decentralization is the best way to elicit local information and thus to implement policies that better fit local realities. In other words, it is the best way for the state to be more efficient.

Reducing Deficits—While Promoting Redistributive Policies

Closely linked to the trust question, the social contract has to rely on redistribution. Indeed, a too-unequal society cannot be one in which people trust one another. Inequalities create rigidities and the willingness to protect social status, impeding social mobility. On the contrary, in a society in which the tax system is sufficiently progressive and redistributive, people are more willing to take risks, innovate, and move up the social ladder.

Concerning deficit reduction, public finances have weakened significantly during and since the recession, as illustrated in figures 5.4 and 5.5. Such a situation is not sustainable in the long run, as illustrated by the current Greek crisis.

Deficit reduction will be costly for everybody, and to make it acceptable (without giving rise to violent social protests), the effort will have to be shared equally—which supposes a fair (that is, progressive) tax increase without excessively cutting social expenditures targeted toward those who need them the most (especially, in the crisis context, unemployment benefits). Moreover, the citizens will be more willing to accept tax increases if

Figure 5.4 General Government Balances of Selected Countries, 2007 vs. 2009

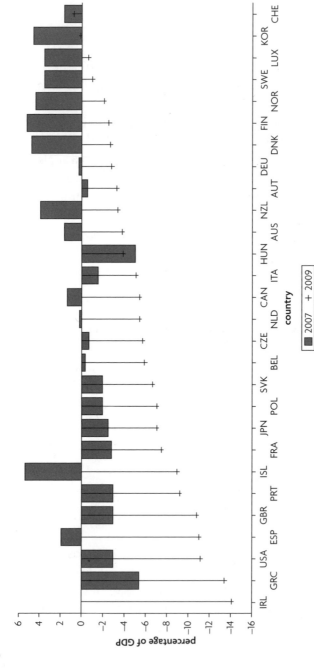

Source: OECD 2010.
Note: GDP = gross domestic product.

Figure 5.5 Gross Government Debt of Selected Countries, 2007 vs. 2009

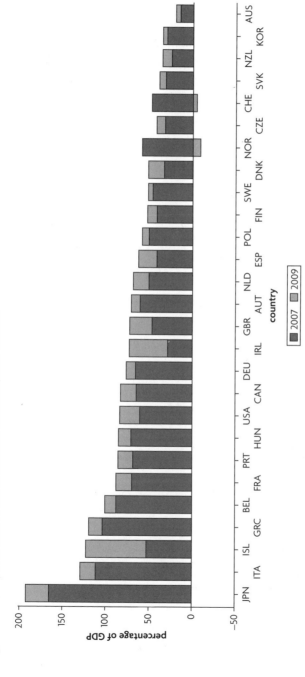

Source: OECD 2010.
Note: GDP = gross domestic product.

they know the government will use fiscal resources efficiently and is not corrupt. Again, this supposes that citizens trust their government.

Let's consider the relevant example of Sweden, which in the 1990s—in only four years—reduced its public deficit from 16 percent to less than 3 percent of its gross domestic product (GDP). And it did so without reducing public education and health services to the Swedish population (services that remain greater today in Sweden than in many other European countries), mainly because of its efficient and progressive tax system.

Fighting Corruption

Finally, an important point to underline is that an efficient state that can guarantee the social contract is one that is noncorrupt and must fight corruption. It is a state that uses the taxpayers' money efficiently and transparently.

The authors' own current research (Aghion et al. 2011) illustrates this dimension of the question. Indeed, the link between taxation and

Figure 5.6 Relation between Taxation and Growth in High-Corruption OECD Countries

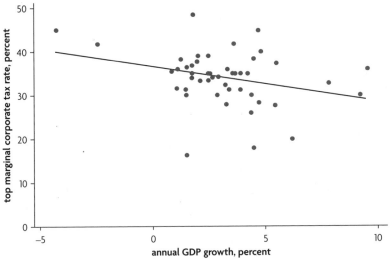

Source: Aghion et al. 2011.

Note: Countries are designated as "high-corruption" based on the corruption index of the *International Country Risk Guide.*

Figure 5.7 Relation between Taxation and Growth in Low-Corruption OECD Countries

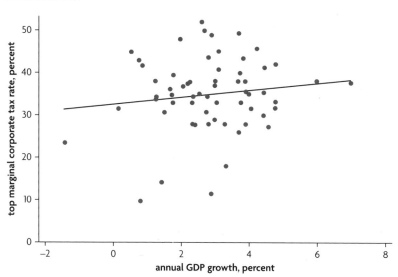

Source: Aghion et al. 2011.
Note: Countries are designated as "low-corruption" based on the corruption index of the *International Country Risk Guide.*

economic growth is a function of the level of government efficiency or of its degree of corruption. For example, among OECD countries, there is a positive correlation between a country's growth rate and the tax burden as measured by top marginal tax rates (on both corporations and individual earned income) in low-corruption countries, and a negative correlation in high-corruption countries, that is robust to the use of different indexes of corruption. In other words, taxation is growth-enhancing for low-corruption countries but not for high-corruption countries. Figures 5.6 (high-corruption countries) and 5.7 (low-corruption countries) illustrate this point.[3]

The authors are now developing this research agenda at the firm level in the United States and find encouraging results going exactly in the same direction. Hence, one has to take this corruption-trust dimension into account to properly evaluate the impact of state intervention on economic growth.

Conclusion

One positive outcome of the recent crisis is to have relegitimized the state's role as a fundamental actor in the growth process—as a regulator that can thereby prevent or limit the effects of financial crises and also as a catalyst of market and firm growth by investing in the knowledge economy and by fostering trust as a guarantor of the social contract. Thus, in our quest for higher economic growth, one should not necessarily think of "more state" versus "less state" but rather of where and how the state should—or should not—intervene.

Notes

1. At the same time, such an intervention must be designed to minimize moral hazard considerations, hence, the importance of introducing further regulations on banks, the financial structure, and also the compensation schemes of employees in the financial sector—as was done, for example, with U.K. Prime Minister Gordon Brown's bailout of English banks in October 2008.
2. See also Aghion et al. (2008).
3. Here, we use the *International Country Risk Guide* index as a measure of corruption. However, the findings are robust to the use of Transparency International's Corruption Perception Index or the World Bank's Worldwide Governance Indicators.

References

Acemoglu, Daron, Philippe Aghion, Leonardo Bursztyn, and David Hemous. 2009. "The Environment and Directed Technical Change." Working Paper 15451, National Bureau of Economic Research, Cambridge, MA.

Acemoglu, Daron, Philippe Aghion, Claire Lelarge, John Van Reenen, and Fabrizio Zilibotti. 2007. "Technology, Information, and the Decentralization of the Firm." *Quarterly Journal of Economics* 122 (4): 1759–99.

Aghion, Philippe, Ufuk Akcigit, Julia Cagé, and William Kerr. 2011. "Taxation, Corruption, and Growth." Unpublished manuscript.

Aghion, Philippe, Yann Algan, Pierre Cahuc, and Andrei Shleifer. 2010. "Regulation and Distrust." *The Quarterly Journal of Economics* 125 (3): 1015–49.

Aghion, Philippe, George-Marios Angeletos, Abhijit Banerjee, and Kalina Manova. 2005. "Volatility and Growth: Credit Constraints and Productivity-Enhancing Investment." Working Paper 11349, National Bureau of Economic Research, Cambridge, MA.

Aghion, Philippe, Philippe Askenazy, Nicolas Berman, Gilbert Cette, and Laurent Eymard. 2008. "Credit Constraints and the Cyclicality of R&D Investment: Evidence from France." Working Paper 2008-26, Paris School of Economics, Paris.

Aghion, Philippe, Antoine Dechezlepretre, David Hemous, Ralf Martin, and John Van Reenen. 2010. "Path Dependence in Clean Versus Dirty Innovation: Evidence from the Automotive Industry." Unpublished manuscript.

Aghion, Philippe, Mathias Dewatripont, Yuosha Du, Ann Harrison, and Patrick Legros. 2010. "Industrial Policy and Competition: Disproving a Fallacy." Unpublished manuscript.

Aghion, Philippe, Mathias Dewatripont, Caroline Hoxby, Andreu Mas-Colell, and André Sapir. 2009. "The Governance and Performance of Research Universities: Evidence from Europe and the U.S." Working Paper 14851, National Bureau of Economic Research, Cambridge, MA.

Aghion, Philippe, David Hemous, and Enisse Kharroubi. 2009. "Credit Constraints, Cyclical Fiscal Policy and Industry Growth." Working Paper 15119, National Bureau of Economic Research, Cambridge, MA.

Aghion, Philippe, and Peter Howitt. 2009. *The Economics of Growth.* Cambridge, MA: MIT Press.

Aghion, Philippe, and Ioana Marinescu. 2008. "Cyclical Budgetary Policy and Economic Growth: What Do We Learn from OECD Panel Data?" *NBER Macroeconomics Annual 2007* 22 (2007): 251–78.

Algan, Yann, and Pierre Cahuc. 2007. *La société de défiance: Comment le modèle social français s'autodétruit.* Paris: Éditions ENS Rue d'Ulm.

———. 2009. "Civic Virtue and Labor Market Institutions." *American Economic Journal: Macroeconomics* 1 (1): 111–45.

———. 2010. "Inherited Trust and Growth." *American Economic Review* 100 (5): 2060–92.

Arrow, Kenneth. 1972. "Gifts and Exchanges." *Philosophy and Public Affairs* 1 (4): 343–62.

Bloom, Nick, Raffaella Sadun, and John Van Reenen. 2009. "The Organization of Firms across Countries." Working Paper 15129, National Bureau of Economic Research, Cambridge, MA.

Cahuc, Pierre, and André Zylberberg. 2009. *Les réformes ratées du Président Sarkozy.* Paris: Flammarion.

Ehrenberg, Alain. 2010. *La société du malaise: Le mental et le social.* Paris: Odile Jacob.

Guiso, Luigi, Paola Sapienza, and Luigi Zingales. 2004. "The Role of Social Capital in Financial Development." *American Economic Review* 94 (3): 526–56.

———. 2006. "Does Culture Affect Economic Outcomes?" *Journal of Economic Perspectives* 20 (2): 23–48.

———. 2009. "Cultural Bias and Economic Exchange" *Quarterly Journal of Economics* 124 (3): 1095–1131.

Jacob, Marcus, and Marcel Tyrell. 2010. "The Legacy of Surveillance: An Explanation for Social Capital Erosion and the Persistent Economic Disparity between East and West Germany." Unpublished working paper, EBS Universität für Wirtschaft und Recht, Wiesbaden and Oestrich-Winkel, Germany; and Zeppelin University, Friedrich-Shafen, Germany.

Knack, Stephen, and Philip Keefer. 1997. "Does Social Capital Have an Economic Payoff? A Cross-Country Comparison." *Quarterly Journal of Economics* 112 (4): 251–88.

La Porta, Rafael, Florencio Lopez-de-Silanes, Andrei Shleifer, and Robert Vishny. 1997. "Trust in Large Organizations." *American Economic Review* 87 (2): 333–38.

OECD (Organisation for Economic Co-operation and Development. 2010. *Economic Outlook No. 87*. Paris: OECD.

Tabellini, Guido. 2010. "Culture and Institutions: Economic Development in the Regions of Europe." *Journal of the European Economic Association* 8 (4): 677–716.

Financial Shocks and the Labor Markets: Should Economic Policy Save Jobs?

Tito Boeri and Pietro Garibaldi

The recent financial crisis, alongside a dramatic rise in unemployment on both sides of the Atlantic, suggests that financial shocks do affect labor markets. In the aftermath of the crisis, unemployment in the United States almost doubled, from peak to trough, within a few quarters (figure 6.1). Its short-run dynamics displayed remarkably larger Okun's elasticity than in previous recessions. U.S. unemployment is now declining at a very low pace, denoting more persistence than in previous recoveries, including the jobless recoveries of the past two decades.

Unemployment in Europe has been consistently lower than in the United States throughout the Great Recession, but the aggregate European Union (EU) figures conceal large cross-country heterogeneity in the responsiveness of unemployment to output changes.

Effect of Labor Market Institutions

Some of these differences in response across the two sides of the Atlantic are arguably linked to the different labor market institutions. For

We are grateful to Philippe Aghion, Stijn Claessens, William Cline, Uri Dadush, and seminar participants at the World Bank conference on "Ascent After Decline: Regrowing Economic Growth," November 19, 2010.

Figure 6.1 U.S. and Euro Area Unemployment Rates, 2000–10

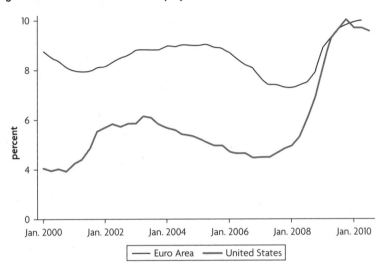

Source: Authors' compilation from European Union Labour Force Surveys (Eurostat database) and the U.S. Current Population Survey (U.S. Bureau of Labor Statistics database).

instance, short-time work schemes[1] have been playing an important role in containing job losses in Germany (where unemployment actually decreased during the recession).

However, other usual suspects for these transatlantic differences in unemployment dynamics seem to have much less explanatory power this time. According to an institutional approach and economic analysis fashionable in the mid-1990s, one could argue that strict employment protection legislation (EPL) in Europe is the smoking gun. High costs of dismissals, according to this perspective, are associated with lower labor market volatility. However, the countries with the strictest EPL, such as Spain, this time experienced the largest increase in unemployment.

European labor markets are today much more flexible on average and are characterized by a dual structure: (a) a flexible temporary fringe alongside (b) a rigid stock of regular contracts. Such a dual structure increased labor market response to adverse business conditions in precisely those countries displaying the strictest employment protection provisions for regular contracts.

Effect of Financial Sector

One should therefore go beyond labor market institutions to understand these asymmetric and largely unprecedented developments. A key factor behind the response of the labor market to the current recession is likely to be in the nature of the shocks that led to the Great Recession. In particular, one should look at the financial markets where the crisis originated and became global after the Lehman bankruptcy in September 2008. Financial markets and the banking sector experienced a credit crunch well into 2009 in both Europe and the United States, as several authors have documented. This global credit crunch is likely to have played a key role in labor market adjustment during the downturn and in the recovery.

Regarding the financial sector, one of the key differences between the two sides of the Atlantic is the degree of financial deepening. A simple empirical measure to account for this difference is the ratio of stock market capitalization to gross domestic product (GDP). Although the size of the financial shocks (measured as losses of stock market capitalization) appear similar in terms of timing and size, the difference in financial deepening between the United States and Europe is striking, as shown in figure 6.2. Whereas U.S. stock market capitalization amounts to some 100 percent of GDP, the same ratio in Europe is about 75 percent.

Boeri, Garibaldi, and Moen (2010) study theoretically and empirically the basic links and transmission mechanisms between the shocks to the financial markets and the labor market. This line of research poses the following questions:

- How does a credit crunch translate into job destruction and larger unemployment?
- Is financial deepening (larger in the United States than in Europe) responsible for the acceleration and increase of the U.S. unemployment-to-output response to the financial shocks of 2008–09?
- How does this explanation cope with the sluggish dynamics of U.S. unemployment during the recovery?
- And how about differences in Okun's elasticities within the EU?

Chapter Objectives and Organization

The goal of this chapter is threefold: First, it reviews the basic facts on unemployment dynamics, financial shocks, and Okun's elasticity over

Figure 6.2 Stock Market Capitalization and Unemployment, Euro Area and United States, 2000–10

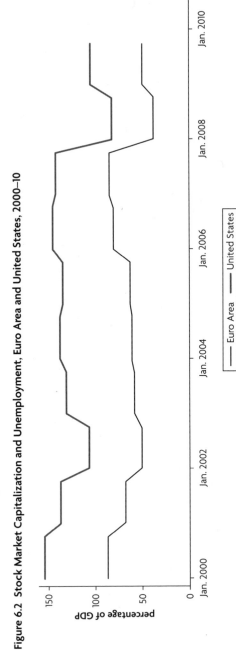

Euro Area —— United States

Sources: World Bank 2010 for data on stock market capitalization; European Union Labour Force Surveys (Eurostat database) and U.S. Current Population Survey (U.S. Bureau of Labor Statistics database) for unemployment data.

the business cycle. Second, it highlights the key mechanisms linking financial markets and labor markets, drawing on the most recent theoretical and empirical research in the area.

Third and foremost, it draws attention to the policy implications of this line of research. It discusses whether intervention in the labor market, in the aftermath of adverse financial shocks, should be conducted directly in the labor market (saving *jobs*) or indirectly through intervention in the financial markets (saving *financial institutions*)—in other words, addressing the trade-off between saving jobs and saving financial institutions. Although there is some evidence that saving jobs can be an effective policy, direct intervention in the labor market should be handled with particular caution because the risk of moral hazard and discretionary industrial policy should not be underestimated.

The chapter proceeds as follows:

- *From the Great Moderation to the Great Volatility* presents key figures on employment and unemployment dynamics throughout the recession.
- *Finance-Labor Interactions* reviews the literature on financial-labor market interactions, drawing on Boeri, Garibaldi, and Moen (2010).
- *Should We Save Institutions or Jobs?* discusses the policy implications of these results, focusing on whether direct intervention in the labor market is an alternative policy to intervention in the financial market, the key action so far taken by policy makers around the globe.
- *Conclusions* summarizes the authors' findings and recommendations.

From the Great Moderation to the Great Volatility

Among the Group of Seven (G-7) nations,[2] the Great Recession resulted in a cumulative GDP decline of 3.7 percent and employment reductions (peak to trough) of 2.1 percent. Thus, the apparent employment-to-output elasticity has been on the order of 0.6—significantly larger than in previous recessions. Even conditioning on output dynamics, which involved sizable falls almost everywhere, the global employment response has been stronger than in previous recessions.

Figure 6.3 Unemployment-to-Output Response in G-7 Countries

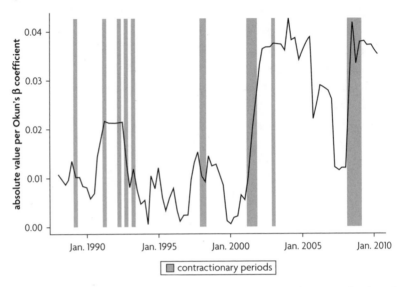

Sources: Authors' estimates based on IMF 2008 for quarterly GDP figures; OECD (Main Economic Indicators) for unemployment data.

Unemployment has also been rising more than in previous contractionary episodes given the magnitude of output decreases. Figure 6.3 displays Okun's Law unemployment-to-output elasticities (in modules), estimated by considering the G-7 as a unique large economy and using a 16-quarter moving window (rolling regression procedure) to allow for time-varying unemployment-to-output elasticities. The 2010Q1 beta coefficient is estimated over the 2007Q1–2010Q1 window from the regression

$$\Delta u_t = c - \beta_t \Delta y_t \%, \tag{6.1}$$

where **y** denotes GDP; **u** is the unemployment rate; and both **y** and **u** are measured at quarterly frequencies.

The first thing to notice is that there is substantial time-series variation in beta coefficients, which suggests that estimates imposing the same elasticity miss a lot of action.

Concerning the responsiveness of unemployment to output during the Great Recession, the message is clear: after the decades of the Great Moderation, we had years of Great Volatility. During the Great

Recession, unemployment has been even more responsive to output changes than during the two oil shocks of the 1970s and previous contractionary episodes (denoted by shaded areas in figure 6.3).

The other aspect of this renewed, even stronger volatility is that a key challenge of the recovery from the Great Recession will be the absorption of high levels of unemployment, notably long-term unemployment. A new Organisation for Economic Co-operation and Development (OECD) Jobs Study (updating OECD 1994) is needed, this time looking not only at Europe but also at the United States.

Needless to say, figure 6.3 conceals substantial cross-country variation in the elasticity of unemployment to output changes. Such cross-country differences are related to the presence of different institutional configurations. Economic theory as well as empirical work (for example, IMF 2010, chapter 4) suggest that labor market institutions—such as EPL, unemployment benefits, and short-time work schemes—affect the unemployment response to output changes. There is also evidence that some of the above institutions have been reformed over time, increasing the flexibility of labor markets and hence unemployment and employment volatility.

In conjunction with these institutional changes, the specific nature of the 2008–09 Great Recession could have affected the labor market response. Assessing the nature of these financial-labor interactions and their relevance in unemployment dynamics is crucial to identify policies that increase the job content of the current recovery.

Most of the interactions discussed below operate on the labor-demand side. Thus, it is useful to begin by looking at the employment-to-output elasticity during the Great Recession and comparing it with previous financial crises involving house price busts. Figure 6.4 displays rolling regression estimates of the employment-to-output elasticity in advanced countries that experienced a sufficiently large number of financial crises and housing busts, enabling us to identify their effect separately from other recessions.

Shaded areas represent financial crises or housing bust episodes according to the taxonomy developed by Reinhart and Rogoff (2009). The figure provides a visual impression that financial crises are indeed associated with greater employment response to output changes. This outcome is confirmed by the average beta coefficients for financial

Figure 6.4 Employment-to-Output Elasticities in Advanced Countries, by Recession Type

absolute value per Okun's βcoefficient

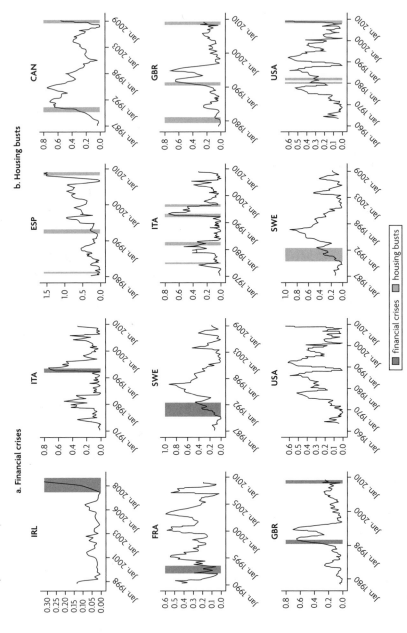

Sources: Authors' estimates based on IMF 2010 for quarterly GDP figures; OECD (Main Economic Indicators) for unemployment data; Reinhart and Rogoff 2009 for taxonomy of financial crises and housing busts.

Notes: CAN = Canada. FRA = France. IRL = Ireland. ITA = Italy. ESP = Spain. SWE = Sweden. GBR = United Kingdom. USA = United States.

Table 6.1 Okun's Betas (Employment-to-Output), Average Period

Country	Overall	Peak-to-peak with financial crisis	Peak-to-peak without financial crisis
Canada	0.336	0.557	—
France	0.286	0.273	0.314
Germany	0.192	—	0.214
Ireland	0.057	0.169	0.050
Italy	0.173	0.287	0.163
Spain	0.445	0.495	0.149
Sweden	0.269	0.300	0.136
United Kingdom	0.184	0.241	—
United States	0.251	0.368	0.265

Sources: Authors' estimates based on IMF 2010 for quarterly GDP figures; OECD (Main Economic Indicators) for unemployment; Reinhart and Rogoff 2009 for taxonomy of financial crises.
Note: — = not available.

crises and other recessions (measured from peak to peak), as displayed in table 6.1.

Finance-Labor Interactions

Why are financial crises more associated than other types of recessions with greater labor market volatility? What are the key channels of interaction between financial and labor markets? Which institutions play a more important role in this respect? Unfortunately, there is a paucity of research on labor-finance interactions.

Theoretical Studies

Most of the theoretical work on finance-labor interactions has dealt with the effects of financial market imperfections on employment adjustment to productivity shocks. There is a range of predictions in this respect.

Some studies view a relatively easy access by firms to financial markets as a substitute for labor market flexibility: firms can borrow to afford the costs associated with labor hoarding during downturns (Belke, Fehn, and Foster 2002; Rendón 2000). In other words, well-developed financial markets make labor market rigidity sustainable for firms. An implication of this view is that well-developed financial markets, coupled with strict EPL, could substantially reduce the cyclical volatility of employment over and beyond the effect of EPL alone.

The polar view is that labor market deregulation goes hand in hand with financial market liberalization (Bertola and Rogerson 1997; Koskela and Stenbacka 2002; Wasmer and Weil 2004). Greater access to financial markets by both firms and workers makes it possible to partly self-insure against labor market risk, thus reducing the demand for employment protection. From a structural standpoint, according to this literature, there should be a political-economic equilibrium in which well-functioning financial markets are associated with less-strict EPL. Countries featuring these flexible equilibria should display more employment volatility over the cycle than countries characterized by rigid labor market institutions and highly imperfect financial markets. Thus, the empirical prediction goes the other way around: deeper financial markets should be associated with more, not less, employment responsiveness to output changes.

Other papers have looked at interactions between financial variables and collective bargaining institutions, particularly the role played by firms' leverage decisions in coping with collective bargaining (Gatti, Rault, and Vaubourg 2010; Monacelli, Trigari, and Quadrini 2010). A general implication of these models is that leverage is a way to contain labor costs or at least to contain the effects that wage increases have on hiring policies. These models also imply that labor-finance interactions could amplify the impact of productivity shocks over the business cycle.

These predictions are not necessarily informative for our purposes because they typically consider the comparative statics of steady-state equilibria and do not analyze the effects of financial crises, which reduce firms' access to credit, taking into account the leverage these firms have at the outset. Financial crises can be framed in this class of models as sudden increases in financial frictions, reducing significantly the scale of financial markets. If these frictions do not increase proportionally with their initial level—in particular, if they increase *less* than proportionally—one should expect to observe larger effects of these crises on employment adjustment in highly leveraged economies and firms.

One strand of literature that offers some insights into the questions of this chapter is the research on financial distress in the context of Chapter 11 bankruptcy procedures. Aghion, Hart, and Moore (1994) and Wruck (1990) argue that financial distress can lead to excessive management control and excessive restructuring even when liquidation could be optimal. Empirical evidence provided by Gilson, John, and Lang (1990) is coherent with such a view.

Empirical Study of "Job Destruction" and "Labor Mobility" Effects

Boeri, Garibaldi, and Moen (2010) tackle the issue more directly and identify two main channels through which financial markets are likely to affect the labor market in the aftermath of an adverse financial shock: the *job destruction* effect and the *labor mobility* effect of the credit crunch. Theoretically, these authors offer a simple matching model, with financial and labor market frictions described by a standard matching function similar to what Wasmer and Weil (2004) originally proposed. Empirically, they use a variety of datasets on both the United States and Europe to ask whether it is possible to identify the two effects outlined by the model.

The research finds some evidence for both types of effects:

- *The job destruction effect.* Leveraged firms may find themselves in a position in which their liquidity is suddenly called back by the lender. This has direct consequences on a firm's ability to run and manage existing jobs. As a result, firms may be obliged to shut down part of their operations and destroy existing jobs. In this sense, the job destruction effect of the credit crunch is essentially a *labor demand-driven* channel of adjustment.

- *The labor mobility effect.* Workers need financial markets to finance their mortgages and real estate investments. Workers who are changing jobs typically need to liquidate and reinvest in real estate in a different part of the country. In such a trade, the quick availability of liquidity is a key requirement. Conversely, when the mortgage market experiences an adverse shock, workers can find it difficult to finance their mobility-related investment, notably the real estate investment. Under these conditions, workers get stuck in the current location and cannot move across jobs in space. This reduction in workers' mobility may increase unemployment and reduce job creation after a recession involving major changes in the spatial allocation of employment opportunities. In this sense, the labor mobility effect of finance is a *labor supply–driven* channel of adjustment.

Boeri, Garibaldi, and Moen (2010) set forth an empirical strategy to test whether the two effects of finance are present in the data. They use a variety of datasets on both the United States and Europe to ask whether it is possible to identify the two effects described above. The empirical strategy is as follows: They draw on two-digit sector-level data on employment and financial market conditions over a large number of OECD countries. Using the United States as a benchmark, they analyze whether sectors with significantly lower leverage ratios relative to the same sector in the United States experienced lower employment-to-output elasticities. This comparison tests the labor-demand channel of adjustment. Drawing on EU-15[3] data from the EU Labor Force Survey, they also estimate whether labor mobility across space is affected by the presence of a mortgage after a housing price bust.

Regarding the job destruction effect, the main results are as follows: Conditional on a financial shock, the more-leveraged sectors and countries experience greater volatility. (The leverage of each sector is measured in terms of both debt-to-assets and debt-to-sales ratios.) From the labor market perspective, after a financial crisis, the so-called nightmare situation arises when firms are highly leveraged and there is a large stock of temporary workers who can be fired "at will," incurring no severance or procedural cost, at contract expiration. Note that in this exercise, the identification comes mainly from time-series variation and results are robust to heteroskedasticity.

Regarding the labor mobility effect, Boeri, Garibaldi, and Moen (2010) estimate probit models using micro data from the European Community Household Panel, a longitudinal survey carried out in the EU-15 in 1994–2001. They study the individual probability of moving in general as well as moving specifically for job-related reasons. The survey allows the use of retrospective information on mobility, and it also includes data on personal characteristics and assets. The authors find that, conditional on a financial shock, the presence of a mortgage reduces labor mobility, notably mobility for labor-market-related reasons.

Should We Save Institutions or Jobs?

More than two years down the road of the Great Recession, financial market reforms still absorb most of the attention. True, the troubles came from financial markets and still need to be fixed. It is also undeniable that too little has been done so far to address the fundamental issues at the core of the crisis: regulatory leaks, institutions that were too big to fail, lax monetary policy, and lack of transparency in accounting rules. But a more important problem is not even being discussed: Were governments right to put so much emphasis on the rescue of financial institutions rather than on the real economy? Should they have been saving jobs instead of the banks and their CEOs who had played a non-marginal role in the crisis?

In most OECD economies, the policy put in place focused mainly on saving financial institutions rather than on saving jobs. During the crisis, the European Commission authorized state aid to banks amounting to some 25 percent of EU GDP, almost 90 percent of which consisted of state guarantees, the rest going toward bank recapitalization, purchase of toxic assets, and ad hoc measures for troubled institutions. The rescue packages for banks in the remaining G-20 countries were also sizable.

Why was so much money spent to rescue the very banks that had contributed to the global crisis? The usual answer is that saving financial institutions also implies saving jobs. Financial institutions are deemed essential in providing long-term finance to firms, and access to bank lending is fundamental to preserve jobs. But so far the policy of rescuing financial institutions has not prevented a huge rise of unemployment and a dramatic fall in bank lending.

There are currently almost 30 million more people unemployed in the G-20 than before the crisis. As shown above, the increase in unemployment has been stronger than what could have been expected from historical experience based on the size of the output fall. Employment losses were also stronger in leveraged sectors and in countries with more heavily indebted firms as employers anticipated a credit squeeze.

Bank lending to the nonfinancial private sector fell by some 10 percent in the United States and by 2–5 percent in the Euro Area and Japan, according to the *Economic Outlook* (OECD 2010). Financial institutions usually argue that this fall is demand-driven: during recessions, fewer firms plan to invest, thus fewer apply for bank loans. Financial institutions cannot support jobs, they usually claim, if firms are not willing to invest in new projects. But are we sure that preventing layoffs is not a worthwhile project on its own?

The recent research by Boeri, Garibaldi, and Moen (2010), as previously discussed, suggests that direct intervention in the sectors more exposed to finance may prevent job destruction. Taken at face value, these findings imply that saving jobs can be an effective way to reduce the adverse impact of financial crises on the labor market.

But, of course, things are not that simple, and great caution is needed for the following reasons:

- Foremost, financial crises tend to have systemic risks. And the first priority of policy makers should indeed be to reduce systemic risks, which can be done only through direct intervention in the financial markets. These interventions must be more selective than in the past, though. Not all bank failures involve systemic risks, and there are ways to support financial institutions involving shareholders and creditors, such as senior bond holders, rather than only taxpayers.
- Saving jobs requires policy makers to choose deliberately the sectors in which intervention is required. This is akin to industrial policy, and we know very well how difficult it is to run a coherent industrial policy without the risks involved by lobbying, corporate politics, and similar practices.
- Saving jobs involves a moral hazard problem not so different from those faced while rescuing financial institutions. Once a job-saving policy is in place, what can prevent that particular sector as well as others from becoming too exposed to financial markets just as a way to anticipate a future rescue package? One possible answer is that such a supervisory role rests on the banking system. Through proper and cautious monitoring of banks' exposure to the protected sectors, banks are potentially in the right position to avoid excessive risk taking on the part of the real sector. In this respect, interactions between labor markets, financial markets, and economic policy would be reinforced.

Conclusions

A stronger governmental hand in preventing private losses from being shifted to taxpayers is essential to free resources for measures that save jobs and ease the reallocation involved in any recession. These measures are much less costly than the measures adopted to support banks throughout the Great Recession. For example, the German *Kurzarbeit*[4] scheme, estimated to have saved up to half a million jobs in 2009, cost "only" €5 billion.

A stronger competition policy is also essential for job creation. Empirical evidence on panels of firms and establishments indicates that the bulk of net job creation comes from startups rather than the expansion of existing business units. Stronger competition policy will also be fundamental in combination with industrial policies, such as those advocated in this chapter.

The first *OECD Jobs Study* (OECD 1994) argued in favor of horizontal policies and reforms of labor market institutions to move Europe toward the United States institutional landscape. The second Jobs Study, to be written after the Great Recession, should instead be much more focused on the U.S. unemployment problems and advocate different types of labor market reforms, notably those reducing the dualism of highly flexible and rigidly contractual labor markets.

The new study could also advocate some role for vertical industrial policy measures targeting those sectors that are subject to the strongest competitive pressures. Stronger competition policies should then make sure that state aid for job creation does not create advantages for incumbents, thus preventing entry of the large-scale startups required to exit the job crisis.

Notes

1. *Kuzarbeit* (German for "short-work") programs in several European countries have avoided layoffs by cutting working hours, with the governments compensating workers for some of their lost income.
2. The G-7 nations comprise Canada, France, Germany, Italy, Japan, the United Kingdom, and the United States.
3. The EU-15 refers to the number of EU-member countries before the accession of 10 candidate countries on May 1, 2004. The EU-15 comprises Austria, Belgium, Denmark, Finland, France, Germany, Greece, Ireland, Italy, Luxembourg, the Netherlands, Portugal, Spain, Sweden, and the United Kingdom.
4. See note 1.

References

Aghion, Philippe, Olivier Hart, and John Moore. 1994. "The Economics of Bankruptcy Reform." In *The Transition in Eastern Europe*, ed. Olivier Blanchard, Kenneth A. Froot, and Jeffrey D. Sachs, 215–44. Chicago: University of Chicago Press.

Belke, Ansgar, and Rainer Fehn. 2000. "Institutions and Structural Unemployment: Do Capital Market Imperfections Matter?" Discussion Paper 190, Department of Economics, University of Hohenheim, Stuttgart.

Belke, Ansgar, Rainer Fehn, and Neil Foster. 2002. "Venture Capital Investment and Labor Market Performance: A Panel Data Analysis." Working Paper 562, Center for Economic Studies and Ifo Institute for Economic Research, Munich.

Bertola, Giuseppe, and Richard Rogerson. 1997. "Institutions and Labor Reallocation." *European Economic Review* 41 (6): 1147–71.

Boeri, Tito, Pietro Garibaldi, and Espen Moen. 2010. "The Labor Market Consequences of Adverse Financial Shocks." Unpublished manuscript, Collegio Carlo Alberto, Moncalieri, Italy, and Bocconi University, Milan.

Eurostat (database). European Commission, Brussels. http://epp.eurostat.ec.europa .eu/portal/page/portal/eurostat/home.

Gatti, Donatella, Christophe Rault, and Anne-Gael Vaubourg. 2010. "Unemployment and Finance: How Do Financial and Labour Market Factors Interact?" William Davidson Institute Working Paper 973, University of Michigan, Ann Arbor.

Gilson, Stuart, Kose John, and Larry Lang. 1990. "Troubled Debt Restructurings: An Empirical Study of Private Reorganization of Firms in Default." *Journal of Financial Economics* 27 (2): 315–53.

IMF (International Monetary Fund). 2008. *World Economic Outlook 2008*. Washington, DC: IMF.

———. 2010. *World Economic Outlook April 2010*. Washington, DC: IMF.

Koskela, Erkki, and Rune Stenbacka. 2002. "Equilibrium Unemployment and Credit Market Imperfections: The Critical Role of Labor Market Mobility." Working Paper 654, Center for Economic Studies and Ifo Institute for Economic Research, Munich.

Main Economic Indicators (database). Organisation for Economic Co-operation and Development, Paris. http://www.oecd.org/document/54/0,3746,en_2649_ 33715_15569334_1_1_1_1,00.html.

Monacelli, Tommaso, Antonella Trigari, and Vincenzo Quadrini. 2010. "Financial Markets and Employment." Paper presented at the conference "Labor Markets after the Great Recession," sponsored by the Kiel Institute for the World Economy and the Federal Reserve Bank of Philadelphia, December 3–4.

OECD (Organisation for Economic Co-operation and Development). 1994. *The OECD Jobs Study*. Paris: OECD.

———. 2010. *Economic Outlook*. Paris: OECD.

Reinhart, Carmen, and Kenneth Rogoff 2009. "The Aftermath of Financial Crises." Working Paper 14656, National Bureau of Economic Research, Cambridge, MA.

Rendón, Silvio. 2000. "Job Creation under Liquidity Constraints: The Spanish Case." Economics Working Paper 488, Universitat Pompeu Fabra, Barcelona.

U.S. Bureau of Labor Statistics (database). Current Population Survey. http://www.bls.gov/cps/.

Wasmer, Etienne, and Philippe Weil. 2004. "The Macroeconomics of Labor and Credit Market Imperfections." *American Economic Review* 94 (4): 944–63.

World Bank. 2010. *Global Development Finance.* Washington, DC: World Bank. http://data.worldbank.org/data-catalog/global-development-finance.

Wruck, Karen Hopper. 1990. "Financial Distress, Reorganization, and Organizational Efficiency." *Journal of Financial Economics* 27 (2): 419–44.

Information Technology, Globalization, and Growth: The Roles of Scale Economies, Terms of Trade, and Variety

Catherine L. Mann

This chapter considers three channels through which globalization of information technology (IT) products may affect economic growth:

- *Terms of trade.* The fall in quality-adjusted prices of IT products favors IT consumers, so net importers (whose consumption exceeds production) experience faster economic growth. But given the fragmentation of IT production into a global supply chain, it is not so simple to measure terms of trade.
- *Economies of scale.* IT production exhibits important economies of scale. For example, a country could specialize in a segment of the supply chain by importing a narrow set of imports (to exploit the terms-of-trade gain) and then exporting a narrow set of IT products (to exploit economies of scale in production). So concentrated trade patterns—and being a net exporter by producing more than consuming—could yield faster growth.
- *Variety.* Availability of a wide variety of IT products is also a potential source of economic gain. Greater variety means that more domestic

users find good matches between products and needs, which increases productivity and growth. The variety of exports might further support growth to the extent that variety increases prices and profits.

Several empirical questions are relevant for policy makers: What are the relative magnitudes of these channels? What data relate economic growth to production, consumption, and international trade in IT products? To catalyze economic growth and enhance performance, should policy makers promote IT exports to exploit economies of scale in production? Or should they promote imports and domestic consumption of a variety of IT products to gain from falling IT prices, get more variety, and through these channels support faster total factor productivity (TFP)?

The chapter explores some of the issues, research, and metrics that can better inform policy makers' approach to these questions, as follows:

- *Measuring Economic Growth: Getting to the Social Surplus Concept* addresses measurement issues and describes a metric and apparatus—"social surplus"—with which to evaluate, in general terms, the relationships between production and consumption of a transformative innovation, and economywide productivity and growth.
- *Data and the Literature on IT and Economic Growth* presents an overview of patterns of IT production, consumption, and trade and reviews the literature on the relationship between IT and growth.
- *International IT Trade and the Social Surplus Measure of Economic Growth* takes the social surplus apparatus to the data on IT production, consumption, and trade to consider the relative importance of economies of scale, variety, and terms of trade for economic well-being and as foundations for growth.
- *Variety and the Dispersion of Country Experience* discusses the correlation of social surplus to the diversity of countries' use of IT and thereby to economic growth relative to peer IT-exporting or IT-importing economies. The analysis suggests that gains to variety in consumption can outweigh gains from economies of scale in production.
- *Policy Implications* sums up the findings' implications for an IT-based economic growth strategy.

Measuring Economic Growth: Getting to the Social Surplus Concept

Productivity and productivity growth are standard ways to measure the foundation of economic growth. A more productive economy is one where resources are allocated efficiently so as to generate the highest amount of output without inflationary strain, resource waste, or environmental degradation. In the long run, a more productive economy can generate more possibilities for consumption and business investment.

Productivity Measures: Labor versus TFP

Labor productivity is output per unit of labor input and is often a key measure of the foundations for economic growth. Increased labor productivity can be achieved without innovation but through increases in the capital stock. Diminishing marginal returns to capital inputs, however, suggest that labor productivity is an incomplete measure of the foundations for economic well-being and growth.

Total factor productivity (also called multifactor productivity) measures the extent to which an economy can generate more output using the same resources. By definition, increased TFP implies innovation and transformation in how resources are combined—observable as new products, changes in business processes, or new workplace practices. Increased TFP also implies increased growth in the sense that the economy can produce more output to allocate toward final demand.

GDP versus GNI and the Role for Terms of Trade and TFP

Gross domestic product (GDP) and GDP per capita are standard measures of economic performance and growth. They incorporate increases in resources and production of new products as well as innovations in business process and workplace practices. But, being aggregates, these measures do not distinguish between components of economic growth—as, for example, between consumption, investment, and net exports.

In a globalized economy with international trade and in an environment of rapid innovation in new products, processes, and practices, the aggregate GDP measure may mask important sources of economic growth that influence the economic well-being of the population. That is, if there is a structural trend in a country's terms of trade, gross national income (GNI) may be a better measure of economic growth. For example, if a country has substantial imports of a product whose international price is falling—which implies that its terms of trade are improving—then real GDP understates the country's real domestic income, its purchasing power, and the economic growth that domestic residents can enjoy.[1] Similarly, if an economy has a structural balance of payments surplus, GDP overstates the extent to which domestic residents enjoy the fruits of economic growth.[2]

Trends in the terms of trade are relevant from the standpoint not only of purchasing power but also of measuring productivity growth. Specifically, there is a mathematical isomorphism between changes in the terms of trade and changes in TFP: an improvement in the terms of trade is equivalent to an innovation that increases TFP and economic growth.[3]

Social Surplus, Transformative Technology, and Economic Growth

TFP is difficult to measure. Social surplus is another way to account for the accumulated gain and economic growth that a country gets as more and more buyers take advantage of a transformative technology (Bayoumi and Haacker 2002, 11–12; Feenstra et al. 2007; Kohli 2004, 2006). From the final consumer's standpoint, innovations that reduce prices yield direct gains, measured as consumer surplus. But purchasing innovative products with falling prices yields indirect gains as well, through cheaper intermediates and changes in production processes. Collectively, the spending power and investment decisions induced by the innovation fall on other parts of the economy, accentuating the value of the transformative technology for overall TFP and growth.

The calculation of how much the overall economy gains from the falling prices associated with an innovation is called "social surplus." Figure 7.1 shows an example of the social surplus apparatus for a transformative technology.

As figure 7.1 illustrates, Social surplus (A + B + C) is larger under the following conditions:

- Higher income elasticity of demand for transformative technology (TT)
- Higher price elasticity of demand for TT

Figure 7.1 Transformative Technology and Social Surplus

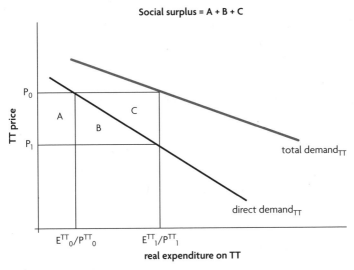

Social surplus = A + B + C

Source: Author.
Note: TT = transformative technology. P = price. E = expenditure.

- Bigger fall in TT price
- Larger initial TT expenditure
- More TT used as intermediates and TT externalities.

The next section reviews the empirical evidence underpinning the facts of IT globalization and the assertions that diffusion of IT products enhances TFP and economic growth. Later, "International IT Trade and the Social Surplus Measure of Economic Growth" calculates social surplus for a set of countries and considers (a) the relationship between social surplus and the extent to which the economy may gain through direct demand for IT, and (b) how the economy may gain through indirect demand for IT.

Data and the Literature on IT and Economic Growth

There is a vast literature on the relationship between IT and measures of economic growth.[4] This paper highlights a small subset of the literature that focuses, first, on the relationship between economies of scale in

IT production and economic growth and, second, on diffusion of variety of IT and economic growth. To give a frame of reference for the literature, we start with some observations based on data on the globalization of IT production and trade. The data have bearing on the issues of economies of scale and variety of IT products in international trade.

Changing Patterns of International Trade and Domestic Expenditure

That the IT industries are greatly globalized in production, investment, and cross-border trade goes without saying. The Organisation for Economic Co-operation and Development's (OECD) *Information Technology Outlook* addresses and quantifies numerous measures of the globalization of the IT industry, for both goods and services. Additional assessments, predominantly for emerging markets and developing economies, can be found in the *Information Economy Report* and the *World Investment Report*, both published by the United Nations Conference on Trade and Development (UNCTAD).[5]

Although the global production of IT goods is highly fragmented, with production sites all over the world, some indicators suggest that production has become more concentrated over time as key producers squeeze the maximum economies of scale in production from factories in the lowest-cost locations.[6] In addition, an increase in exporters' revealed comparative advantage for information and communication technology (ICT) goods during the 1990s (OECD 2008, 94–95) also points to some concentration of global production of specific parts and components, even as the production process of a wider variety of "final" ICT goods remains highly fragmented.

IT Exporters. Data on the IT goods trade, as table 7.1 shows, exhibit both rapid changes in ranking among the top exporters and importers and changes in trade concentration. The bottom line is that the sum of China and Hong Kong SAR, China, exploded from 2 percent of global exports (ranked 14th) in 1990 to 15 percent of global exports (ranked 1st) in 2004. On the import side, China and Hong Kong SAR, China, moved from 9th-ranked, with 4 percent of global imports, to top-ranked with 20 percent of global imports.

Table 7.1 Global IT Trade Patterns, by Economy, 1990–2004

	Rank	Economy	Share of world trade (percent)	Cumulative share (percent)
			a. 1990	
Exports	1	Japan	20.4	20.4
	2	United States	19.3	39.7
	3	United Kingdom	7.7	47.4
	4	Germany, Federal Rep.	7.4	54.8
	5	Singapore	6.7	61.5
	14	China and Hong Kong SAR, China	1.7	n.a.
Imports	1	United States	20.6	20.6
	2	Germany, Federal Rep.	9.7	30.3
	3	United Kingdom	9.0	39.3
	4	France	6.5	45.8
	5	Italy	4.5	50.3
	9	China and Hong Kong SAR, China	3.9	n.a.
			b. 2000	
Exports	1	United States	17.0	17.0
	2	Japan	14.1	31.1
	3	Singapore	9.8	40.9
	4	Korea, Rep.	6.6	47.5
	5	Taiwan, China	6.4	53.9
	9	China and Hong Kong SAR, China	4.2	n.a.
Imports	1	United States	20.3	20.3
	2	China and Hong Kong SAR, China	10.0	30.3
	3	Japan	6.7	37.0
	4	Singapore	6.7	43.7
	5	Germany	5.9	49.6

(continued next page)

Table 7.1 (continued)

	Rank	Economy	Share of world trade (percent)	Cumulative share (percent)
			c. 2004	
Exports	1	China and Hong Kong SAR, China	15.2	15.2
	2	United States	11.0	26.2
	3	Singapore	8.7	34.9
	4	Japan	7.9	42.8
	5	Germany	6.9	49.7
	6	Taiwan, China	6.4	n.a.
Imports	1	China and Hong Kong SAR, China	20.1	20.1
	2	United States	14.8	34.9
	3	Germany	6.5	41.4
	4	Singapore	6.2	47.6
	5	Japan	5.8	53.4

Sources: Mann 2006, table 2.2a; original data from the United Nations Commodity Trade Statistics Database (Comtrade).
Note: n.a. = not applicable.

There were other changes in the trade landscape, even if not so dramatic. Between 1990 and 2004, the cumulative share of the top three exporters fell from 47 percent to 35 percent, suggesting less trade concentration.

The top three IT-exporting economies also changed over the 1990–2004 period: Japan dropped from being the top exporter (with 20 percent of world exports) in 1990 to fourth (with 8 percent) in 2004. China and Hong Kong SAR, China, rose from 14th (with 1.7 percent of world exports) in 1990 to first (with 15 percent) in 2004. The United States remained the second-largest exporter (with 19 percent of world exports) in 1990 but with only 11 percent in 2004. The United Kingdom was the third-largest exporter in 1990 but dropped to 10th in 2004. Singapore rose from fifth-largest in 1990 to third-largest in 2004.

IT Importers. On the import side, concentration has changed little, but the rankings have changed. The top-three importers accounted for about 40 percent of world imports from 1990 through 2004. The United

States was the top-ranked importer in 1990, accounting for about 20 percent of world imports—about the same as what China and Hong Kong SAR, China, accounted for with its top ranking in 2004. China and Hong Kong SAR, China, doubled its share of global imports from only 4 percent of imports in 1990 to 10 percent by 2000, and then doubled its share again to reach 20 percent in 2004. The United States slipped to second by 2004 with 15 percent of world imports. Among the other top-ranking importers, Germany, Japan, and Singapore rounded out the top-five list in both 2000 and 2004, albeit in changing order.

IT Expenditures. An interesting question is whether countries that rank highly in global trade also rank highly in domestic expenditure on IT. A quick look at the data in table 7.2 indicates that deep involvement in global production and international trade in IT does not necessarily correlate with a country's domestic spending on IT.

For example, the United States accounted for 45 percent of global expenditure on IT in 2000, shrinking to 36 percent by 2008. Both shares, though, were substantially larger than the U.S. share of global IT trade. Germany's and Japan's shares of global IT trade, however, were somewhat closer to their shares of domestic IT expenditure. China and Hong Kong SAR, China, quadrupled its share of global expenditure between 2000 and 2008, ranking sixth in global expenditure by 2008, but its share of expenditure remained quite small relative to that economy's importance in global trade.

If an economy's share of world trade and its share of global expenditure were the same, it would suggest a balanced expansion path for that economy overall. When economies have higher shares of global trade than of global expenditure, that suggests that IT is relatively more important as a production platform for growth through international trade than through domestic use. On the other hand, if the share of expenditure is greater than the share of trade, that suggests that domestic business use of IT in the economy is the basis for growth.

Gains from Producing IT versus Using IT

We turn now to a review of selected empirical studies on the relationship between IT and economic growth. The research agenda started

Table 7.2 Global IT Expenditure Patterns, by Economy, 2000–08

Rank	Economy	Share of world (%)
	a. 2000	
1	United States	45.1
2	Japan	15.9
3	Germany	6.4
4	United Kingdom	6.1
5	France	4.8
8	China and Hong Kong SAR, China	1.5
	b. 2004	
1	United States	39.0
2	Japan	10.7
3	Germany	7.3
4	United Kingdom	7.0
5	France	6.0
6	China and Hong Kong SAR, China	3.3
	c. 2008	
1	United States	36.2
2	Japan	9.1
3	Germany	7.2
4	United Kingdom	6.4
5	France	5.8
6	China and Hong Kong SAR, China	5.2

Sources: Author's calculations; data from World Information Technology and
Services Alliance (WITSA).

with a focus on how the ICT-producing sector generates economic growth though high estimated TFP and economies of scale in production.[7] Van Ark (2005), using 1979–2002 data, shows that TFP in the ICT-producing sector is higher than it is in other sectors: 8 percent in the ICT-producing sector versus 3 percent in the ICT-using sectors. Chun and Nadiri (2008) find that in the United States (using 1978–99 data), economies of scale in ICT production account for 30 percent of TFP in the ICT-producing sector.

From a policy-making perspective, however, looking to the ICT-producing sector for growth creates some problems. First, if the source of growth is production of ICT, then the sector must keep growing as a share of the economy to continue the overall expansion of economic activity. Second, if economies of scale in production are that important for TFP, any small country must produce primarily a narrow set of products for export because domestic demand is unlikely to absorb all that is produced. Globalization of ICT production—and the rising share of the production complex of China and Hong Kong SAR, China, as noted in the previous statistics—means tough competition in export markets. Finally, if growth from ICT comes only from producing ICT, then any country without an ICT sector would appear to be doomed to slow growth.

These conundrums encouraged researchers to look more deeply into how ICT was being *used* in an economy. Van Ark's (2005) closer examination of the ICT-producing versus ICT-using sectors reveals that TFP in ICT-using industries increased 250 percent versus only 30 percent in ICT-producing industries (comparing data from 1979–95 and 1995–2002, respectively). Mun and Nadiri's (2002) research using U.S. data shows that networked IT deployed in an ICT-using sector (particularly in services) that linked forward to customers and backward to suppliers contributed importantly to cost reductions and TFP gains for the ICT-using sectors.

The research on ICT-using sectors found quite a bit of variation across countries in the TFP growth associated with ICT use. Explaining this variation can inform policy making. One line of research looked at domestic institutions, human capital, and competition. Several research papers suggest that flexible labor markets enhance the impact of ICT on productivity growth, with more product-market competition having a similar and complementary result (Gust and Marquez 2000; OECD 2003b; and van Ark, Inklaar, and McGuckin 2003 focus on continental Europe). If businesses cannot (or have no incentive to) change product mix or change what workers do, then buying IT is just an additional cost of doing business rather than an enhancement to the business (see case examples in Mann, Eckert, and Knight 2000).

Further, if ICT investment takes place in a business environment lacking in strong international competition, productivity growth also lags (Shih, Kraemer, and Dedrick 2007).

Another line of research, particularly relevant for developing countries, finds that there needs to be a balance between human capital and investment in ICT before domestic use of ICT yields higher productivity and growth (Dewan and Kraemer 2000; Pohjola 2001; Sciadas 2005; Seo and Lee 2006).

A different direction for research focuses on how variety in products relates to TFP. Research on all types of products (not just ICT) finds that increased export variety is associated with 40 percent of the difference in measured TFP across countries. Feenstra and Kee (2008) attribute the bulk of this finding to variety in trade in electronics products. On the import side, a higher variety of all types of imports accounts for about 25 percent of TFP growth in developing countries (Broda, Greenfield, and Weinstein 2006). The way this works is that, with an insufficient variety of ICT products, the business community may find only poor matches to its needs and would use less ICT, resulting in lower productivity and growth.

In sum, even though TFP is higher in the ICT-producing sector and economies of scale in production are quite important, the results of research on the relationship between ICT and economic growth increasingly point away from production of ICT and more toward how ICT is used by businesses in an economy and what features of the economy are most conducive to that use. With globalized production of ICT, where quality-adjusted prices are falling, international trade offers a more compelling avenue to buy ICT. Thus, international trade in ICT may play a particularly important role in TFP growth in the ICT-using sectors.

International IT Trade and the Social Surplus Measure of Economic Growth

Despite the obvious relationships, little of the literature on IT and growth addresses the nexus of international IT trade and economic growth. However, just as the domestic focus shifted from the IT-producing sector to the IT-using sectors, this section shifts the focus from the domestic sources of growth to the global sources of growth from international IT trade.

With increased globalization of production and international trade, the decline in quality-adjusted prices of IT products has different implications for producers of exported IT versus consumers of imported IT. But this fragmentation of production around the world enables some countries to establish significant economies of scale in production of certain IT products. How do the terms of trade balance against the economies of scale, and what role is there for variety in supporting economic growth?

International IT Trade and Social Surplus: The Hypothesis

Information technology is a transformative technology. Its quality-adjusted global price is falling, which should promote imports and greater use of the technology—resulting in gains to social surplus, productivity, and economic growth. Yet special economic zones in some countries focus on production for export rather than domestic use.

Whereas production and export of IT products obviously should not directly harm an economy,[8] declining prices for IT products means that the terms of trade (export prices compared to prices of imported products) are moving against these producers. Thus, the gains to the domestic economy that do come from producing IT for export (through economies of scale, for example) are partly offset by the opportunity cost of not using those resources to produce IT (or other) products with increasing value in domestic markets or in international trade. How important is production versus consumption for getting the gains from IT, considering the trade dimension?

The apparatus of social surplus is a crucial ingredient to investigating the relationship between economic growth and being an IT producer versus an IT buyer (or falling somewhere in between, as do most economies). The first step estimates social surplus for a set of countries. The second step uses the net of production and expenditure as a measure of international IT trade. The final step considers why countries differ from each other beyond being net producers (exporters) or net consumers (importers) of IT.

Figure 7.2 sets out the hypotheses, based on the previous literature, concerning the roles of the following factors:

- *Terms of trade.* The quality-adjusted falling prices of IT favor IT consumers and importers. Based on terms of trade alone, social surplus should be negatively correlated with the difference between production and expenditure (or imports), as shown by the negative sloped dash line.
- *Economies of scale.* However, economies of scale favor high-volume IT producers, who are probably also exporters. TFP is positively associated with the scale of production of IT products. So social surplus may be higher for high-volume producers and exporters, which tilts the solid black line up, creating a U-shaped relationship between social surplus and the production – expenditure (trade) balance.
- *Variety.* Research suggests that greater variety of IT products, including imports, used by business supports TFP and social surplus.

Figure 7.2 Growth and International IT Trade: The Hypotheses

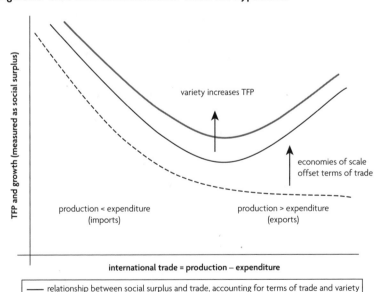

Source: Author.
Note: TFP = total factor productivity. Social surplus is the calculation of overall economic gain from the falling prices associated with an innovation.

A greater variety of exports likely achieves relatively higher prices (fewer of the products are low-margin commodities), which offsets the otherwise deleterious terms-of-trade effect for exporters. Therefore, all else equal, increased variety would tend to shift the U-shaped curve further upward.

Given this set of hypotheses, what do the data reveal?

Patterns of IT Trade and Social Surplus: The Evidence

The first step is to calculate social surplus. Following the previous discussion in the *Measuring Economic Growth* section, the main ingredients to this calculation are data for each economy's (a) real GDP, (b) real IT prices, (c) real production of IT, and (d) real domestic expenditure on IT. The estimated price and income elasticities of demand for IT also are needed.[9]

Social surplus is calculated as the average for 2000–07 for 36 economies, as shown in figure 7.3. The figure shows the relationship between

Figure 7.3 Growth and International Trade in IT: The Calculations

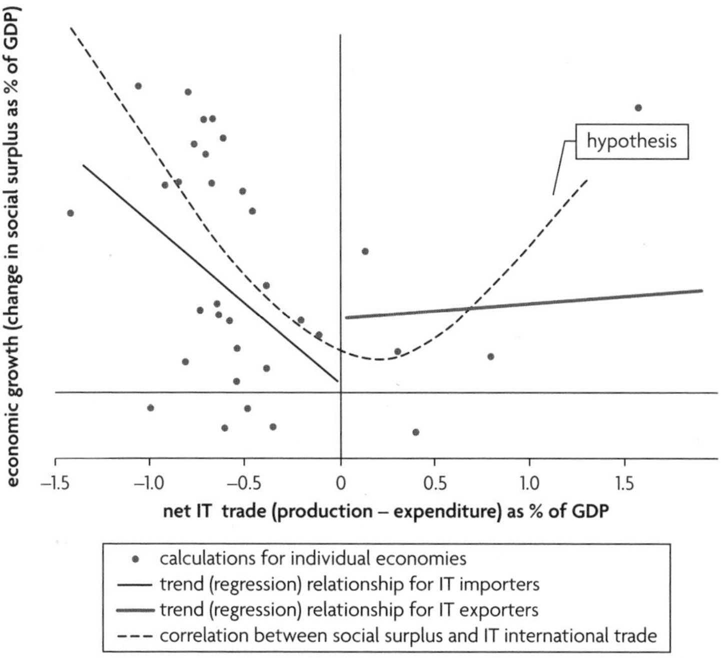

Source: Mann 2009.

this metric of economic growth (social surplus as a share of GDP) and trade in IT products (measured as production less expenditure, as a share of GDP for the years 2003–06, averaged). The linear segments show the linear trend (regression) relationship for importers taken alone and for exporters taken alone.

Overall, the collection of estimated data points for individual economies matches the basic hypothesis that importers of IT (production < expenditure) enjoy relatively higher social surplus (TFP and growth) than economies that are exporters of IT (production > expenditure). But the significant dispersion of the economies around the average regression relationship bears further examination.

Figure 7.4 shows the two sides of the previous diagram along with more economy-specific detail. These calculations reveal several important points that bolster the empirical research already cited and partly support the hypothesis that social surplus and imports of IT products are positively related through the terms of trade.

IT Importers. First, consider the importers (see figure 7.4, panel a) to be those economies where IT expenditure exceeds IT production. For these economies, falling IT prices increase social surplus because more consumers accumulate the benefits of falling IT prices, both directly and indirectly, as IT diffuses through the economy.

The trend line in figure 7.4, panel a, reveals the positive relationship between social surplus and imports of IT: the larger the (negative) gap between production and expenditure on IT hardware (for example, imports), the greater the increase in social surplus (for example, accumulated gain to buyers from declining IT hardware prices). The trend relationship is somewhat greater than unity (–1.5), indicating that a 1 percent increase in IT imports (production less expenditure) is associated with a 1.5 percent increase in social surplus. This greater-than-unitary association is consistent with other research already cited on the productivity-enhancing diffusion benefits and externalities associated with using IT.

These estimates of social surplus use data from the 2000s and can be compared to Bayoumi and Haacker's (2002) estimates using data from the 1990s as discussed in Mann (2009). First, the relationship between social surplus and imports is stronger in the 2000s than in the 1990s

Figure 7.4 Social Surplus and IT Trade in Selected Economies, 2000–07

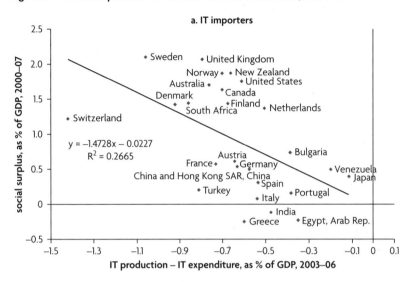

a. IT importers

$y = -1.4728x - 0.0227$
$R^2 = 0.2665$

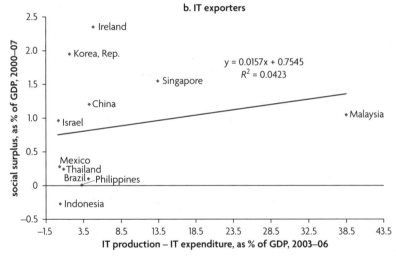

b. IT exporters

$y = 0.0157x + 0.7545$
$R^2 = 0.0423$

Source: Author.

(for example, a steeper slope of –1.5 versus –0.9). This implies that the translation of IT imports into social surplus, productivity, and economic growth has been stronger in the recent decade than during the 1990s. This is a bit surprising because the quality-adjusted decline in IT prices actually slowed in the 2000s compared with the 1990s (from about 11 percent per year to about 8.5 percent per year).[10] That the relationship is strengthening suggests that more economies are getting greater social surplus gains from their IT expenditures and imports. In other words, economies on average are experiencing greater changes in products, processes, and practices by using IT over the past decade than during the dot-com decade.

Second, around the trend line is quite a dispersion of experience of individual economies. Some of the dispersion could be due to greater variety of imports or IT expenditures, which accentuates social surplus gains. Some dispersion could also be due to institutional and business environment factors that affect the relationship between IT diffusion and productivity growth, as discussed in the literature. The next section will address these points further.

IT Exporters. Now consider the exporters, where IT production exceeds IT expenditure (see figure 7.4, panel b). For these economies, two forces directly influence the underlying IT prices associated with the social surplus calculation. On the one hand, the terms of trade should worsen for exporters of IT hardware, reducing social surplus. On the other hand, cost efficiencies from economies of scale in production may offset the terms-of-trade effect and increase social surplus.

In fact, the estimated trend coefficient near zero (0.0157) suggests that there is virtually no relationship between being an exporter and social surplus, which was also the case using data from the 1990s.[11] However, the observation that the trend line cuts the y-axis at around 0.76 percent indicates that an economy does gain social surplus from being a producer and exporter; it is just that there is not a strong relationship between the magnitude of production, exports, and social surplus. Therefore, the hypothesized negative relationship between social surplus and just the terms of trade is not, on average, supported by the data for exporters. As suspected, it appears that economies of scale do offset the pure terms-of-trade effect.

As was the case for importers, for exporters as well there is quite a bit of dispersion around the trend line, including some economies where a high production share of GDP appear to be associated with substantial economies-of-scale gains that outweigh terms-of-trade losses from exports (Malaysia). But for others (Indonesia), the terms-of-trade loss appears to outweigh any economies-of-scale gain, in that social surplus for Indonesia is estimated to be negative.

Finally, considering both panels a and b of figure 7.4 together suggests that many importers and exporters have similar estimated social surplus (between 0 and 0.5). Clearly net production (production less expenditure) as a proxy for international trade cannot be the whole story. The next section considers the role for variety in IT trade.

Variety and the Dispersion of Country Experience

In both panels of figure 7.4, the trend regression line shows the average social surplus and trade relationship for a particular set of economies. Those above the regression line have a greater-than-average calculated social surplus from IT production less expenditure (whether an importer or exporter), whereas those below the trend line have a less-than-average calculated social surplus from their production and expenditures on IT.

Earlier research on the roles for institutions and for labor and product market flexibility found that countries with more-rigid markets (such as the continental European economies) tended to have lower TFP growth associated with ICT; these economies lie below the regression line in figure 7.4, panel a. Countries that tended to have faster TFP growth from ICT investments lie above the regression trend line (for example, Australia, Finland, and the United States). The social surplus calculation appears to map well to the diversity of country experiences in using ICT.

For exporters (see figure 7.4, panel b), countries such as China, Ireland, Israel, the Republic of Korea, and Singapore are high-TFP countries where calculated social surplus is more than the average among IT exporters. Other exporters (such as Brazil, Mexico, the Philippines, and Thailand), while still enjoying positive social surplus, are growing less quickly than the average within their peer group of exporters. For at least some of these countries, previous research points to difficulties with the infrastructural environment, which is less supportive of domestic use of IT.

Research indicated that, in addition to institutional factors, labor and product market competition, and infrastructure, variety could be an important factor relating to social surplus. How much can variety in IT trade explain the dispersion of country experience around the trends?

Variety: Measurement and Country Experience

Variety can be measured in several ways. This work uses the Herfindahl (H) index.[12] For each country, the value of 178 varieties of IT exports and imports from the United Nations Comtrade database are allocated to five larger groups based on the OECD (2003a) categorization: other ICT, computers, components, telecommunication, and audio-visual. For example, the components category includes 62 varieties of components. The Herfindahl index for components measures whether a country's export (import) trade flows are about equally distributed among all 62 individual varieties (H close to 0) or whether one particular variety of export (import) accounts for nearly all of the trade (H close to 1).

What might the H index reveal about a country's pattern of trade? Hs close to 1 for one or more of the five categories suggest that imports (exports) of a particular IT variety account for nearly the whole value of trade in that category. Systematically high Hs in the computer and component categories may point to the country being part of the global value chain rather than having much production designed to satisfy domestic demand. Export Hs close to 1 might be associated with deleterious terms of trade, whereas import Hs close to 1 would be associated with positive terms-of-trade effects, especially if trade is concentrated in a few intermediate inputs.

Systematically low Hs in the "other ICT" and audio-visual categories may be associated with a greater variety of products that have embedded ICT (such as medical devices, control instruments, and set-top boxes). Greater variety may support innovation in business processes and workplace practices in that business consumers are more likely to find products to meet their needs and to use in order to change business processes and workplace practices.

Figure 7.5 shows Herfindahl indexes for three countries with different patterns of trade and social surplus:

- *Indonesia* is an exporter with lower-than-average social surplus (lying below the trend line) for exporters and a high concentration of trade in computer exports. A concentrated export pattern with

Figure 7.5 Variety vs. Concentration in Product Trade, Selected Countries

average of 1999 and 2006 Herfindahl indexes

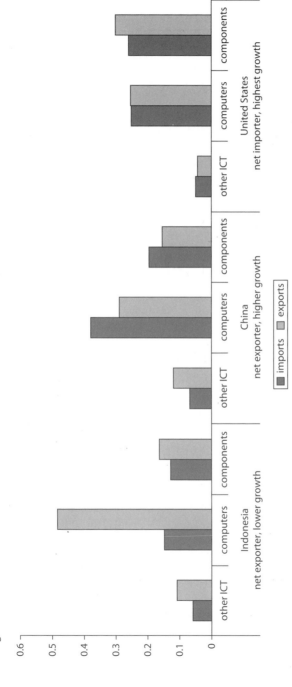

lower-than-average social surplus suggests that economies of scale in production do not outweigh the terms-of-trade effect.

- *China* is also an exporter but with higher-than-average social surplus (lying above the trend line) for exporters. Although China's computer exports are somewhat concentrated, it has an even greater concentration of component imports. Therefore, China is more likely to achieve higher-than-average social surplus by importing and getting the benefits of the terms of trade on components than by producing at economies of scale for export.
- *The United States* is an importer with higher-than-average social surplus (lying above the trend line) for importers and a moderate concentration of both exports and imports in computers and components. Notably, however, it has a lot of variety (low H) of both imports and exports of "other ICT" products. On the import side, greater variety may meet more business needs and support TFP. On the export side, greater variety is consistent with some market power in trade associated with an ability to price above cost, therefore offsetting the otherwise deteriorating terms of trade.

A systematic assessment of how variety is related to the dispersion of countries around the mean, thus a comparison with their peers, involves an econometric estimation. Table 7.3 reports on a simple regression relating the deviation of countries' experience from the average of their peer group and the Herfindahl measures of variety.

The difference between the individual country data points and the trend regression lines in the previous charts represents the country-specific deviation from the average relationship for all the countries measured. Positive (negative) residuals represent countries above (below) the social surplus average, whether importers or exporters. Are these residuals related to variety in exports and imports of the five categories of ICT trade?

This simple evidence regarding the role for variety is stronger for countries that have negative residuals—those with below-average social surplus, whether as exporters or imports. On the import side, a high import concentration (particularly of components and telecommunications) reduces the negative residuals, which is consistent with the countries benefiting from terms of trade. However, a high export

Table 7.3 Country Deviation from Trend Line and Export and Import Concentration

	a. Countries below average (negative residuals)				b. Countries above average (positive residuals)		
	Coefficients	Standard error	T-stat		Coefficients	Standard error	T-stat
Intercept	1.97848375	0.47832930	4.136238	Intercept	0.302610986	0.8974011	0.337208
Import concentration				Import concentration			
Computers	−0.06804930	0.37851722	−0.179780	Computers	0.082895698	1.4377481	0.057657
Components	−8.80131440	2.55014584	−3.451300	Components	−0.547320875	1.9650254	−0.278530
Telecoms	−1.36409183	0.71022729	−1.920640	Telecoms	−0.447041594	1.2689741	−0.352290
Audio-visual	−0.41073959	0.77676283	−0.528780	Audio-visual	0.748854012	3.1948530	0.234394
Export concentration				Export concentration			
Computers	0.23293815	0.47546042	0.489921	Computers	0.355216222	0.8466289	0.419565
Components	3.38250904	1.34515425	2.514588	Components	1.436379223	0.9121335	1.574747
Telecoms	−0.15029666	0.34159160	−0.439990	Telecoms	0.449863745	0.6655635	0.675914
Audio-visual	0.82114370	0.28915735	2.839782	Audio-visual	−1.250264029	1.0623114	−1.176930

Source: Author.

concentration (particularly components and audio-visual) increases the residuals, moving the country further away from the average social surplus. This finding suggests that the economies of scale do not outweigh terms of trade and variety. For countries with positive residuals (social surplus above average), the extent of variety in trade does not seem to be an important factor in explaining how a country differs from its peers. This may be because many of these countries already have a relatively high variety of both imports and exports.

Policy Implications

What are the implications of these findings for economic growth?

First, becoming part of the global supply chain of IT production to gain economies of scale may be a jumping-off point for higher growth. Countries that neither produce nor consume much IT are the least well-off in terms of social surplus and growth.

Second, a growth strategy that focuses on production mainly for export in the international supply chain gives up the potential gains to growth that come from importing, consuming, or producing domestically a wide variety of IT products. Therefore, for most countries, a high variety of traded IT products (both exports and imports) is associated with higher TFP and therefore higher growth. This variety of IT products, as used in the domestic economy, is associated with more-widespread diffusion of IT throughout the economy—and with higher TFP, higher GDP per capita, and growth.

Therefore, an IT-based growth strategy might start with being a part of the international supply chain to gain economy-of-scale benefits and later mature to import and produce the variety of products appropriate for domestic needs. Appropriate infrastructure and institutions—and a domestic business environment that is conducive to transformation of economic activities—enhances the likelihood that this variety of IT products yields higher growth.

Notes

1. See United Nations (2008) for general discussion of the terms-of-trade effect on GDP versus GNI. See also Feenstra et al. (2007) for a further discussion of real production versus real expenditure measures and their implications for welfare

analysis. Kohli estimates overall terms-of-trade effects for 26 countries (2004) and Canada (2006).

2. The balance of payments surplus presumably is invested and thus there is an intertemporal trade-off between the generation today and future generations.

3. See Crafts (2004) and Diewert and Morrison (1986) for mathematical details of this isomorphism, and see Morrison and Diewert (1991) for examples using Japanese and U.S. data.

4. The term "information technology" can include any combination of hardware, software, services, and communications. In specific empirical analysis, the included set can influence the results. Where it does, the text will be more explicit; otherwise the generic term IT will be used.

5. Global fragmentation of production of IT services has begun relatively recently, and has started out more concentrated (India), but promises to become more globally disbursed. See, for example, the discussions in the *Information Technology Outlook* (OECD 2008, 87) and *Information Technology Report* (UNCTAD 2007).

6. See Mann (2006, 33)—on apparent concentration of production by U.S. multinationals in low-cost locations—and Reed Electronics Research data.

7. Herein, much of the extant research includes telecommunications (C) as well as information technology (IT) products, thus ICT.

8. Assuming that the targeting of certain sectors does not lead to corruption or other inefficient activities.

9. Mann (2011) gives more details on the construction of the data and calculation of each country's social surplus. Among important points in the construction of social surplus: Calculations consider only IT hardware, not communications and not software. Communications is not addressed primarily because many countries still have publicly owned communications networks, making market forces less important in production, spending, and pricing decisions. Data on international trade in software products and associated prices are not available. Moreover, calculations in Bayoumi and Haacker (2002) show, for the time period of their study, that the main contributor to social surplus is the price and expenditure dynamic for IT hardware.

10. The calculations for net price decline for each economy incorporate domestic price changes and exchange rate changes, but the dominant feature driving the data is the IT price decline in the U.S. data.

11. Removing Malaysia from the sample changes the trend coefficient to 0.093, so it does not alter the overall observation.

12. The Herfindahl index is often used in industrial-organization investigations to assess the extent of market competition among several firms—for example, "four-firm concentration ratio." Here one can use it to assess the extent to which a country imports or exports a wide variety of detailed products or is specialized in importing or exporting just a few products. For more details on the construction of the Herfindahl indexes, see Mann (2011).

References

Bayoumi, Tamim, and Markus Haacker. 2002. "It's Not What You Make, It's How You Use IT: Measuring the Welfare Benefits of the IT Revolution across Countries." Working Paper 02/117, International Monetary Fund, Washington, DC.

Broda, Christian, Joshua Greenfield, and David E. Weinstein. 2006. "From Groundnuts to Globalization: A Structural Estimate of Trade and Growth." Working Paper 2512, National Bureau of Economic Research, Cambridge, MA.

Chun, Hyunbae, and M. Ishaq Nadiri. 2008. "Decomposing Productivity Growth in the U.S. Computer Industry." *Review of Economics and Statistics* 90 (1): 174–80.

Comtrade (United Nations Commodity Trade Statistics Database). United Nations, New York. http://comtrade.un.org/db.

Crafts, Nicholas F. R. 2004. "Social Savings as a Measure of the Contribution of a New Technology to Economic Growth." Working Paper in Large-Scale Technological Change 06/04, London School of Economics, London.

Diewert, W. Erwin, and Catherine J. Morrison. 1986. "Adjusting Output and Productivity Indexes for Changes in the Terms of Trade." *Economic Journal* 96 (383): 659–79.

Dewan, Sanjay, and Kenneth L. Kraemer. 2000. "Information Technology and Productivity: Evidence from Country-Level Data." *Management Science* 46 (4): 548–62.

Feenstra, Robert C., Alan Heston, Marcel P. Timmer, and Haiyeng Deng. 2007. "Estimating Real Production *and* Expenditures across Nations: A Proposal for Improving the Penn World Tables." Policy Research Working Paper 4166, World Bank, Washington, DC.

Feenstra, Robert, and Hiau Looi Kee. 2008. "Export Variety and Country Productivity: Estimating the Monopolistic Competition Model with Endogenous Productivity." *Journal of International Economics* 74 (2): 500–18.

Gust, Christopher, and Jaime Marquez. 2000. "Productivity Development Abroad." *Federal Reserve Bulletin* 86 (October): 665–81.

Kohli, Ulrich. 2004. "Real GDP, Real Domestic Income, and Terms-of-Trade Changes." *Journal of International Economics* 62 (1): 83–106.

———. 2006. "Real GDP, Real GDI, and Trading Gains: Canada 1981–2005." *International Productivity Monitor* 13 (Fall): 46–56.

Mann, Catherine L. 2006. *Accelerating the Globalization of America: The Role for Information Technology.* Washington, DC: Peterson Institute for International Economics.

———. 2009. "ICT, Trade, and Innovation: The Channels of Contribution." Prepared for the OECD Working Party of the Trade Committee, June 2009.

———. 2011. "Information Technology, Globalization, and Growth: Role for Scale Economies, Terms of Trade, and Variety. Working Paper 27, Department of

Economics and International Business School, Brandeis University, Waltham, Mass.

Mann, Catherine L., Sue E. Eckert, and Sarah Cleeland Knight. 2000. *Global Electronic Commerce: A Policy Primer*. Institute for International Economics: Washington, DC.

Morrison, Catherine, and Erwin Diewert. 1991. "Productivity Growth and Changes in the Terms of Trade in Japan and the United States." In *Productivity Growth in Japan and the United States*. National Bureau of Economic Research Studies in Income and Wealth Series, ed. Charles R. Hulten, 201–27. Chicago: University of Chicago Press.

Mun, Sung-Bae, and M. Ishaq Nadiri. 2002. "Information Technology Externalities: Empirical Evidence from 42 U.S. Industries." Working Paper 9272, National Bureau of Economic Research, Cambridge, MA.

OECD (Organisation for Economic Co-operation and Development). 2003a. "A Proposed Classification of ICT Goods." Paper of the Working Party on Indicators for the Information Society, DSTI/ICCP/IIS(2003)1/Rev 2, OECD, Paris.

———. 2003b. *The Source of Economic Growth in OECD Countries*. Paris: OECD.

———. 2008. *Information Technology Outlook 2008*. Paris: OECD.

Reed Electronics Research (database). RER (Reed Electronics Research), Oxon, U.K. http://www.rer.co.uk/.

Pohjola, Matti. 2001. "Information Technology and Economic Growth: A Cross-Country Analysis." In *Information Technology, Productivity, and Economic Growth: International Evidence and Implications for Economic Development*, ed. Matti Pohjola. Oxford, U.K.: Oxford University Press.

Sciadas, George, ed. 2005. *From the Digital Divide to Digital Opportunities: Measuring Infostates for Development*. Publication prepared by Orbicom (International Network of UNESCO Chairs in Communications) and ITU (International Telecommunication Union). Montreal: Claude-Yves Charron and NRC Press Canada.

Seo, Hwan-Joo, and Young Soo Lee. 2006. "Contribution of Information and Communication Technology to Total Factor Productivity and Externalities Effects." *Information Technology for Development* 12 (2): 159–73.

Shih, Eric, Kenneth L. Kraemer, and Jason Dedrick. 2007. "Research Note: Determinants of Country-Level Investment in Information Technology." *Management Science* 53 (3): 521–28.

UN (United Nations). 2008. "Price and Volume Measures." In *System of National Accounts, 2008*, 295–323. New York: European Commission, International Monetary Fund, Organisation for Economic Co-operation and Development, United Nations, and World Bank.

UNCTAD (United Nations Conference on Trade and Development). 2000–08. *World Investment Report*. New York and Geneva: UNCTAD.

———. 2007. *Information Economy Report 2007–2008*. New York and Geneva: UNCTAD.

van Ark, Bart. 2005. "Does the European Union Need to Revive Productivity Growth?" Groningen Growth and Development Centre Research Memorandum GD-75, University of Groningen, Netherlands.

van Ark, Bart, Robert Inklaar, and Robert McGuckin. 2003. "'Changing Gear'—Productivity, ICT, and Service Industries: Europe and the United States." In *The Industrial Dyanmics of the New Digital Economy*, ed. Jens Froslev Christensen and Peter Maskell, 56–100. Cheltenham, U.K.: Edward Elgar.

WITSA (World Information Technology and Services Alliance). 2000–08. "Digital Planet." Biennial report, WITSA, Selangor, Malaysia.

8

Innovation-Driven Growth: Analytical Issues and Policy Implications

Paolo Guerrieri and Pier Carlo Padoan

The Great Recession has left permanent scars on the global economy. The Organisation for Economic Co-operation and Development (OECD 2009) estimates that output in the advanced economies may have decreased by as much as 3 percent as a consequence of the recession. Although potential growth is more difficult to pin down, it has probably also been affected. The same estimates indicate that average potential growth in the OECD areas may have been cut by as much as 0.5 percent. These results are the consequence a number of factors (OECD 2009):

- In several countries, the recession has significantly increased structural unemployment (or, in some cases, the duration of unemployment). Structural unemployment can also affect potential output because a protracted separation from work implies a permanent loss of skills.
- The recession has destroyed capital stock following an increase in risk aversion, which will hold investment back. This factor, too, may result in loss of embodied knowledge and consequent negative impact on productivity.
- Total factor productivity (TFP) may have been affected as a result, for example, of the closure of several companies and the loss of their stock of knowledge, both tangible and intangible.

Return to Growth Requires Innovation

Once the global economy has completed its recovery from the Global Recession, it will not return to business as usual. Not only will potential output levels be lower but the economy's composition is also bound to change because a number of companies will have been thrown out of business. Indeed, history shows that after deep recessions (especially those associated with severe banking crises), growth is bound to be weak or even to stagnate for a considerable time (Reinhart and Reinhart 2010).

Taking potential output back to precrisis levels—and even more important, boosting the rate of output growth—will require not just policy support of household consumption and business investment but also reallocation of resources toward new products and sectors.

To put it differently, to leave behind the consequences of the Great Recession, the global economy will have to pursue new sources of growth. Almost by definition, therefore, innovation must be a key component of the return to growth. Of course, this is not new. What *is* new, at least in part, is the way we look at innovation.

Jones and Romer (2009) recently restated the argument that growth is fundamentally driven by ideas and that ideas grow with the number of personal interactions. In a nutshell, as populations grow, ideas grow and, with them, output grows. This fascinating concept, which needs to be better explored and developed, could be restated as follows: innovation, the process through which ideas generate growth, is increasingly becoming the main driver of growth. However, innovation itself is changing—and in a way that could make the link between ideas and growth even stronger. So to understand how ideas generate growth, one must understand how the new process of innovation is developing.

Chapter Overview and Structure

Innovation Is Changing discusses new features of the innovation process such as open innovation, global innovation chains, and the role of technology platforms such as the Internet and how all these features interact in a general purpose technology (GPT) framework.

The European Innovation and Productivity Slowdown explains that these new features are particularly relevant to the slowdown of European growth and productivity over the past two decades. In particular, the new-economy story linked with information and communication technology (ICT) is useful to assess European trends.

Challenges for Modeling addresses this question: as innovation changes, how and to what extent does innovation modeling need to be updated, in addition to how does one relate it to economic growth? Moving in this direction implies moving away from the traditional, growth accounting, linear relationship toward a systemic approach to modeling innovation. Some initial examples show how this can be done by suggesting how knowledge globalization can be considered, based on the recognition that there are multiple and interacting channels of innovation diffusion.

A Dynamic Structural Model of Innovation and Growth briefly describes the main features of a structural growth model that moves toward a systemic approach by including elements of the new paradigm of innovation. It also offers examples of how to endogenize the role of ICT in the economic system.

Policy Simulations Exercises shows how this structural model of endogenous growth, innovation, and business services can simulate the impact of several policy interventions on economic system performance and economic growth, particularly in European countries.

Concluding Remarks summarizes the chapter's primary points and their implications for future innovation policy.

Innovation Is Changing

No longer is innovation simply a linear progression from scientific research to discovery and thereafter to technological improvements, finished products, and those products' diffusion across society. Today, innovation is a much broader phenomenon comprising more complex and interactive processes (OECD 2008). Ultimately such processes underlie the relationship between ideas and people. Innovation—the production and application of ideas—prospers with the amount of personal interactions. This process of interaction, in turn, is enhanced by the following elements (OECD 2008):

- *Increasingly open collaboration* alongside competition among innovative actors
- *A new geography of innovation* where global dimensions and local links interact, often in complex ways, to determine innovation-based

comparative advantage—or, in other words, where the geographical extension of markets also extends global-local interaction

- *Intangible assets* that both produce and are facilitated by interactions, requiring a closer look at nontechnological innovation and a look beyond research and development (R&D) because investment in intangibles and the role of services are rising
- *Technological platforms such as ICT*, which are becoming as important as, or even more important than, framework conditions in fostering innovation by supporting networks and interactions.

Innovation Is Increasingly Open

Confronted with mounting global competition and rising R&D costs, companies are increasingly collaborating with external partners—whether suppliers, customers, or universities—to stay abreast of developments, expand their markets, tap into a larger base of ideas and technology, and get new products or services to market before their competitors (OECD 2008).

In almost all cases, this more-open approach to innovation does not come for free but rather entails entering into partnerships or exchanges that can imply the (often significant) payment of license fees between companies for intellectual property.

Larger firms innovate more openly than smaller firms. Innovation survey data indicate that large companies are four times more likely than small and medium-size enterprises to collaborate on innovation.

The degree of openness in innovation also differs across firms and industries, depending on factors such as the importance of the technology, the strategy of the firm, the characteristics of the industry, and so on. Collaboration on innovation is important in manufacturing as well as in services. Industries such as chemicals, pharmaceuticals, and ICT typically show high levels of open innovation. Companies traditionally seek to retain their core capabilities and determine what to outsource or with whom to collaborate. Their core competencies (in technology and markets) are developed internally, but open innovation may be a faster, less risky alternative to in-house development when the objective is to diversify (in terms of technology or markets).

As the practice of open innovation expands and new forms of knowledge sharing and exchange between firms, individuals, and institutions occur, "knowledge markets" are emerging. Using various mechanisms and platforms, buyers and sellers can pool trade data, information, contacts, and know-how. Intellectual property (IP) exchanges and patent pools, consortia, networking, matching or brokering services, clearinghouses, knowledge warehouses, and auctions are all alternative ways of managing and deriving value from intellectual assets.

Innovation Is Going Global

Innovation is going global, including in services. It relies on new global innovation chains, but innovation takes place in localities. Indeed, geographical proximity matters in global networks as well as in collaboration because companies seem to prefer innovation partners that are nearby. So a challenge is to understand better the interactions between the global and local dimensions (OECD 2008).

Open innovation interacts with global innovation. The rising cost and risk of innovation and the growing trend toward open models of innovation have fueled a decades-long trend toward the globalization of innovation. Multinational enterprises (MNEs), in particular, have increasingly shifted R&D activities across borders within their global value chains and relied on cross-border partners for new products, processes, and access to markets and skilled human capital. Although the networks may be global, the nodes of innovation—clusters of expertise—continue to be local but are increasingly interconnected, thanks to MNEs and new networking tools such as ICTs. One important implication is that the channels of knowledge transmission are several and complex. They are also often complementary because they involve trade, investment, services, and skills as well as intangible knowledge. They all contribute to progress toward global knowledge markets.

Intangibles and Services Matter

The role of business services in innovation-driven growth is a novel feature. Business services, including communications, financial services, and insurance—both domestically produced and imported— grow with output and with technology, reflecting the fact that the share of "advanced" services in the economy increases with technology accumulation (Guerrieri and Padoan 2007). Services act as drivers and multipliers of innovation-driven growth. The literature has so far devoted little attention to the tertiary, or service, sector as a driver of technology accumulation, while empirical analyses have focused almost entirely on the interaction between technology accumulation and growth of the manufacturing sector.

One must also consider the role of manufacturing sector composition in producing and trading business services (Milgrom and Roberts 1990). This role can be interpreted both as the direct stimulus from a higher level of intermediate demand and as the result of knowledge flows associated with forward links or spillovers. Moreover, with globalization, technological change leads to a splintering process by which services (in particular, business services) spring from the increased technical and social division of labor within production—in turn, engendering a strong interdependence between manufacturing and service activities. Therefore, service-driven globalization of innovation is also important.

The rising importance of services calls into question how we observe and measure innovation advances. We usually consider patent citations to be a direct measure of innovation output. However, traditional technological variables, such as R&D expenditures and patents, do not entirely capture innovation in business services. In fact, although manufacturing sectors spend more on R&D and generate more patents than service sectors do, if technological innovation is understood as affecting marketing, training, and other activities, many services are more technology-intensive than generally considered. At the same time, the diffusion of knowledge-intensive service industries is deeply affected by the parallel diffusion and implementation of the new ICT systems.

GPT, ICT, and the Green Economy

Technological platforms such as ICT, as well as the green economy, are becoming just as important as, if not even more important than, framework conditions in fostering innovation. The history of innovation can be narrated also as the history of GPTs (general purpose technologies such as electricity, the steam engine, or the Internet) and innovation platforms that sometimes require the interaction of several technologies (Bresnahan and Trajtenberg 1995).

The Internet is the great facilitator of our times, a GPT that has allowed the development of a number of technology platforms. The data show the effects, outlining three features on which the Internet has been established:

- *Convergence.* The rapid decline in price of computing and communications has both contributed to and caused a shift toward the Internet—the global platform to deliver voice, video, and data services.
- *Creativity.* Over a short period, the Internet and its ability to network ICT has spurred an outpouring of creativity that has turned businesses upside down and driven economic growth (Bresnahan, Brynjolfsson, and Hitt 2002).
- *Confidence.* The Internet requires a minimum set of agreed-on regulations for protection from IP piracy and to help ensure profitable investment.

Networked innovation processes, underpinned by the spread of broadband Internet connections, enable much larger participation in the innovation process, opening it beyond the realm of corporate R&D laboratories to include users, suppliers, and consumers. So the Internet and open and global innovation go closely together. Tapping into this source of ideas offers a potentially important new factor that supports and boosts innovation while representing an important contribution to demand-side policies for innovation (Lipsey, Carlaw, and Bekar 2006).

The intangible, information-based nature of services gives the generation and use of ICTs a central role in innovation activities and performance that patents cannot entirely capture (Hempell, van der Wiel, and van Leeuwen 2004). The role of ICTs as enabling technologies is also at the basis of the reverse product cycle model to describe the dynamics of the innovation process in services. In this view, during the first stages of the reverse product cycle, services use ICT to enhance back-office efficiency. Subsequent learning leads to process and product innovations. Finally, the industrial sector begins to use information technologies as they increase information-intensive activities. ICTs also allow for the increased transportability of service activities by making it possible for services to be produced in one place and consumed simultaneously in another. Last but not least, nontechnological innovation is growing, thanks to ICT, but it is also reflecting its interaction and complementarity with technological innovation through the key role of organizational change in the implementation of ICTs (Arvanitis 2004; Bayo-Moriones and Lera-López 2007).

The European Innovation and Productivity Slowdown

The changes in innovations described above are closely related to Europe's main problem today: the longer-term weakening of European growth.

After World War II, European economies enjoyed a three-decade period of rapid catch-up with the United States in terms of GDP per capita that confirmed the conventional "convergence" view (predicting that less-advanced economies grow faster than more-advanced ones). By the early 1990s, however, this catch-up process paused before being inverted during the second part of the 1990s and the first part of the 2000s, when output per head and per working hour grew more slowly in Europe than in the United States (EC 2010). Annual average growth in GDP per head (the single best measure of economic performance) reached 2.3 percent in the United States in 1996–2005, compared with 1.8 percent in the Euro Area.

The persistently high GDP-per-head differential with the United States mainly reflects fewer hours worked in Europe. In the Euro Area, fewer people work, and the employed work far fewer average hours. However, the crucial factor that has weakened European GDP growth per head is slower growth in labor productivity (GDP per hour worked)—the single most important driver of long-term potential output and living standards. As shown in figure 8.1, despite a slight catching-up in employment and hours worked, the EU still has a substantial income gap with the United States, two-thirds of which is explained by lagging productivity (EC 2010).

Particularly worrisome for the Euro Area countries was the trend in TFP growth (growth that is not accounted for by increases in labor and capital inputs). Data show that TFP growth has steadily declined in the Euro Area since the 1970s, with TFP growth halved in 1995–2005 compared with the 1980s and early 1990s. In the United States, by contrast, TFP growth has accelerated since 1995 to nearly double the Euro Area

Figure 8.1 Real Income Sources in Europe and Japan Compared with the United States, 2007

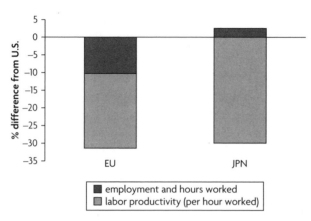

Source: EC 2010.
Note: EU = European Union. JPN = Japan.

rate. These trends suggest that the Euro Area growth slowdown was not just a conjunctural phenomenon but also closely related to its poor long-term performance (EC 2010).

Technology and Market Rigidities

Of course, many factors have contributed to these outcomes, and there is considerable uncertainty about the root causes of Europe's relatively poor performance. A common view is that Europe has become uncompetitive because of its rigidities (highly inflexible labor markets, barriers to free competition, and taxes). There is no doubt that despite recent reforms in key areas—especially the labor market and the red tape that affects business—the Euro Area countries remain far more regulated than the United States. There is a need for labor market reforms aimed at increasing the flexibility that would allow real wages to better reflect productivity. Increasing employment rates among women and youth can add significantly to the labor force and strengthen potential output. Although it is unclear to what extent it accounts for the performance gap, the lack of structural reforms appears to explain part of the story (EC 2007).

Another factor contributing to the slowdown in European productivity growth is what one could call the technological explanation. More specifically, one should emphasize the strong impact on productivity from innovation and innovation-related investment, notably in intangible assets. OECD data show that in the decade 1996–2006, more than two-thirds of productivity growth came from these sources in advanced economies (OECD 2008). In particular, the new-economy story linked with the ICT diffusion comes nearest to explaining European trends, although many important issues remain unclear, including the relationship between ICT and the overall policy framework.

Empirical investigations (based on a standard cross-section growth framework) of the impact of ICT on growth yielded results that appear to strongly support the technological story (see, for instance, Inklaar, O'Mahony, and Timmer 2005). The evidence does point to lower ICT growth and shares of ICT in total investment and GDP since 1995 in key European economies than in the United States. Therefore, the slowdown of productivity growth in Europe since 1995 is seen to be the result of the delayed introduction of ICT or its inefficient use.[1] As shown in various growth accounting studies, the growth contribution from ICT diffusion in Europe, while positive, has not been enough to counteract the overall tendency for productivity growth to decline at the same time it accelerated in the United States (Inklaar, O'Mahony, and Timmer 2005).

Innovation and Structural Factors

Studies have confirmed that, in addition to the role of ICT-producing sectors, strong productivity growth in many U.S. service industries (for example, retail distribution, transport, construction, and financial and professional services) explains most or all of the difference between U.S. and European productivity growth since 1995 (van Ark, O'Mahony, and Timmer 2008). Productivity in such industries (which also make up a large share of U.S. output) has boomed in the United States but has stayed roughly constant or grown very slowly in Euro Area countries because European barriers to entry and corporatist protections result in massive inefficiencies (van Ark, Inklaar, and McGuckin 2003).

That story would be the most consistent with the view that emphasizes Europe's general structural rigidities, reinforcing the argument for structural reform of services. A recent European Commission report "A New Strategy for the Single Market," offers the complete list of service regulatory changes that would cut the chains holding down Europe's productivity and growth (Monti 2010). Service sector liberalization enhances the impact of innovation and innovation diffusion, hence amplifying productivity growth.

Europe's relatively low take-up and inefficient use of ICT technologies was also the result of these service, product, and labor market rigidities. A series of OECD studies sees delayed ICT diffusion as perhaps the most important manifestation of the deficiencies of European institutions (OECD 2008). The European Commission takes a similar view (EC 2010).

Therefore, in the case of Europe, returning potential output to precrisis levels and, even more importantly, boosting the rate of output growth requires enhanced interaction of innovation and structural policies.

Challenges for Modeling

Modeling the impact of innovation on growth, productivity, and employment performance must take into account (a) the interaction between technological and organizational changes, and (b) the crucial role of institutions in favoring or hampering ICT diffusion across countries. The literature on technological paradigms (Freeman and Perez 1988; Freeman and Soete 1987; Perez 1988) and the neoclassical literature on ICTs agree that major innovations such as ICT generate imbalances in the system and that it takes time to exploit their full potential. Moreover, such innovations also involve organizational and social changes if a new techno-economic paradigm is to be established.

The Traditional Model

As innovation is changing, we must ask how and to what extent we must update the way we model innovation and relate it to economic growth. At the aggregate level, innovation is traditionally modeled through the standard growth accounting model (Barro and Sala-i-Martin 1995):

$$Y = AKH \text{ (in labor units)}, \qquad (8.1)$$

Where Y is output; K is physical capital; H is human capital; and A is the residual (TFP).

In this framework, the relationship between innovation and growth is linear and follows one causation pattern. Inputs such as R&D spending (both private and public) and investment in human capital can lead to more innovation outputs (possibly measured by patents) and hence to TFP growth (A).

This is a useful first approximation tool. Aghion and Howitt (2006) recently expanded the framework in a number of ways, as follows:

> New growth theory has linked productivity growth to innovation . . . in turn motivated by the prospect of above normal returns that successful innovators can realise. The theory suggests that innovation, and therefore productivity growth, should be . . . fostered by:
>
> • better protection of intellectual property rights to allow successful innovators to benefit from their endeavour
> • financial development, as tight credit constraints will limit entrepreneurs' ability to finance new innovative projects
> • better education, as this will improve the ability to innovate and/or imitate leading edge technologies
> • macroeconomic stability, which allows for a lower, risk-adjusted interest rate that will enable entrepreneurs to invest more in growth-enhancing projects.

It is straightforward to extend the traditional model to take some aspects of new growth theory into account, including some of the points raised earlier.

This linear model can be augmented as follows:

$$Y = AKHTIW, \tag{8.2}$$

where Y is output; K is physical capital; H is human capital; T is technology, or measurable knowledge; I is ICT investment; W is a set of global (international) factors; and A is the residual, standing in for nonmeasurable knowledge.

A New Modeling Strategy

The new features of innovation mentioned above call for further steps. In particular, they require a systematic approach to innovation in which the structure of the system and the links among the variables need to be considered explicitly to better account for the process of idea production, which is taken as the major source of growth. Needless to say, this is a challenging task.

A starting point is this: what can be modeled in a way that is amenable to empirical testing? Given the nature of the idea production process, the modeling strategy should take into account as much interaction as possible among the different factors involved in such a process. This strategy, in turn, suggests a system approach to modeling innovation.

To move from a single equation to a system representation, the first step, again, is the standard growth accounting relationship (in its augmented version, as shown in equation [8.2] above):

$$Y = AKHTIW.$$

The second step is to endogenize (in part) the variables entering the growth equation to suggest how, and to what extent, the features of the new innovation paradigm recalled above can be related to the growth accounting framework:

$$K = K(H, I, W, F, C, \ldots), \tag{8.3}$$

Where physical capital K depends on human capital H; ICT investment I (H and I may be complementary given that ICT is a GPT); global relations W, capturing factors related to global value chains; "framework conditions" F, including macroeconomic policy and financial market conditions; and social capital C, largely related to the role of social networks as facilitators of the production and diffusion of knowledge (which partly captures open innovation effects because social capital facilitates collaboration among innovators).

Investment in human capital depends on the following: physical capital (as a proxy of business requirements for skills, making the two variables, in principle, complements rather than substitutes); ICT investment (again as a complement); elements related to global factors, including international skill migration; the business-university relationship U; and investment in education E:

$$H = H(K, I, W, U, E, \ldots). \tag{8.4}$$

Intangibles are partly captured by human capital (skills) and partly by services S. Services (both domestic and imported business services) grow with output and with technology, reflecting the idea that they represent an important intermediate input and that the share of "advanced" services in the economy increases with technology accumulation. Services are also a function of the expansion in ICT investment I and of the structure of the economy, according to how the manufacturing sector is oriented toward the use of services in production. This relationship can be proxied by the composition of human and physical capital. Finally, regulation R, if excessively tight, has a negative impact on the production of services, both domestic and imported:

$$S = S(Y, T, I, H, K, R). \tag{8.5}$$

Measurable knowledge T (identified by patents) depends on human capital, investment in R&D (RD), intellectual property protection (IP), global knowledge chains and outsourcing, ICT investment, university-business links, framework conditions, and nonmeasurable knowledge A. This "sketchy" relationship would also *partly* capture open innovation effects through the impact of social capital C for reasons explained above. Through output Y and physical capital K, we can *partly* take into account user-driven innovation to the extent that this reflects consumer needs and business needs:

$$T = T(H, RD, IP, W, I, U, F, A, ... Y, K, C). \tag{8.6}$$

Factors in ICT Adoption and Diffusion

One now moves to adoption and diffusion of ICT. As mentioned, ICT is a GPT and, as such, it cannot be modeled simply by considering it an additional factor of production. A fully satisfactory way of modeling GPT- and ICT-driven growth requires an endogenous determination of ICT investment.

Suggestions on how to endogenize ICT investment can be derived from the literature on the digital divide. There is widespread agreement that the digital divide is mostly due to the differences in countries' economic wealth. Another widely considered factor is human capital (Trinh, Gibson, and Oxley 2005). The argument is that skilled workers are more capable of learning how to use new technologies and more flexible with respect to their job assignments. Because the adoption of ICT often requires a reorganization of the firm—or nontechnological innovation—a firm with a high share of skilled workers can implement information technologies more easily.

The impact of regulation on ICT adoption has also received much attention in the literature. In general, all kinds of restrictions, regulations, or constraints that limit the decisions of an economic agent drive the economy to a suboptimal equilibrium (Conway, Janod, and Nicoletti 2005; Conway and Nicoletti 2006).

Demographic factors such as the age structure of the population and the size of the urban population have also been taken into account. The idea is that ICT has larger diffusion among younger people and that the urban population tends to adopt more ICT (Internet and computer) because of network economies. Another variable that has been extensively investigated is the degree of openness. The justification is that technological spillovers from and toward other countries could be an important factor in supporting the adoption of ICT. Finally, because some sectors are more ICT-intensive than others, the possibility that economies' sectoral composition determines different rates of investment in ICT has also been investigated. A large service sector as a share of GDP is usually associated with a high rate of ICT adoption, while a large agriculture sector as a share of GDP is associated with low rates of ICT adoption.

In conclusion, the factors determining ICT diffusion include complementarity with physical and human capital; R&D investment; consumer behavior as captured by output Y; measured and unmeasured knowledge (T, A); and the regulatory stance R. The role of social capital in the development of cultural networks associated with Internet use could be important to capturing *part* of open and user-driven innovation effects:

$$I = I \ (H, K, T, RD, Y, R, C, A, \dots). \tag{8.7}$$

Modeling a Global Knowledge Pool

As argued earlier, a country's capacity to innovate increasingly depends on the capacity to interact and link with the global system, both in terms of attracting foreign activities and in terms of projecting activities abroad. What we are trying to model here is the structure of a global knowledge pool, itself evolving over time.

The model requires taking into account several elements of the global innovation chain: trade, investment, human capital, labor flows, and intangible assets. Also, although countries tend to be seen as more or less integrated in the global innovation chains, we are really looking at networks of *companies*, big and small. So it is a tough call to identify what to measure and what determines it.

Interestingly, both local and global variables matter: factor endowments such as physical human capital; the Internet; knowledge (both measurable and nonmeasurable); the policy environment; framework conditions; intellectual property; the regulatory framework; and, at the aggregate level, the distance to the technology frontier (following Aghion and Howitt 1998, 2006). The latter could be seen as a dynamic factor such as distance (Dist) that evolves over time under the effect of several variables (Guerrieri, Maggi, and Padoan 2009):

$$W = W(K, H, I, ... T, A, ... F, R, IP,... Dist). \qquad (8.8)$$

Finally, nonmeasurable knowledge depends on factor endowment and investment in knowledge, including human and physical capital; R&D; the Internet; and measurable knowledge. Institutional networks are represented by international links; business-university links; social capital; policy conditions (including framework conditions, regulation, and IP); and consumer behavior as captured by output:

$$A = A (T, I, H, K, RD, ... W, U, C, ... F, R, IP, ... Y). \qquad (8.9)$$

Toward an Innovation Ecosystem Model

The set of relationships shown in equations (8.2)–(8.9) is, at best, a sketchy "system." To move toward an innovation ecosystem, one would have to introduce at least two more elements:

- *Dynamics.* One can think of a model in which variables adjust to a (partial) equilibrium value at different speeds. For example, ICT investment would, most likely, move faster than physical capital K. So different speeds would generate different overall system dynamics with complex outcomes in terms of convergence, divergence, or multiple equilibria (Krugman 2009).
- *Evolution.* Relationships among variables, reflecting relationships among actors and institutions, evolve over time. Some get stronger, others get weaker—further complicating the picture.

The next challenge: how can one move from a theoretical framework (still in implicit form) to a system amenable to empirical analysis?

A Dynamic Structural Model of Innovation and Growth

One way forward is through a dynamic system approach that can be modeled and estimated rigorously to capture the systemic nature of innovation. What follows briefly describes the main features of a model that moves in the direction sketched above (for full details, see Guerrieri 2009; Guerrieri, Maggi, and Padoan 2009; Guerrieri and Padoan 2007).

This model develops the system approach, including some elements of the new paradigm of innovation discussed above: international dimensions, services, and ICT. It is specified and estimated as a set of continuous-time dynamic equations, shown in table 8.1, where *Dlog* stands for the derivative with respect to time; hence, the variables in the left column represent the rate of change of the endogenous variables.

Output growth Y is a function of (exogenous) labor L; capital K accumulation; endogenous accumulation of technology (measurable knowledge) T; and business services (both domestic Sh and imported Sm).

As previously mentioned, business services, including communication, financial services, and insurance—both domestically produced and imported—grow with output and technology and depend on the structure of the economy (STR).

The intangible, information-based nature of services gives the generation and use of ICT a central role in innovation activities and performance. Services and ICT interact. ICT also allows for the increased

Table 8.1 Dynamic Model Equations

Output	$Dlog Y = f1(T, Sh, Sm, K, L)$	(8.10)
Domestic services	$Dlog Sh = f2(Y, T, STR, I, R)$	(8.11)
Imported services	$Dlog Sm = f3(Y, T, STR, I, R)$	(8.12)
Technology	$Dlog T = f4(HK, HKR, Sh, Sm, Y, Dist)$	(8.13)

Source: Authors.

Note: Dlog = derivative with respect to time. Y = consumer behavior as captured by output. Sh = domestic business services. Sm = imported business services. T = technology. K = physical capital. L = labor. STR = structure of the economy. I = information and communications technology. R = regulation. HK = domestic human capital. HKR = foreign human capital. Dist = distance.

transportability of service activities by making it possible for services to be produced in one place and consumed in another. Hence, provision of services is independent from proximity to the final user.

This model formulation recognizes the role of a global knowledge pool—implying that domestic technology grows with output; services; domestic human capital (HK); and, through diffusion, foreign technology. However, the amount of foreign-produced technology that can be used domestically is limited by distance (Dist) and absorption capacity in the receiving country proxied by human capital in such a country (HKR).

The impact of distance is allowed to vary over time to the extent that technological progress reduces the cost of technology diffusion. Technological accumulation (specified by patents accumulation) also depends on imports of services—another channel of knowledge diffusion.

Regulation (R) affects the production and import of services, hence growth, in two ways: (a) domestic regulation intensity depresses the production of services and (b) uniform (and low) levels of regulation across countries (a level playing field) favor the production and import of services.[2]

In modeling the international transmission of technology, we assume that technology accumulation, as measured by patents (Pat), is equal to domestic and (part of) foreign technology that flows from other countries, as shown in the following three-country example:

$$Tt1 = Tt{-}11 + Pat11 + Pat21 + Pat31, \tag{8.14}$$
$$Tt2 = Tt{-}12 + Pat12 + Pat22 + Pat32, \tag{8.15}$$
$$Tt3 = Tt{-}13 + Pat13 + Pat23 + Pat33, \tag{8.16}$$
$$Dlog\text{Pat ij} = f5(\text{HK, HKR, Sh, Sm, Y, Dist}). \tag{8.17}$$

The model can be expanded by endogenizing ICT investment. An augmented version of the model (Guerrieri 2009; Guerrieri and Padoan 2007) introduces an equation for ICT investment:

$$\Delta log\,\text{ICT}_{it} = \delta\alpha - \delta log\,\text{ICT}_{it\text{-}1} + \delta\beta Z_{it} + \eta_i + \varepsilon_{it}, \tag{8.18}$$

where the vector of variable Z characterizing the steady-state equilibrium includes the variables services, GERD (government expenditure on R&D), researchers, and regulation.

The assumption is that human capital and investments in R&D increase ICT investments, while regulation tends to depress them. Furthermore, the structure of the economy is a relevant factor to understand the different rate of investment in ICT; in particular, countries in which the service sector constitutes a larger share of GDP usually display higher ICT investment. Another finding is that regulation can prevent or discourage investment in IT equipment.

Policy Simulations

This model enables simulation of the impact of several policy interventions on a set of endogenous variables such as services, innovation, and economic growth. The analysis is carried out on a panel of 10 countries (Austria, Denmark, Finland, Germany, Italy, Japan, the Netherlands, Sweden, the United Kingdom, and the United States) over the period 1992–2005.[3]

Other studies have looked at similar issues. The European Commission (EC 2007) investigated the causes of the lower performance of European countries with respect to the United States in terms of TFP growth and identified three policy areas that can contribute to increases in European growth and jobs: building knowledge, strengthening competition, and enhancing flexibility. In particular, using the QUEST model, such studies have shown that

- actions to support R&D investment could significantly raise economic and productivity growth in Europe;
- competition is crucial for both the level and growth rate of productivity; and
- enhanced flexibility is needed to smoothly adjust production structures toward further specialization and diversification into new areas of relative comparative advantage.

Previous studies had also shown the importance of decreasing regulation for European Union (EU) growth (Bayoumi, Laxton, and Pesenti 2004). The gains would amount to as much as a 7 percent increase in GDP and a 3 percent productivity increase. Simulations by the European Commission (2003) have shown that deregulation alone (that is, bringing the level of EU product market regulation down to the U.S. level) would not be enough but should be accompanied by an increase in R&D, education, and ICT spending to close the European gap with the United States in per capita GDP. The combination of these measures could increase the potential growth rate by 0.5–0.75 percent per year over 5 to 10 years.

Finally, Guerrieri et al. (2005) have shown that, in the long run, growth in Europe is best supported through stronger technology accumulation, itself supported by larger availability of human capital. In the medium term, a better regulatory environment, more ICT investment, and a deeper integration can provide a stronger boost to growth.

The results of the policy simulations just reviewed are all based on models with exogenous ICT expenditure. However, firms' incentives to adopt new technologies depend on the business environment in which they operate, the level of human capital and complementary R&D expenditure, and the structure of the economy (for example, its sectoral composition). The model presented here is enriched with an endogenous representation of ICT to simulate the impact of changes in regulation and human capital on ICT investment, services (domestic and imported), and technological innovation and growth in Europe.

The methodology for the simulations is reported in Guerrieri and Padoan (2007) and Guerrieri (2009). Given the historical initial values of the variables (the last available value for all the variables) and the parameter estimates, the authors run a baseline scenario to construct various scenarios, and compare each of these scenarios with the baseline.

Policy Scenarios

The different scenarios address the following questions:

1. *What happens if the level of regulation decreases by 20 percent in all European countries?* The simulation decreases by 20 percent the equilibrium starting values of regulation (R).
2. *What happens if there is a deeper integration of services (harmonization of regulations) in EU countries?* The simulation decreases the value of R by 20 percent (as in scenario 1) in any country up to the point where the value of REG in Europe is 80 percent of the original value.[4]

3. *What happens if human capital increases in all European countries?* The simulation increases by 5 percent the equilibrium starting values of human capital.
4. *What happens if EU countries implement structural changes?* To simulate structural change (that is, a better business environment), the parameters are changed to increase the impact of (a) ICT on service and (b) service on both ICT and technology.
5. *What happens if the EU countries delay reforms?* To assess this effect, the simulation reduces the level of regulation by 20 percent, assuming that this deregulation takes 10 years to occur.
6. *In a composite scenario (combining scenarios 1 and 3), what is the impact of a simultaneous decrease in regulation and increase in human capital?*

Figures 8.2–8.7 report the results of the policy simulations on the endogenous variables of our model. Simulation results confirm that deeper European integration in the market for services does significantly contribute to growth and that services are a powerful driver of growth, as shown in figure 8.2. Services and, hence, growth are also boosted as the impact of regulation is eliminated.

The overall effect on GDP of the increase in human capital (operating through its positive impact on technology) is larger than the effect of the change in regulation (operating through its positive impact on services), as figure 8.3 illustrates.

Changes in both regulation and human capital affect output growth indirectly through their impact, respectively, on services (domestic and imported) and on technology. Both policy measures have a negligible impact at the beginning of the simulation period (for the first five years), but the impact increases over time, as figures 8.2 and 8.3 illustrate.

Another interesting result is that although the decrease in regulation and the harmonization of regulation across Europe have a similar impact (recall that the magnitude of the change in regulation is the same in the two scenarios), harmonization outperforms deregulation in its impact on services (and, in particular, on imported services). Meanwhile, deregulation is more effective than harmonization in its impact on technology (see figure 8.2, panel d). On the other hand,

Figure 8.2 Effects of Deregulation and Harmonization on Selected Variables

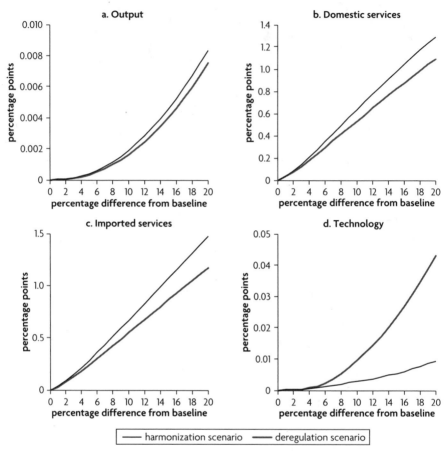

Source: Authors.

Note: Each line represents the percentage difference from the baseline scenario. If y_{base} is the sum of the output produced in all EU countries in the baseline scenario, and y_B is the sum of the output produced in all EU countries under scenario 2 (regulatory harmonization), then the gray line (deregulation) is $100 \times (y_B - y_{base}) / y_{base}$. The same applies to all variables.

harmonized regulation across countries brings more benefits for economic growth than does deregulation. For the same decrease in regulatory barriers, the overall effect on output is higher with harmonization across countries. This result is consistent with the idea that there are important benefits for harmonization, especially in the European single market for the production and trade of services—an area that remains subject to different national regulation and degrees of protection across Europe and advanced countries.

Figure 8.3 Effect of a 5 Percent Increase in Human Capital on Selected Variables

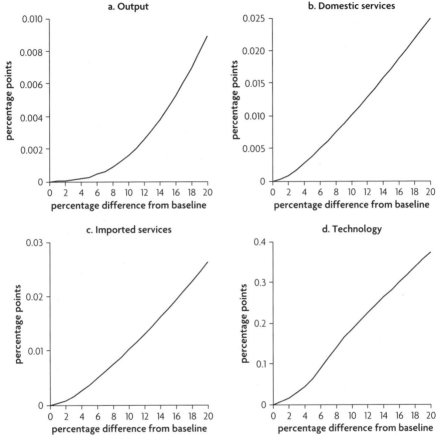

Source: Authors.

Technology accumulation is enhanced especially by human capital accumulation, as figure 8.3 shows. The stock of technology is higher when the stock of human capital increases in both sending and receiving countries. Furthermore, higher investment in education (which can be considered a key public policy strategy) boosts human capital accumulation, hence ICT, and hence output growth. This last result sends an important message about the interaction between technology accumulation and growth. The ultimate driver of growth is technology accumulation, and the latter is strongly supported by human capital accumulation. However, in such a mechanism, a complex transmission mechanism is involved. This confirms the need for a systemic approach to understand the relationship between innovation and growth.

If ICT is endogenous, policy can affect ICT only indirectly, albeit in a number of ways. Higher ICT investment, which can be boosted by a number of policy strategies (such as more investment in human capital, more investment in R&D, and an appropriate regulatory framework), provides powerful additional stimuli to growth, as shown in figure 8.4.

The magnitude of changes in the regulation scenario is much higher than the impact of the increase in ICT investment. In other words, decreased and harmonized regulation across Europe, when combined,

Figure 8.4 Comparative Effects of Policy Scenarios on Output

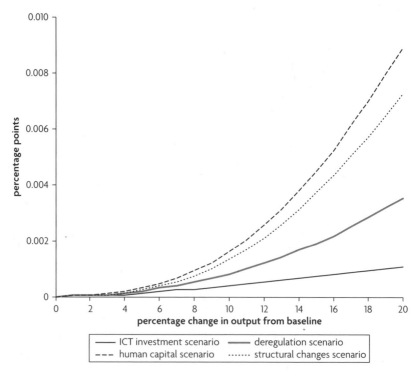

Source: Authors.
Note: Each line represents the percentage difference from the baseline scenario. If y_{base} is the sum of the output produced in all EU countries in the baseline scenario, and y_B is the sum of the output produced in all EU countries under the scenario 2 (regulatory harmonization), then the black line is: $100 \times (y_B - y_{base}) / y_{base}$. The same applies to all scenarios.

have a much greater impact on ICT adoption (or use) than increased ICT investment does. Both decreasing regulation and homogenizing *regulation* across Europe lead to about a 10 percent increase in ICT adoption, while increasing *investment* leads to an increase in ICT of about 2 percent.

A key objective of any growth agenda is to increase ICT investment. In this model, the result can be better reached only through deep changes in the general environment in which European firms operate, as shown in figure 8.5.

In particular, reforming the economic structure (the share of advanced services) positively affects ICT investment as well as services, technology, and GDP (as figure 8.5 illustrates). This is not surprising because ICTs are technologies that affect almost all industries of the economy and have important repercussions on firms' organization. Therefore, their virtuous interaction with the "facilitating factors" is crucial not only for ICTs to exert their positive impact on the economy but also for creating the incentives for firms to restructure and reorganize themselves.

Furthermore, the costs of delays in implementing policy reforms mount quickly. In particular, by comparing reforms implemented now with reforms of similar size that are implemented over a longer period, figure 8.6 shows that delay exacts substantial costs in terms of lower growth, less development of the service sector, and less technology accumulation.

Finally, the policy simulations offer another relevant message for innovation and growth policy: economies cannot rely on a single instrument to boost innovation and, through it, productivity and growth. Our simulation results, for instance, show that output growth can be significantly increased if the availability of business services and the accumulation of knowledge are enhanced. Such results can be obtained by improving the regulatory environment, deepening service market integration, and increasing and improving human capital accumulation.

It is also interesting to observe that, when the two measures (deregulation and human capital increase) are taken simultaneously, their joint impact is larger than the sum of the two effects taken separately. The simultaneous decrease in regulation and increase in human capital

Figure 8.5 Impact of Structural Changes on Selected Variables

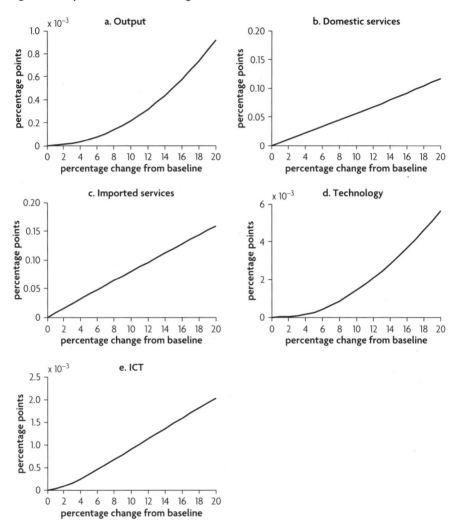

Source: Authors.
Note: The simulation of structural change shows the increased impact of (a) ICT on *services* and (b) of *services* on both ICT and technology. ICT = information and communication technology.

exerts the largest impact on all the endogenous variables, as figure 8.7 shows.

Coordinated policies would therefore bring about greater gains because joint implementation of policies generates effects that are greater than the sum of those obtained by implementing policies individually.

Figure 8.6 Cost of Delaying Deregulation

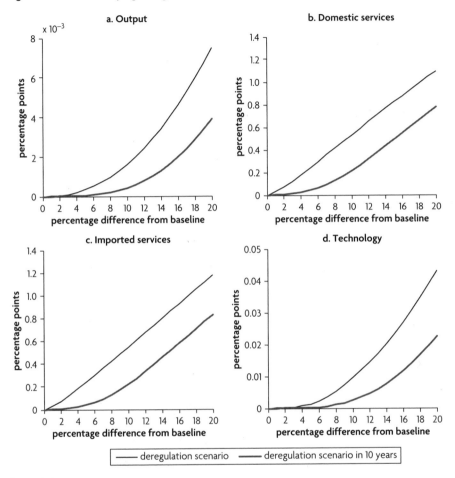

Source: Authors.
Note: Each line represents the percentage difference with respect to the baseline scenario. If y_{base} is the sum of the output produced in all EU countries under the baseline scenario, and y_B is the sum of the output produced in all EU countries under scenario 2 (regulatory harmonization), then the black line is $100 \times (y_B - y_{base}) / y_{base}$. The same applies to all variables.

Concluding Remarks

To leave behind the legacy of the Great Recession, all major economies—and particularly Europe—will have to pursue new sources of growth, and innovation will have to be a key component of a return to sustained growth. However, as the process of innovation evolves and becomes more complex, our understanding of the process must also evolve to

Figure 8.7 Aggregate Effect of Coordinated Policies: Increasing Human Capital and Deregulation

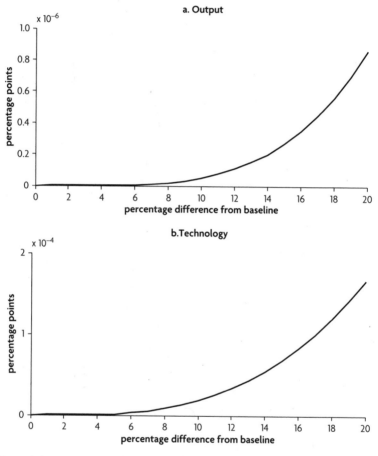

Source: Authors.

Note: y_{base} is the sum of the output produced in all EU countries under the baseline scenario, and y_B is the sum of the output produced in all EU countries. Let us further define $\psi A = 100 \times (y_B - y_{base}) / y_{base}$ as the percentage gain obtained by implementing scenario 1 (deregulation). For all variables, the black line = $\psi(A+B) - (\psi A + \psi B)$. For broadband only: $\psi A = BBNDB - BBND_{base}$.

identify the appropriate policy strategies. In so doing, we need to better understand how features such as open innovation, global innovation chains, and the role of technology platforms such as the Internet interact and how they can be modeled.

Moving in this direction implies moving away from the traditional, growth accounting, linear relationship toward a systemic approach to modeling innovation. In this chapter, we have offered some initial examples of how this can be done. We have suggested ways to take knowledge globalization into account, based on the recognition that there are multiple, interacting channels of innovation diffusion. We have offered examples of how to endogenize ICT in the economic system.

These new features are particularly relevant to European countries, which have suffered slower GDP growth per capita over the past two decades. Particularly worrisome for the Euro Area countries was the steadily declining trend in labor productivity (GDP per hour worked) and TFP growth. Although many factors have contributed to these outcomes, there is considerable uncertainty about the root causes of Europe's relatively poor performance. A relevant contributing factor, however, is the European technological gap and, in particular, the slow adaptation of European economies to the new-economy paradigm linked with ICT diffusion.

In this regard, the policy simulation results in this chapter offer some interesting messages for innovation and growth policy:

- *The model simulations confirm the following:*
  - Innovation and technology accumulation are enhanced, especially by human capital accumulation, because a larger stock of human capital enhances technology accumulation (and hence growth) while also promoting international knowledge diffusion.
  - Business services are a powerful driver of growth, and deeper integration in the European market for producers of services does indeed significantly contribute to growth.
  - Delays in implementing policy reforms are costly. In particular, delay in completing reforms causes substantial costs in terms of lower growth, less development of the service sector, and less technology accumulation and innovation.
- *Improvements in economic structure are effective in stimulating ICT diffusion and innovations.* In particular, the economic structure (the share of business and advanced services) has a positive impact on ICT investment and positively affects services, technology, and GDP.

Because of ICT's nature as a GPT, ICT introduction requires not only a specific investment in ICT equipment but also, even more important, a number of facilitating factors to generate the appropriate environment for ICT diffusion. For example, business services are intensive ICT users; hence, a widespread presence of such services in the economy enhances the impact of ICT on overall performance.

- *A single instrument is insufficient to boost innovation and thereby productivity and growth* because a joint implementation of policies generates effects that exceed the sum of those obtained by implementing policies separately. For instance, our results show that EU output growth can be significantly increased by enhanced availability of business services, accumulation of knowledge, and ICT diffusion. Such results can be obtained by improving the regulatory environment, by deepening integration in service markets, and by increasing and improving human capital accumulation.

Notes

1. Many studies have shown large differences across European countries in the production and use of ICT. Two, or possibly three, groups of national patterns can be identified (Schreyer 2000). Within Europe, Daveri (2000) identifies laggards (Italy, Spain, and to a lesser extent, France and Germany) and fast adopters (Finland, the Netherlands, Sweden, and the United Kingdom).

2. The level of regulation is computed by means of three different indices: (a) an index of regulatory conditions in seven nonmanufacturing sectors (*regulation*, time series, and cross-sectional data) constructed by Conway and Nicoletti (2006); (b) the OECD index of administrative burdens on start-ups (*absu*, cross-sectional data) taken from Conway, Janod, and Nicoletti (2005); and (c) an index measuring the flexibility of the labor market (*labor*, cross-sectional data). For all regulation indices, a higher value of the index means a tighter level of regulation (Guerrieri 2009).

3. This section draws heavily from the two research reports conducted for the European Commission by the College of Europe, Bruges: Guerrieri and Padoan (2007) and Guerrieri (2009).

4. Basically, the magnitude effect on scenarios 1 and 2 is the same; the difference is that, in scenario 1, regulation decreases uniformly everywhere, while in scenario 2 it decreases in some countries such that the variance of the variable across countries decreases (harmonization in regulation).

References

Aghion, Paul, and Peter Howitt. 1998. *Endogenous Growth Theory*. Cambridge, MA: MIT Press.

————. 2006. "Joseph Schumpeter Lecture—Appropriate Growth Policy: A Unifying Framework." *Journal of the European Economic Association* 4 (2–3): 269–314.

Arvanitis, Spyridon. 2004. "Information Technology, Workplace Organization, Human Capital, and Firm Productivity: Evidence for the Swiss Economy." In *The Economic Impact of ICT: Measurement, Evidence, and Implications*, ed. Organisation for Economic Co-operation and Development (OECD), 183–212. Paris: OECD.

Barro, Robert, and Xavier Sala-i-Martin. 1995. *Economic Growth*. New York: McGraw-Hill.

Bayo-Moriones, Alberto, and Fernando Lera-López. 2007. "A Firm-Level Analysis of Determinants of ICT Adoption in Spain." *Technovation* 27 (6–7): 352–66.

Bayoumi, Tamim, Douglas Laxton, and Paolo Pesenti. 2004. "Benefits and Spillovers of Greater Competition in Europe: A Macroeconomic Assessment." Working Paper 10416, National Bureau of Economic Research, Cambridge, MA.

Bresnahan, Timothy F., Erik Brynjolfsson, and Lorin M. Hitt. 2002. "Information Technology, Workplace Organization, and the Demand for Skilled Labor: Firm-Level Evidence." *Quarterly Journal of Economics* 117 (1): 339–76.

Bresnahan, Timothy F., and Manuel Trajtenberg. 1995. "General Purpose Technologies: 'Engines of Growth?'" *Journal of Econometrics* 65 (1): 83–108.

Brynjolfsson, Erik, and Lorin Hitt. 2003. "Computing Productivity: Firm-Level Evidence." *Review of Economics and Statistics* 85 (4): 793–808.

Conway, Paul, Véronique Janod, and Giuseppe Nicoletti. 2005. "Product Market Regulation in OECD Countries, 1998 to 2003." Economics Department Working Paper 419, Organisation for Economic Co-operation and Development, Paris.

Conway, Paul, and Giuseppe Nicoletti. 2006. "Product Market Regulation in Non-manufacturing Sectors in OECD Countries: Measurement and Highlights." Economics Department Working Paper 530, Organisation for Economic Co-operation and Development, Paris.

Daveri, Francesco. 2000. "Is Growth in Europe an ICT Story Too?" Working Paper 168, Innocenzo Gasparini Institute for Economic Research, Bocconi University, Milan.

EC (European Commission). 2007. "The EU Economy: 2007 Review." *European Economy* No. 8. Brussels: EC.

————. 2010. "EUROPE 2020, A New Growth Agenda." EC, Brussels. http://ec.europa.eu/europe2020/index_en.htm.

Freeman, Christopher, and Carlota Perez. 1988. "Structural Crises of Adjustment, Business Cycles, and Investment Behaviour." In *Technical Change and Economic*

Theory, ed. Giovanni Dosi, Christopher Freeman, Richard Nelson, Gerald Silverberg, and Luc Soete, 38–66. London: Pinter Publishers.

Freeman, Christopher, and Luc Soete. 1987. *Technical Change and Full Employment.* Oxford, U.K.: Blackwell.

Guerrieri, Paolo. 2009. "Using State-of-the-Art Models and Tools for the Assessment of ICT Impacts and Growth and Competitiveness in a Low-Carbon Economy." Report prepared for the European Commission, College of Europe, Bruges.

Guerrieri, Paolo, Bernardo Maggi, Valentina Meliciani, and Pier Carlo Padoan. 2005. "Technology Diffusion, Services, and Endogenous Growth in Europe: Is the Lisbon Strategy Useful?" *Rivista di Politica Economica* 95 (1): 271–317.

Guerrieri Paolo, Bernardo Maggi, and Pier Carlo Padoan. 2009. "A Continuous Time Model of European Growth, Integration and Technology Diffusion: The Role of Distance." *Economic Modelling* 26 (3): 631–40.

Guerrieri, Paolo, and Pier Carlo Padoan, eds. 2007. "Modelling ICT as a General Purpose Technology: Evaluation Models and Tools for Assessment of Innovation and Sustainable Development at the EU level." Report prepared for the European Commission, *Collegium* 35, College of Europe, Bruges, Belgium.

Gust, Christopher, and Jaime Marquez. 2002. "International Comparisons of Productivity Growth: The Role of Information Technology and Regulatory Practices." International Finance Discussion Paper 727, Board of Governors of the U.S. Federal Reserve System, Washington, DC.

Hempell, Thomas, Henry van der Wiel, and George van Leeuwen. 2004. "ICT, Innovation, and Business Performance in Services: Evidence for Germany and the Netherlands." In *The Economic Impact of ICT: Measurement, Evidence and Implications,* ed. Organisation for Economic Co-operation and Development (OECD), 131–52. Paris: OECD.

Inklaar Robert, Mary O'Mahony, and Marcel P. Timmer. 2005. "ICT and Europe's Productivity Performance: Industry-Level Growth Account Comparisons with the United States." *Review of Income and Wealth* 51 (4): 505–36.

Jones, Charles I., and Paul Romer. 2009. "The New Kaldor Facts: Ideas, Institutions, Population, and Human Capital." Working Paper 15094, National Bureau of Economic Research, Cambridge, MA.

Krugman, Paul. 2009. "The Increasing Returns Revolution in Trade and Geography." *American Economic Review* 99 (3): 561–71.

Lipsey, Richard G., Kenneth I. Carlaw, and Clifford Bekar. 2006. *Economic Transformations.* Oxford, U.K.: Oxford University Press.

Milgrom, Paul, and John Roberts. 1990. "The Economics of Modern Manufacturing Technology, Strategy, and Organization." *American Economic Review* 80 (3): 511–28.

Monti, Mario. 2010. "A New Strategy for the Single Market: At the Service of Europe's Economy and Society." Report to the President of the European Commission, José Manuel Barroso, European Commission, Brussels.

http://ec.europa.eu/commission_2010-2014/president/news/press-reseases/pdf/20100510_1_en.pdf.

Organisation for Economic Co-operation and Development (OECD). 2008. *Open Innovation in Global Networks.* Paris: OECD.

———. 2009. *Economic Outlook No. 86*, OECD, Paris.

Perez, Carlota. 1988. "New Technologies and Development." In *Small Countries Facing the Technological Revolution*, ed. Christopher Freeman and Bengt-Ake Lundvall, 85–97. London: Pinter.

Reinhart, Carmen M., and Vincent R Reinhart. 2010. "After the Fall." Paper presented at the Federal Reserve Bank of Kansas City Economic Policy Symposium, Jackson Hole, WY, August 27.

Schreyer, Paul. 2000. "The Contribution of Information and Communication Technology to Output Growth: A Study of the G-7 Countries." Science, Technology, and Industry Working Paper 2000/2, Organisation for Economic Co-operation and Development, Paris.

Trinh, Le, John Gibson, and Les Oxley. 2005. "Measures of Human Capital: A Review of the Literature." Working Paper 05/10, New Zealand Treasury, Wellington.

van Ark, Bart, Robert Inklaar, and Robert H. McGuckin. 2003. "'Changing Gear'— Productivity, ICT and Service Industries: Europe and the United States." In *The Industrial Dynamics of the New Digital Economy*, ed. Jens Froslev Christensen and Peter Maskell, 56–99. Cheltenham, U.K.: Edward Elgar.

van Ark, Bart, Mary O'Mahony, and Marcel Timmer. 2008. "The Productivity Gap between Europe and the United States: Trends and Causes." *Journal of Economic Perspectives* 22 (1): 25–44.

Index

Boxes, figures, notes, and tables are indicated with b, f, n, and t following the page number.

A

Abbas, S. M., 82n30
accountability, 157
ACE (allowance for corporate equity), 120, 123
Acemoglu, Daron, 184, 185, 187, 193
"adding-up problem," 13
advanced economies. *See* developed countries
Africa, infrastructure expenditures in, 139, 146, 173n6
Africa Infrastructure Country Diagnostic (AICD), 173n6
African Development Bank, 172n5
African Union, 168
Aghion, Philippe, 12, 23, 112, 181, 182, 184, 189, 210, 258
AICD (Africa Infrastructure Country Diagnostic), 173n6
Algan, Yann, 190
allowance for corporate equity (ACE), 120, 123

allowance-trading incentives, 168
Andres, Luis, 157
Argentina, regulatory framework in, 156
Arnaud, Camille, 172n2, 173n14
Arrow, Kenneth, 189–90
Arslanalp, Serkan, 111
ASEAN+3, 51, 82n25
Auriol, Emmanuelle, 169
Australia, infrastructure expenditures in, 142, 173n12
Austria, current account imbalances in, 45
autonomous growth, 30n1, 31n7
Aziz, Iwan, 50
Azumendi, Sebastian, 157

B

balance of payments, 243n2
Basel Committee on Banking Supervision, 9b, 76
Bastani, Spencer, 128n11

Bayoumi, Tamim, 234, 243n9
Belgium, infrastructure expenditures in, 160–61
Bertaut, Carol, 81n9
Biancini, Sara, 169
Blanc-Brude, Frederic, 172n2, 173n14
Blomquist, Sören, 128n11
BNDES (Brazilian Development Bank), 15
Boeri, Tito, 25, 201, 203, 211, 212, 214
bonds for infrastructure finance, 136, 149, 151
Brazil
    domestic financing in, 15
    financial openness ranking of, 83n40
    infrastructure investment in, 136
    private infrastructure financing in, 148
    U.S. Federal Reserve loans to, 14
Brazilian Development Bank (BNDES), 15
Briceño-Garmendia, Cecilia, 146
Burger, Philippe, 154

C

Caballero, Ricardo, 54, 56
Cagé, Julia, 12, 23, 112, 181
Cahuc, Pierre, 190
Canada
    fiscal policy in, 91
    infrastructure expenditures in, 141
Canuto, Otaviano, 3, 30n2
capital adequacy ratio, 76
capital gains taxes, 118–21
capitalization rates, 44
carbon pricing, 113, 117–18, 184–85, 187
Caulkins, Jonathan P., 168
C-efficiency, 114
central banks, 18, 77, 104. *See also* *specific banks*
CGD. *See* Commission on Growth and Development

Chiang Mai Initiative, 51, 82n25
China
    current account imbalances in, 18–19, 36, 46–49, 62, 65f, 68f, 70–75, 71–74f, 81n18
    economic growth in, 13, 14
    export diversification in, 15
    financial openness ranking, 83n40
    growth scenarios, 70–75, 71–74f
    ICT trade in, 224, 225–26t, 226–27, 229, 237
    infrastructure expenditures in, 143
    private infrastructure financing in, 148
    trade concentration in, 240
Chinn, Menzie, 12, 13, 18, 35, 52, 53
Chun, Hyunbae, 228
Claessens, Stijn, 29
Clean Air Act (U.S.), 168
clean innovations, 112, 185
climate change
    fiscal policy and, 89, 111–12
    green taxes, 116–18
    infrastructure expenditures and, 145
    innovation and, 23–24
    knowledge economy and, 184–87
Cline, William, 13
collective bargaining, 191–92, 210
Commission on Growth and Development (CGD), 11, 15, 173n5
compliance to tax policy, 114, 125–26
concentration rates for ICT trade, 26, 219–20, 232–33, 238–42, 239f, 241t
congestion pricing, 118
Congressional Budget Office (U.S.), 91
contingent cash transfers, 108
contributory principle modernization, 109–10
convergence of technology, 253
Conway, Paul, 276n2
corporate savings rate, 47, 48
corporate taxes, 119–20

corruption
    current account imbalances and, 53
    infrastructure projects and, 111
    social contract and, 24, 196–97,
        196–97f, 198n3
Corruption Perception Index (Trans-
        parency International), 198n3
cost-plus regulatory regimes, 163, 168
Cottarelli, Carlo, 19, 87
countercyclical regulation, 76–77, 184
cream skimming risks, 161–62
cross-boundary coordination, 18, 19
currency swap lines, 19, 51, 78, 82n25
current account imbalances, 6, 18–19,
        35–86, 37f
    in China, 46–49, 70–75, 71–74f
    in East Asian countries, 49–51
    empirical analyses of, 52–75, 55t,
        57–61t, 79–80
    in Euro area, 41–46, 41f, 42–43t
    in oil-exporting nations, 52
    policy challenges, 36–52
    policy implications, 75–78
    predictions, 62–75, 63–68f, 70–74f
    in U.S., 37–41, 38f, 69–70, 70f

D

Daveri, Francesco, 276n1
debt in fiscal policy, 96–104, 97–98f,
        127n2
decentralization, 193
Dechezlepretre, Antoine, 184
deficits
    fiscal policy, 96–104, 97–98f
    social contract and, 193–96, 194–95f
deforestation, 117
deleveraging, 5, 38–39
demographic changes
    economic growth and, 16
    fiscal policy and, 89, 92, 93f, 94
    information technology adoption
        and, 261

dependency ratios, 54, 56
Deutsche Bank, 47, 158
developed countries
    fiscal policy, 90–91, 90f, 92–93f,
        95–97f
    infrastructure expenditures in, 139
developing countries
    autonomous growth in, 31n7
    infrastructure expenditures in, 136,
        138
    private infrastructure financing
        in, 149
    procurement policies in, 163
development banks, 154
Dewatripont, Mathias, 189
dirty innovations, 112, 185
disability allowances, 108
dispersion rates for ICT, 237–42
DLA Piper, 148
Dudley, William, 31n8

E

ease of doing business, 276n2
East Asian countries
    current account imbalances in, 49–51
    domestic financing in, 15
    economic growth in, 14
    import substitution policies in, 188
ECB (European Central Bank), 4
economic growth measurement
    GDP vs. GNI, 221–22
    productivity measures, 221
    social surplus and, 222–23, 223f
    terms of trade and, 221–22
    transformative technology and,
        222–23, 223f
economies of scale, 26, 219, 228, 232
education funding, 23, 182–89,
        183f, 186t
Eichengreen, Barry, 12, 13, 18, 35, 40
electricity infrastructure, 140
El-Erian, Mohamed, 12

emerging economies
    carbon pricing in, 117
    current account imbalances
        in, 51
    fiscal policy, 91–95, 93–95f
    infrastructure projects in, 136
    petroleum subsidies in, 112
    value added taxes in, 116
employment protection legislation
    (EPL), 202
Engel, Eduardo, 153
environmental agencies, 167
EPEC (European PPP Expertise
    Centre), 148
equity markets, 14
Erceg, Christopher, 82n30
Estache, Antonio, 21, 111, 135, 163,
    174n19
Euro area
    current account imbalances in,
        41–46, 41f, 42–43t
    financial sector in, 203
    growth challenges in, 4
    labor markets in, 212
    productivity in, 28
    unemployment in, 25, 201
European Central Bank (ECB), 4
European Climate Exchange, 165
European Commission, 265
European Community Household
    Panel, 212
European Monetary Union, 42
European PPP Expertise Centre
    (EPEC), 148
exchange rates
    current account balances and, 40,
        50, 81n7
    current account imbalances
        and, 47
    G-20 reform goals for, 9b
exports
    diversification of, 15, 26, 219–20,
        232–33, 238–42, 239f, 241t

    exchange rates and, 50
    of ICT, 224, 226, 236–37
external rebalancing, 7, 9b

F

Farhi, Emmanuel, 54, 56
FAT (financial activities tax), 124
Fay, Marianne, 172n5, 173n5
Federal Reserve (U.S.), 14, 40
Feenstra, Robert, 242n1
financial activities tax (FAT), 124
financial openness, 53, 83n40
financial sector
    capitalization of, 44
    current account imbalances and, 76
    Great Recession impact on, 14
    G-20 reform goals for, 9b
    labor markets and, 203, 204f,
        209–12
    regulatory framework for, 18
    taxation of, 123–24
Finland, current account imbalances
    and, 45
fiscal consolidation
    in Euro area deficit countries,
        42–44, 42t
    growth impact of, 31n11, 103–4
fiscal policy, 19–21, 87–133
    current account imbalances and, 19,
        77–78
    G-20 goals, 9b
    infrastructure investments, 146–54
    macroeconomic dimension, 20, 88,
        89–104
        advanced economies, 90–91, 90f,
            92–93f, 95–97f
        deficits and debt, 96–104, 97–98f
        emerging economies, 91–95,
            93–95f
        fiscal adjustment's impact on
            growth, 103–4
        public debt, 99–103, 101–2f

microeconomic dimension, 20, 88,
    105–26
    climate change expenditures,
        111–12
    infrastructure investment, 110–12
    innovation expenditures, 110–12
    petroleum subsidies, 112–13
    public spending policies, 105–13
    renewable resource subsidies, 113
    subsidies, 112–13
    tax policy, 113, 114–26
    welfare reform, 106–10
    policy challenges, 88–89
Fischer, Ronald, 153
flat tax, 125
food prices, 14
foreign-currency-denominated
    borrowing, 77
foreign exchange reserves, 78
Foster, Vivien, 146
France
    fiscal policy in, 91
    infrastructure expenditures in, 140
fuel prices, 14
Fullerton, Don, 129*n*17, 168

G

G-7, 205–6, 206*f*
G-20
    economic growth goals, 8–11, 9*b*
    financial sector reform agenda, 78
    infrastructure expenditures, 21, 135
Galetovic, Alexander, 153
Garibaldi, Pietro, 25, 201, 203, 211,
    212, 214
GDP (gross domestic product),
    221–22
general purpose technology (GPT), 248,
    252–54
*The General Theory of Employment,
    Interest and Money*
    (Keynes), 136

Germany
    corruption in, 160
    current account imbalances in, 19,
        41, 41*f*, 42, 45, 62, 64*f*, 67*f*
    fiscal policy in, 91
    ICT trade in, 225–26*t*, 227
    infrastructure expenditures in,
        143–44
    labor markets in, 215, 215*n*1
    public-private partnerships in,
        174*n*16
Giavazzi, Francesco, 103
Gilson, Stuart, 211
"Global Economic Prospects 2011"
    (World Bank), 31*n*9
"Global Financial Stability Report"
    (IMF), 6
Global Infrastructure Index (S&P),
    32*n*12, 149, 173*n*13
globalization
    economic growth and, 3
    fiscal policy and, 89
    of information technology
        production, 229, 243*n*5
    of innovation, 249–50
    tax policy and, 121–23
GNI (gross national income),
    221–22
Gourinchas, Pierre-Olivier, 54, 56
governance reforms, 169
government role, 22–24, 181–200
    in development process, 11–12
    in infrastructure, 154–65
    as knowledge economy investor, 23,
        182–89, 183*f*, 186*t*
    in national saving, 48–49
    social contract and, 23, 24,
        189–97
GPT (general purpose technology), 248,
    252–54
Great Recession of 2008–09
    labor markets impact of, 205–9
    systemic shocks from, 14

Greece
    current account imbalances and,
        41, 41*f*, 42
    macroeconomic instability in, 99
    sovereign debt crisis in, 4
Green, Stephen, 48
green taxes, 116–18
green technology, 112, 165–68, 185.
        See also clean innovations
gross domestic product (GDP), 221–22
gross national income (GNI), 221–22
guarantee risks, 162–63
Guasch, J. Luis, 157, 163
Guerrieri, Luca, 82*n*30
Guerrieri, Paolo, 27, 29, 247, 266
Gust, Christopher, 82*n*30

H

Haacker, Markus, 234, 243*n*9
Hall, David, 153
Hart, Olivier, 210
Hausmann, Ricardo, 4
Hayek, F. A., 173*n*9
health care reforms, 91, 107
Herfindahl index, 238–42, 243*n*12
higher education, investment in,
        182, 183*f*
Hines, James R., Jr., 128*n*14
Holland, Stephen, 166
home ownership, 113
Hong Kong SAR, ICT trade in, 224,
        225–26*t*, 226–27, 229
horizontal differentiation, 188
household saving, 8, 38, 45–46, 50,
        81*n*18
housing markets, 14, 108
Howitt, Peter, 258
human capital, 29, 260–61, 269–70, 275

I

Iceland, macroeconomic instability
        in, 99

ICT. *See* information and communica-
        tion technologies
Idzelis, Christine, 151, 174*n*19
IFC (International Finance Corpora-
        tion), 14, 82*n*29
Iimi, Atsushi, 163
ILO (International Labour Organiza-
        tion), 142
IMF. *See* International Monetary Fund
imports
    concentration rates for, 26, 219–20,
        232–33, 238–42, 239*f*, 241*t*
    of ICT, 226–27, 234–36
incentives, tax policy, 121
income taxes, 48, 129*n*16
India
    carbon pricing in, 117
    domestic financing in, 15
    private infrastructure financing
        in, 148
Indonesia
    current account imbalances in, 50
    ICT trade concentration in, 238, 240
industrial policy, 24, 187–89
information and communication
        technologies (ICT), 17, 26–27,
        219–46
    adoption rates, 260–61
    concentration rates, 238–42,
        239*f*, 241*t*
    diffusion rates, 260–61
    dispersion rates, 237–42
    economic growth measurement
        and, 221–23
    expenditures on, 227, 228*t*
    exporters of, 224, 226, 236–37
    fiscal policy and, 127*n*1
    global knowledge pool and, 261–62
    importers of, 226–27, 234–36
    international trade patterns and,
        224–27, 225–26*t*, 230–37,
        232–33*f*, 235*f*
    literature review, 223–30

policy implications, 242
social surplus and, 230–37,
  232–33*f*, 235*f*
Information Economy Report
  (UNCTAD), 224
Information Technology Outlook
  (OECD), 224
infrastructure, 21–22, 135–78
demand for, 138–41, 139*t*
fiscal policy and, 110–12, 146–54
government role in, 154–65
greening of, 165–68
institutional coordination, 167–68
long-term changes, 136–37
needs, 139–40, 139*t*
planning for, 160–61
policy coordination needs, 165–66
policy implications, 137
political economy of, 172
private sector financing, 148–49,
  150*f*, 171–72
procurement processes and, 143–44,
  159–60
regionalization of large projects,
  168–70
regulatory framework for, 156–59,
  158*t*, 166–67
risk assessments, 151–53, 161–63
short-term responses, 135–36
supply, 141–45
transparency of fiscal costs, 159
inherited trust, 190
innovation, 17, 27–29, 247–79
dynamic structural model,
  263–65, 263*t*
ecosystem model, 262–63
in Euro area, 254–57, 255*f*
evolution of, 249–54
fiscal policy and, 110–12
general purpose technologies, 252–54
globalization of, 251
intangibles and, 251–52
modeling of, 257–63

open collaboration in, 249, 250–51
policy simulations, 265–73, 268–70*f*,
  272–74*f*
regulatory framework and, 256–57
in service sector, 251–52
institutional framework
G-20 goals for, 9*b*
infrastructure and, 167–68
labor markets and, 201–2, 212–14
trust investments and, 190
intangible assets, 250, 252
intellectual property (IP), 251
Inter-American Development Bank,
  173*n*5
interest rate growth differential, 97
internal rebalancing, 7, 9*b*
international competition and
  cooperation. *See* policy
  coordination
International Finance Corporation
  (IFC), 14, 82*n*29
International Labour Organization
  (ILO), 142
International Monetary Fund (IMF)
on China's current account
  imbalances, 49
economic growth projections,
  81*n*14
on Euro area current account
  imbalances, 4, 43
on financial sector taxation, 124
on fiscal consolidation, 104
on G-20 growth goals, 8
on industrial policy, 188
on pension costs, 107
on policy coordination, 10
on UK current account deficits, 46
on U.S. current account deficit,
  40–41
Internet, 28, 252–54
investment climate, 188
investment tax credits, 45
in-work tax credits, 108

Ireland
    current account imbalances and, 41,
        41*f*, 42
    ICT trade in, 237
    macroeconomic instability in, 99
    sovereign debt crisis in, 4
Israel, ICT trade in, 237
Italy
    current account imbalances and,
        41, 41*f*
    fiscal policy in, 91
Ito, Hiro, 12, 13, 18, 35, 52, 53

J

Janod, Véronique, 276*n*2
Japan
    current account imbalances in,
        49–50, 62, 64*f*, 67*f*
    economic growth projections in, 6
    export promotion in, 188
    fiscal policy in, 91
    ICT trade in, 225–26*t*, 226–27
    infrastructure investment in, 136
Jensen, Olivia, 172*n*2, 173*n*14
job creation, 144–45, 154
job destruction, 25, 211–12
John, Kose, 211
Jones, Benjamin, 129*n*15
Jones, Charles I., 248

K

Kamin, Steve, 81*n*9
Kandiero, Tonia, 172*n*5
Kawai, Masahiro, 50
Keen, Michael, 19, 87, 129*n*15, 129*n*20
Keynesian policies, 136
Kleven, Henrik, 129*n*21
knowledge economy
    climate-change policy and, 184–87
    education policy and, 23, 182, 183*t*
    government role in, 182–89,
        183*f*, 186*t*
    industrial policy and, 24, 187–89
    innovation and, 251
    macroeconomic stabilization and,
        183–84
    market liberalization, 182–83
knowledge sharing, 251
Kohli, Ulrich, 243*n*1
Korea. *See* Republic of Korea
Kose, M. Ayhan, 29
KPMG, 140
Krelove, Russell, 129*n*20
Kumar, Mohan, 100
Kurzarbeit (Germany), 215, 215*n*1
Kydland, Finn E., 173*n*9

L

Labor Force Survey (EU), 212
labor hoarding, 209
labor markets, 24–26, 201–17
    demand-driven adjustments, 211
    employment protection
        legislation, 202
    financial sector and, 203, 204*f*,
        209–12
    Great Recession of 2008–09 impact
        on, 205–9
    institutional framework and, 201–2,
        212–14
    job destruction effects, 211–12
    labor mobility effects, 211–12
    supply-driven adjustments, 211
labor mobility, 25, 129*n*21, 211–12
labor unions, 191–92
Lamberte, Mario, 50
Landais, Camille, 129*n*21
Lang, Larry, 211
Latin America. *See also specific countries*
    economic growth in, 14
    import substitution policies in, 188
    infrastructure expenditures in, 139
    private infrastructure financing
        in, 163

legal framework, 53
Leipziger, Danny M., 3, 17, 30, 30n1
liberalization
    of financial markets, 210
    of trade, 23, 182–83
liquidity ratio, 76
Lu, Feng, 47–48
Lyon, Andrew B., 129n17

M

Ma, Guonan, 82n21
Maastricht Treaty, 128n8
macroeconomic dimension of fiscal
        policy, 89–104
    advanced economies, 90–91, 90f,
        92–93f, 95–97f
    deficits and debt, 96–104, 97–98f
    emerging economies, 91–95, 93–95f
    fiscal adjustment's impact on growth,
        103–4
    public debt, 99–103, 101–2f
macroprudential regulation, 18
management autonomy, 157
Mann, Catherine L., 26, 219, 234, 243n9
Mansur, Erin, 166
manufacturing
    current account imbalances and, 40
    growth models based on, 36
    innovation and, 252
marginal effective corporate tax rate
        (MECTR), 119–20
McDermott, Shaun P., 168
means testing, 108–9
Mexico
    financial openness ranking, 83n40
    U.S. Federal Reserve loans to, 14
Micheletto, Luca, 128n11
microeconomic dimension of fiscal
        policy, 105–26
    climate change expenditures, 111–12
    infrastructure investment, 110–12
    innovation expenditures, 110–12

petroleum subsidies, 112–13
public spending policies, 105–13
    subsidies, 112–13
    tax policy, 113, 114–26
    welfare reform, 106–10
MNEs (multinational enterprises),
        28, 251
mobility of capital, 119
"modern tradables," 13
Moen, Espen, 203, 211, 212, 214
monetary policy, 9b, 213
Moore, John, 210
moral hazard, 198n1, 214
Morisson, Mary, 173n5
mortgage-interest tax breaks, 113
multifactor productivity. *See* total factor
        productivity (TFP)
multinational enterprises (MNEs),
        28, 251
Mun, Sung-Bae, 229
Mutual Assessment Process (G-20), 8

N

Nadiri, M. Ishaq, 228, 229
National Audit Office (UK), 163
National Commission on Fiscal
        Responsibility and Reform
        (U.S.), 113
Netherlands, current account
        imbalances in, 45
Newell, Graeme, 158
New Partnership for Africa's Develop-
        ment (NEPAD), 168, 172n5
Nicoletti, Giuseppe, 276n2
nontariff trade barriers, 188
nontechnological innovation, 250,
        253, 260
Norregaard, John, 129n20

O

O'Boyle, William, 17, 30
Obstfeld, Maurice, 40

oil-exporting nations, 36, 52
Organisation for Economic Co-operation
    and Development (OECD)
    on administrative burdens on new
        businesses, 276n2
    on current account imbalances, 39
    deficit reductions and, 197
    economic growth projections, 247
    employment study, 207, 215
    financial sector and labor markets
        in, 213
    on information technology, 224, 257
    infrastructure expenditures and,
        141–42, 172n3
    on infrastructure investment
        needs, 139
    on productivity growth, 256

P

Padoan, Pier Carlo, 27, 29, 247, 266
Pagano, Marco, 103
patent pools, 251
path dependence, 184
Peng, Hsu Wen, 158
pensions
    reforms, 91, 93f
    taxes on private pensions, 120–21
    welfare reform and, 106–7
petroleum subsidies, 112–13
Philippines, current account imbalances
    in, 50
Pinto, Brian, 3
planning for infrastructure, 160–61
policy coordination
    current account imbalances and, 19
    financial regulation, 18
    G-20 goals for, 9b
    ICT innovation and, 272
    IMF agenda for, 10
    infrastructure, 165–66
    tax policy, 121–23, 122f, 126
policy gap, 114

political economy of infrastructure
    expenditures, 22, 161, 172
Pollitt, Michael G., 166, 167
Portugal
    current account imbalances and, 41,
        41f, 42
    infrastructure investment in, 136
    macroeconomic instability in, 99
    sovereign debt crisis in, 4
PPI. See private participation in
    infrastructure
PPIAF (Private-Public Infrastructure
    Advisory Facility), 174n20
PPPs. See public-private partnerships
Prasad, Eswar, 53
Prescott, Edward C., 173n9
Price-Adjusted Major Currencies Dollar
    Index (Federal Reserve), 40
price-cap regulatory regimes, 163
private participation in infrastructure
    (PPI), 22, 140, 148–50, 150f,
    171–72
Private-Public Infrastructure Advisory
    Facility (PPIAF), 174n20
procurement processes, 143–44, 159–60
productivity measures, 221
progressive income taxes, 129n16
property taxes, 116
public debt and fiscal policy, 99–103,
    101–2f
public-private partnerships (PPPs), 111,
    149, 153, 161, 169, 174n16
public spending policies, 105–13
    infrastructure investment, 110–12
    innovation expenditures, 110–12
    subsidies, 112–13
    tax policy, 113
    welfare reform, 106–10

Q

quantitative easing (QE), 4, 7, 50
QUEST model, 265

R

regionalization of large infrastructure
projects, 168–70
regulatory framework
coordination of, 166–67
countercyclical regulation, 76–77
current account imbalances
and, 76
financial sector, 18, 213
information technology adoption
and, 261, 264, 266, 276n2
for infrastructure, 146, 156–59, 158t,
166–67
labor markets, 210
social contract and, 24, 191–92, 192f
Reinhart, Carmen, 16
renewable resource subsidies, 113
Republic of Korea
currency swap lines and, 51
export promotion in, 15, 188
ICT trade in, 237
infrastructure expenditures in, 143
U.S. Federal Reserve loans to, 14
research and development (R&D), 23,
121. *See also* innovation
reserve adequacy, 62
reserve pooling arrangements,
19, 51, 78
retirement age, 128n10
retraining workers, 23
risk allocation renegotiation, 163
risk assessments, 151–53, 161–63
risk sharing, 106
Rodrik, Dani, 4, 13, 15
Rogoff, Kenneth, 16, 40
Romer, Paul, 248
Rua, Gisela, 40
Russian Federation, tax policy in, 125

S

Saez, Emmanuel, 129n21
sales taxes, 116

S&P Global Infrastructure Index,
32n12, 149, 173n13
Saudi Arabia, tax policy in, 114
saving glut hypothesis, 53
savings rate, 8, 38, 45–46, 50, 81n18
sectoral subsidies, 189
services sector
fiscal policy and, 128n13
innovation and, 252, 256–57,
266, 275
Sessions, David N., 144
"short work" programs, 215, 215n1
sickness allowances, 108
Siemens, 152
Singapore
current account imbalances in, 62,
65f, 68f
ICT trade in, 225–26t, 226–27, 237
skilled workers, 260–61
small and medium-sized
enterprises, 121
social contract
corruption and, 196–97, 196–97f
decentralization and, 193
deficit reduction and, 193–96,
194–95f
government role in, 189–97
regulatory framework and,
191–92, 192f
social relationships and, 192–93
trust investments and, 24,
189–93, 191f
social relationships, 192–93
social surplus
economic growth measurement and,
222–23, 223f, 243n9
ICT and, 230–37, 232–33f, 235f
SOEs (state-owned enterprises), 48,
82n19
South Asia
economic growth in, 14
infrastructure expenditures in, 139
South Korea. *See* Republic of Korea

Spain
  corruption in, 160
  current account imbalances and, 41,
      41*f*, 42
  infrastructure investment in, 136
  public-private partnerships in,
      174*n*16
  sovereign debt crisis in, 4
Spence, Michael, 30
state-owned enterprises (SOEs), 48,
      82*n*19
state role. *See* government role
Stern Review (Stern), 112
Stevans, Lonnie K., 144
stimulus packages
  current account imbalances and, 38
  fiscal policy and, 20
  infrastructure projects and, 135–36,
      142, 149, 160
  macroeconomic stabilization and, 184
Strauss-Kahn, Dominique, 31*n*5
subprime crisis, 40, 81*n*13
Subramanian, Arvind, 15
Sub-Saharan Africa
  economic growth in, 14
  infrastructure expenditures in, 142
subsidies
  for clean technology innovations,
      185, 186
  fiscal policy and, 112–13
  industrial policies and, 189
  infrastructure financing and, 147
Summers, Lawrence H., 128*n*14
super-rich, taxation of, 124–25
swap lines, 19, 51, 78, 82*n*25
Sweden
  deficit reduction in, 196
  tax policy in, 119

T

tagging, welfare targeting by, 109
Takagi, Shinji, 50

targeting welfare
  by means testing, 108–9
  by tagging, 109
tariffs
  industrial policy and, 188
  infrastructure expenditures and, 157,
      173*n*12
tax-exempt bonds, 151
tax planning, 126
tax policy, 114–26
  capital gains taxes, 118–21
  carbon pricing, 117–18
  compliance improvements, 125–26
  congestion pricing, 118
  corporate taxes, 119–20
  financial sector taxation, 123–24
  green taxes, 116–18
  implementation improvements,
      125–26
  incentives, 121
  international competition and
      cooperation, 121–23, 122*f*, 126
  investment tax credits, 45
  private pension taxes, 120–21
  progressive income taxes, 129*n*16
  property taxes, 116
  public spending policies and, 113
  super-rich, taxation of, 124–25
  value added taxes, 114–16, 115*t*
technology accumulation, 29, 269, 275
Tenorio, Vyvyan, 151, 174*n*19
terms of trade
  current account imbalances and, 53
  economic growth measurement,
      221–22
  information technology and, 26, 219,
      232, 236
Terrones, Marco E., 29
TFP. *See* total factor productivity
Thailand
  current account imbalances, 50
  financial openness ranking, 83*n*40
Thomas, Charles, 81*n*9

Thorbecke, William, 50
Tomain, Joseph P., 166
"too big to fail" problem, 22, 158,
    181, 213
total factor productivity (TFP)
    Euro area slowdown in, 254
    ICT and, 26, 28, 221, 228
    industrial policies and, 189
    innovation and, 247
trade finance, 14
trade openness, 23, 53, 182–83
trade patterns
    for ICT, 224–27, 225–26t, 230–37,
        232–33f, 235f
    infrastructure investments and,
        168–69
training workers, 23
transformative technology (TT),
    222–23, 223f, 231
transparency
    financial sector, 213
    infrastructure costs, 159
    regulatory rule-making process, 157
Transparency International, 198n3
transport infrastructure, 140, 149
Treasury Department (U.S.), 188
trust investments, 24, 189–93, 191f
TT. See transformative technology
Turkey, private infrastructure financing
    in, 148
twin deficit hypothesis, 53
Tyers, Rod, 47–48

U

unemployment, 8, 16, 201–2, 202f.
    See also labor markets
unemployment assistance, 108
unions, 191–92
United Kingdom
    current account imbalances in,
        45–46, 62, 63f, 66f
    economic growth projections in, 6

exchange rates and, 81n11
fiscal policy in, 91
ICT trade in, 225–26t, 226
infrastructure expenditures in, 162,
    163, 173n12
means testing in, 108
private infrastructure financing in,
    151–52
public-private partnerships in,
    174n16
regulatory framework in, 166
tax policy in, 116, 125
United Nations Conference on
    Trade and Development
    (UNCTAD), 224
United States
    alternative scenarios, 69–70, 70f
    carbon pricing in, 117
    current account imbalances in,
        18, 37–41, 38f, 62, 63f, 66f,
        69–70, 70f
    economic growth projections in, 6
    financial sector in, 203
    fiscal policy in, 91
    ICT trade in, 225–26t, 226–27, 240
    infrastructure expenditures in, 143,
        144, 151
    labor markets in, 212
    productivity in, 28
    quantitative easing policy in, 4, 7
    regulatory framework in, 156,
        167–68
    tax policy in, 114, 125
    unemployment in, 25, 201
utilities infrastructure, 149

V

value added tax (VAT), 114–16, 115t,
    123–24, 161
van Ark, Bart, 228, 229
variety in ICT trade, 26, 219–20,
    232–33, 238–42, 239f, 241t

W

Washington consensus, 188
Wasmer, Etienne, 211
Weil, Philippe, 211
welfare reform, 106–10
  contributory principle
    modernization, 109–10
  health care costs, 107
  pension costs, 106–7
  targeting
    by means testing, 108–9
    by tagging, 109
Woo, Jaejoon, 100
worker retraining, 23
World Bank
  growth and development paradigm,
    13–14
  on industrial policy, 188

Worldwide Governance Indicators,
    198n3
World Economic Outlook (IMF),
    6, 104
World Investment Report
    (UNCTAD), 224
Worldwide Governance Indicators
    (World Bank), 198n3
Wren-Lewis, Liam, 174n19
Wruck, Karen Hoppes, 211

Y

Yepes, Tito, 172n5, 173n6
Yi, Wang, 82n21

Z

Zoellick, Robert, 31n10